Essentials of a Successful Biostatistical Collaboration

Essentials of a Successful Biostatistical Collaboration

Editor

Luigi Salvay

scitus academics

Essentials of a Successful Biostatistical Collaboration
Edited by **Luigi Salvay**

ISBN: 978-1-68117-697-0
Library of Congress Control Number: 2016958857

SCITUS Academics LLC,
616, Corporate Way, Suite 2, 4766,
Valley Cottage, NY 10989

www.scitusacademics.com

Notice

Printed in United States of America on Acid Free Paper

Preface

There has been an explosive growth in the development of statistical methodology over the past several decades. Research in both medicine and public health, in which the involvement of biostatisticians has increased dramatically during this period, has been both a beneficiary of this new methodology as well as a source of new problems. Biostatisticians are specialists in the evaluation of data as scientific evidence. They understand the generic construct of data and they provide the mathematical framework that transcends the scientific context to generalize the findings. Their expertise includes the design and conduct of experiments, the mode and manner in which data are collected, the analysis of data, and the interpretation of results. Meaningful generalization of experimental results requires the application of an appropriate mathematical framework for the scientific context. The validity of research results depends on this application and the reproducibility of the experimental methods. Biostatisticians use mathematics to enhance science and bridge the gap between theory and practice.

Essentials of a Successful Biostatistical Collaboration provides information in promoting and developing biostatistical methodologies and applications in health and medical research. It provides an overview of common functions expected of a collaborating biostatistician. The book delivers valuable information on where to look for information and material on sample size and statistical techniques commonly used in clinical research, trials, samples and on how best to communicate with clinicians. It also covers the best practices to adopt in terms of project, time, and data management; relationship with collaborators; etc. The intention of this book is to presents valued information to biostatisticians and other quantitative scientists with the necessary skills, and knowledge, to collaborate effectively with clinicians in the healthcare field.

Table of Contents

1

CHAPTER

Mathematical Models for Translational and Clinical Oncology

Ralf Gallasch, Mirjana Efremova, Pornpimol Charoentong, Hubert Hackl and Zlatko Trajanoski

Biocenter, Division of Bioinformatics, Innsbruck Medical University, Innrain 80, 6020 Innsbruck, Austria

ABSTRACT

In the context of translational and clinical oncology, mathematical models can provide novel insights into tumor-related processes and can support clinical oncologists in the design of the treatment regime, dosage, schedule, toxicity and drug-sensitivity. In this review we present an overview of mathematical models in this field beginning with carcinogenesis and proceeding to the different cancer treatments. By doing so we intended to highlight recent developments and emphasize the power of such theoretical work.

We first highlight mathematical models for translational oncology comprising epidemiologic and statistical models, mechanistic models for carcinogenesis and tumor growth, as well as evolutionary dynamics models which can help to describe and overcome a major problem in the clinic: therapy resistance. Next we review models for clinical oncology with a special emphasis on therapy including chemotherapy, targeted therapy, radiotherapy, immunotherapy and interaction of cancer cells with the immune system.

As evident from the published studies, mathematical modeling and computational simulation provided valuable insights into the molecular mechanisms of cancer, and can help to improve diagnosis and prognosis of the disease, and pinpoint novel therapeutic targets.

INTRODUCTION

Cancer is still one of the leading causes of death in the world and major efforts have been undertaken to improve diagnosis and therapy of common cancer types. Recently developed technologies (i.e. next generation sequencing) give us unprecedented opportunities to study individual cancer samples at the molecular level and to identify genomic variants and rearrangements [1]. This information will build the basis for the stratification of patients, and for personalized or precision medicine. The increasing complexity of the generated data utilizing various high-throughput technologies for characterizing the genome, epigenome, transcriptome, proteome, metabolome, and interactome pose considerable challenges and therefore plethora of bioinformatics methods and tools for the analysis have been developed [2]. However, the real value of the disparate datasets can be truly exploited only if the data is integrated and will then enable one to comprehensively study molecular mechanisms of cancer cells.

One possibility for data integration is the use of mathematical models. Modeling has been successfully applied in physiology for many decades but only recently the quality and the quantity of biomolecular data became available for the development of causative and predictive models. Due to their importance in cancer mathematical models have also been in the focus of theoretical investigators. For example application of theoretical techniques and the postulation of the "two hit" hypothesis in the early 70s led to the identification of tumor-suppressor genes [3]. Later, in a landmark paper it was shown that cancer results from evolutionary processes occurring within the body [4].

In the context of translational (i.e. from bench to bedside, or in other words: transforming scientific discoveries arising from laboratory to clinical applications) and clinical oncology, mathematical models can provide novel insights into tumor growth and progression, into tumor-related processes such as angiogenesis, the immune response, and the interaction with the tumor microenvironment, and into the development of drug resistance. Furthermore, modeling can support the clinical oncologists in the design of the treatment regime, dosage, schedule, toxicity and drug-sensitivity. Common treatments against the different types of cancers include surgery, radiation therapy, chemotherapy, targeted therapy or combinations of those to limit the progression of malignant disease, eradicate tumor cells and prolong survival. The information gained from mathematical models can also help in the development and efficacy of clinical trials and treatment protocols, and can accelerate the progress of clinical research in fighting cancer.

To the best of our knowledge there is currently no review study on mathematical models focusing on translational and clinical oncology applications except for a similar attempt made by Swierniak et al. [5] few years ago. We therefore initiated this work to provide an overview of the field and stimulate the discussion and the development of novel models. While mechanistic models have proven extremely valuable and provided novel insights, there are not considered here and we refer the readers to recent reviews [6, 7, 8]. Given the wealth of published studies using mathematical models in cancer, we by no means intended to provide a comprehensive picture. Rather, we selected several topics we believe are of relevance for the readers. Wherever possible, we refer to additional reviews in order to guide interested researchers.

We first highlight mathematical models for translational oncology comprising epidemiologic and statistical models, mechanistic models for carcinogenesis and tumor growth, as well as evolutionary dynamics models [9], which can help to describe and overcome a major problem in the clinic: therapy resistance. Next we review models for clinical oncology. It should be noted that a survey of application of modeling results in clinics was beyond the scope of this review. Rather, we provide an overview of the models with a special emphasis on therapy including chemotherapy, targeted therapy, radiotherapy, immunotherapy and interaction of cancer cells with the immune system. Table 1 shows the specific categories and the publications used in this work.

Table 1. Categories and mathematical models in translational and clinical oncology reviewed in this paper

Translational oncology	Clinical oncology
Biological processes	Treatment options
Carcinogenesis	Chemotherapy
[3,10-17]	[61-70]
Tumor-growth	Targeted therapy
[18-27]	[58,72,73,75-78]
Clonal evolution	Radiotherapy
[37,38,41-46]	[79-81]
Therapy resistance	Tumor immune-cell interaction/ immunotherapy
[47-59]	[82-88]

MATHEMATICAL MODELS FOR TRANSLATIONAL ONCOLOGY

Carcinogenesis and tumor-growth models

Early models that aimed to explain the dynamics of cancer progression were based on experimental and epidemiological data, which indicated that the cancer incidence is often rapidly increased with age and simple patterns could be observed at the population level. Fisher and Hollomon [10] presented a multicellular model in which mutations occur in different cells within the same cell population and only the combination of all mutations leads to cancer development. As an alternative to this theory, Nordling [11] suggested that mutations must occur sequentially in the same cell for transformation into cancer cell.

Most mathematical models of cancer progression descend from Armitage and Doll's [12] multistage theory, which include major concepts for how to think about incidence, carcinogenesis, and progression. The theory states that carcinogenesis progresses through series of genomic alterations in a single cell and the age-specific incidence of cancers is predicted to increase with a power of age that is one less than the number of alterations. Two other studies, using data comparing inherited and noninherited cases in colon cancer [13] and retinoblastoma [3], provided additional empirical evidence for the multistage theory. Knudson used a statistical analysis of the incidence of retinoblastoma in children to explain the role of tumor suppressor genes in sporadic and inherited cancers. This work was later extended to a two-stage stochastic model for the process of cancer initiation and progression [14], which lead to important subsequent work [15, 16] that helped with characterization of other suppressor genes such as APC in colon cancer and TP53, which is mutated in several human tumors.

Even though these models provided accurate descriptions of cancer incidence data, they were unable to relate the data with the functional changes associated with tumor progression. Since then the understanding of the molecular mechanisms underlying tumor initiation and progression has improved [17] and mechanistic models that use biological knowledge and biophysical laws to quantify and predict cancer progression were developed.

The growth and development of solid tumors occurs in two stages – avascular and vascular. The early spatio-temporal models [18, 19] of avascular tumor growth describe the interactions between tumor cell population and nutrients and calculate the nutrient concentrations as a function of tumor spheroid radius that is changing due to the rate of cell proliferation. Significant progress was made with the development of new models [20, 21] that introduced the interrelated concepts of cell movement and pressure.

Since tumor induced angiogenesis i.e. the growth of a network of blood vessels, is a crucial component of solid tumor growth, the basic models have been expanded to account for tumor growth during angiogenesis and the increase of tumor availability associated with the expanding vasculature. In order to make a transition from avascular to vascular growth, tumors may secrete diffusible substances called tumor angiogenic factors (TAF). The earliest continuum models of tumor angiogenesis [22] describe the growth of a capillary network in terms of capillary tip densities and capillary sprout densities in response to TAF. The mathematical models in angiogenesis have mostly focused on describing endothelial cell migration and proliferation through the extracellular matrix [23, 24, 25, 26, 27]. A comprehensive overview of models in this area can be found in [28]. Mathematical modeling of blood flow in tumor-induced capillary networks has been described in more recent studies [29, 30, 31].

The concept that the successful formation of a tumor depends on vascularization has resulted in developing cancer therapies designed to inhibit the tumor vasculature in order to deprive the tumor from oxygen and nutrients. Several models have focused on exploring the efficiency of such antiangiogenic treatments [32, 33, 34]. Using methods of optimal control theory to analyze drug dosing and treatment strategies these studies showed that the combination with other forms of therapy would be beneficial.

Clonal evolution models and therapy resistance

An important conceptual breakthrough in understanding cancer lies in Darwinian and ecological theories: cancer progression is an evolutionary process that results from accumulation of genetic and epigenetic variations in somatic cells [35, 36]. Experimental evidences and recent advances in genetic sequencing technologies – that allowed identification of the genetic alterations in a cancer cell - have revealed the complexity and heterogeneity of cancer progression and have stimulated the use of evolutionary-based approaches in the study of cancer.

Several methods of population dynamics and evolutionary game theory were applied to account for the elementary principles of evolution that lead to tumor initiation and progression. In the earliest models, mutations accumulate in a population of constant or variable size, and they consider only one or two mutations [37, 38]. Newer models are now being used to investigate how the sequence and timing of mutations and the environmental conditions influence tumor progression [39, 40]. An in-depth review of models that describe the evolutionary dynamics of cancer can be found in [41].

Several studies have focused on the waiting time to cancer development, which may be defined as the time from the first presence of neoplasm, until a critical number of hits (driver mutations) are accumulated and initiate the growth of carcinoma. Beerenwinkel et al. [42] developed one of the first models that was based on genomic studies of colorectal cancer patients. They related the waiting time to the population size, mutation rate, and the advantage of the driver mutations and showed that selective advantage of mutations has the largest effect on the evolutionary dynamics of tumorigenesis. In a similar manner, Bozic et al. [43], by fitting their model to glioblastoma and pancreatic cancer data, estimated that driver mutations give an average fitness advantage of 0.4%.

Another characteristic of evolutionary processes is the influence of the local cellular environment on the tumor progression. The progress of tumor is characterized not only by the genetic and epigenetic changes accumulating in the cells, but also by the dynamic interactions between cells within the tumor and between the cells and the constantly changing microenvironment. The microenvironment provides a selective fitness landscape that includes competing for limited resources and active intracellular (initiation of cell proliferation and cell death) and extracellular control mechanisms (the immune system) that aim to restore homeostasis.

There are several studies that utilize mathematical modeling to predict and quantify the interactions of the tumor cells with the surrounding environment during tumor progression [44,45]. Gatenby et al. [46] developed a model of carcinogenesis according to which the tumor cells have to overcome six microenvironment barriers that appear as tumor cells proliferate. They proposed that the nature and sequence of the alterations during carcinogenesis are determined by the specific microenvironmental properties that prevent proliferation within changing adaptive landscapes.

An important clinical problem in cancer research that can be analyzed using modeling techniques is the development of resistance to targeted therapies. Resistance to drugs may develop as a consequence of genetic events such as point mutations or gene amplifications. The emergence of resistance to therapy as a result from a single mutational effect has been first introduced in a model of Coldman and Goldie [47]. More recent studies have also used point mutations to explain the evolutionary dynamics of drug resistant cancer cells [48, 49, 50, 51]. Other models studied gene amplification as one of the mechanisms that has a strong influence on the evolution of drug resistance [52, 53, 54, 55, 56].

Foo et al. [57] designed a methodology that can be used to investigate optimal drug dosing schedules to avoid resistance conferred by one (epi)genetic mutation. In a recent study, Diaz et al. [58] showed that tumors became resistant to anti-EGFR antibodies as a result of emergence of resistance mutations in KRAS and other genes that were present in clonal subpopulation within the tumors before the initiation of the treatment. Analyzing data from 20 melanoma patients who received targeted therapy, Bozic et al. [59] found that simultaneous administration of two drugs is much more effective than sequential therapy. The improved understanding of the evolutionary dynamics of cancer provided by these models can have practical implications in the design and administration of new cancer therapeutics.

In summary, using the overwhelming amount of generated knowledge in tumor biology, mathematical modelers have succeeded in formalizing this knowledge and make it usable for simulations. Moreover, the published models represent a unique basis for testing novel hypotheses which are otherwise difficult or even impossible to test. For example, it is very difficult to obtain samples from early cancer stages or longitudinal samples in order to study the development of tumor heterogeneity. The models presented above enable researchers to address questions which were previously not possible and by using iterative cycles of simulations and experimentation ultimately lead to novel knowledge (Figure 1). Moreover, the maturity of the tools and the availability of data in public databases are additionally supporting the translation of this knowledge into clinical practice.

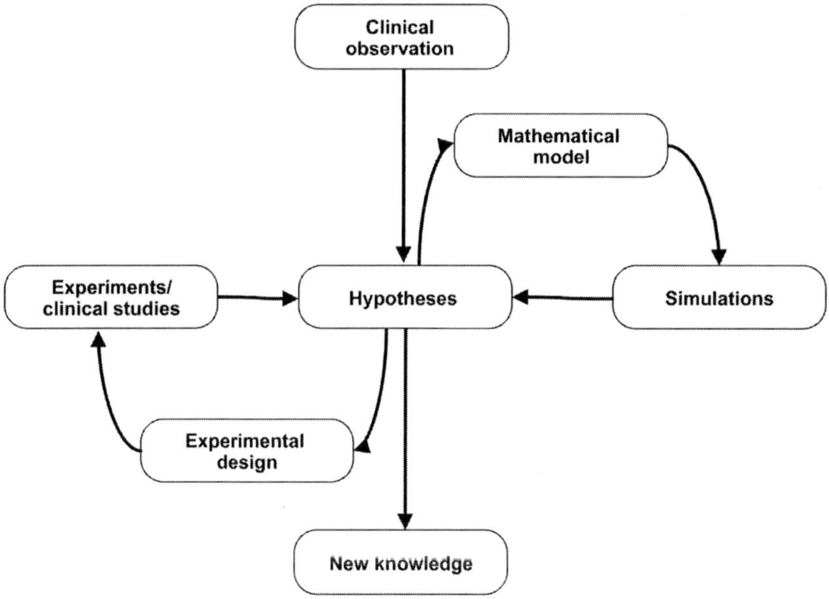

Figure 1. Cycles of experiments and modeling for gaining new knowledge. Experiments and clinical studies are closely coupled with mathematical modeling and simulations and require multiple cycles of iterations.

MATHEMATICAL MODELS FOR CLINICAL ONCOLOGY

Chemotherapy and targeted therapy

Chemotherapy is widely used therapy against cancer. Proliferating cells undergo different phases during the cell cycle including DNA replication and cell division and different chemotherapeutic compounds are affecting cells in different phases. The greatest challenge associated with chemotherapy is that not only cancer cells but also normal dividing cells are affected. In contrast, targeted cancer therapy [60] is aimed at specific molecular targets and is therefore more effective and has fewer side effects.

Fister et al. [61] developed a model that try to solve the problem of maximizing the effect on cancer cells but also maximizing the survival of the host cells. The mathematical model shows that if shorter periods of treatment are used it is possible to use higher doses of the drug and destroy more cancer cells without causing excess damage to the host cells. A more complex model is the cellular automaton model of Byrne et al. [62]. It is a multi-scale model that has a vascular layer, a cellular layer and an intracellular layer. With this model it is possible to get detailed spatio-temporal information about the tumor and the healthy tissue. In general three results are possible with the model; the tumor is eliminated, the tumor continues grow, or an oscillation. It is possible to combine different treatments in one model. The model of de Pillis et al. [63] based on a previous model [64] combines different treatments and shows that if the chemotherapy is stopped a system with a undetectable tumor can return to a high tumor state.

The combination of different treatments is one possibility to eliminate the patient's tumor. Jackson et al. [65] introduced two different types of cells and investigated the tumors response to different chemotherapeutic strategies. It was possible to estimate the largest size of a tumor that can be eradicated by a bolus injection. With only one cell population the results of bolus and continues drug were similar. With two populations, one of them drug resistant, the continuous infusion increased the time to cure. This indicates that it is important to tailor treatment strategies.

Another interesting aspect is the use of growth factors in the model from Panetta and Adam [66]. They showed that the use of growth factors in their model increases the cell killing up to 20%. Based on the model of Anderson and Chaplain [27] McDougall [29] developed a model where the blood viscosity, pressure drop and mean capillary radii can be varied of the surrounding vessels of a solid tumor can be analyzed. The model shows that if there are highly interconnected vessels around the tumor there is a low drug delivery to the tumor itself. It shows that it is important to consider the vasculature around the tumor to find the optimal chemotherapy strategy.

The strategy of chemotherapy in combination with other treatments is being increasingly used. Powathil addressed this in recent publications [67, 68, 69] and showed ways to simulate and improve protocols of chemotherapy. It was demonstrated that the cytotoxic effect is dependent on many factors like timing of the drug delivery, time delay between the doses, heterogeneities of the cell cycle, the spatial distribution of the tumor and the surrounding microenvironment. It is noteworthy that these issues have been also investigated in older studies, e.g. using models of phase-specificity of chemotherapeutic drugs published in the 1990s [70]. In this section different methods were shown to model chemotherapy and effects that can lead to a better treatment strategy.

Most targeted cancer therapies use monoclonal antibodies directed against tumor-specific surface proteins or small-molecule drugs against intracellular targets (e.g. tyrosin kinases) [71]. Billy et al. [72] developed a model that simulates a treatment on the angiogenesis of tumors by gene therapy. The gene therapy is delivered by adenoviruses and influences, the antagonist of vascular endothelial growth factor, endostatin. The simulation showed that there is a critical treatment dose which is important to improve the efficacy.

TGF-β is a cytokine that has an immunosuppressive effect. In the model of Kirschner et al. [73] it was shown that a treatment with initial delivery of double stranded RNA into tumor cells that is cut by the enzyme Dicer into 21–23 segments known as siRNA inhibits TGF-β production and leads to a controlled oscillatory tumor behavior. Using a combination of experimental data and a mathematical model about the resistance against the monoclonal antibody panitumumab based on the Luria-Delbrück model [74], Diaz et al. [58] tested the development of mutations conferring resistance to the antibody. The simulation results suggested a combination of therapies where at least two pathways will be required. The use of ex-vivo activated alloreactive cytotoxic-T-lymphocytes (CTL) is another possibility to direct target the tumor. Kronik et al. [75] developed a mathematical model to investigate the effect of directly administrated CTL to glioblastomas. They showed that most sensitive parameters were the death rate of CTLs, the initial size of the tumor and the maximal growth rate.

Nanda et al. [76] developed a mathematical model simulating the drug imatinib mesylate that was approved in 2002 by the FDA for use in newly diagnosed cases of chronic myelogenous leukemia. The results show that a high dosing level from the beginning is optimal. Another interesting aspect of targeted therapy is the use of oncolytic viruses. Wein et al. [77] showed in their model that a single intratumoral injection in a solid tumor is not enough to effectively spread the virus. Also important is the suppression of the immune-mediated clearance of the virus. In the work of Mok et al. [78] two additional modifications are shown through mathematical modeling of herpes simplex viruses first the decreasing of the binding affinity of the virus and second the effective diffusion coefficient of the virus through degradation of the tumor extracellular matrix.

RADIOTHERAPY

The aim of radiotherapy is to destroy the tumor cells but not the host cells. This is possible if the tumor cells are more sensitive to irradiation than the host cells. Mathematical modeling can show strategies and improve treatment protocols to obtain an optimal patient treatment. In this sense Rockne et al. [79] present a model to investigate the response to various schedules and dose distribution on a virtual tumor. The advantage in the mathematical simulation is that the effect of radiation can be observed continuously. The model suggests that a radiation dose on daily basis is more effective than several treatments per day.

Another important aspect is the general response of cells to radiation. Richard et al. [80] used a cellular automaton model to investigate these mechanisms after low doses of radiation. Enderling et al. [81] developed a model that simulates the recurrence after radiotherapy. In the 2D simulations it was shown that if pre-malignant cells reside in the breast post-surgery and survive radiotherapy this cells could be the reason for a recurrence.

Tumor immune-cell interaction and immunotherapy

The immune system plays an important role in tumor progression. Immune processes with different components like chemokines, cytokines or different cell types that work together are highly complex and intertwined. Mathematical modeling has already provided deeper insights and helped to get fundamental knowledge and improve patient's treatment. For example De Boer et al. [82] developed a detailed model where they were able to show tumor regression and tumor growth dependent on the antigenicity of tumor-immune interaction. Tumour-infiltrating cytotoxic lymphocytes (TICLs) play an important role in tumor-immune interaction. Matzavinos et al. [83] developed a spatio-temporal model to investigate the interaction of TICLs and tumors. It is possible to simulate the spatio-temporal dynamics of TICLs in a solid tumor. Kirschner et al. [84] developed a model that includes immunotherapy with cultured immune cells that have anti-tumor reactivity and additionally IL-2. In simulations a total eradiation of the tumor was only possible with the immune therapy. In the model of de Pillis et al. [85] the cytolytic effectiveness of tumor specific T-cells was the most sensitive parameter. Following the simulation results the efficacy of the CD8+ T cells and the response to immunotherapy was correlating.

One therapy against superficial bladder cancer is the treatment with Bacillus Calmette-Guerin (BCG). Rentsch et al. [86] showed with their mathematical model that the dose of BCG and the treatment interval have a positive correlation of tumor extension. Wei [87] investigated this immunotherapy with a mathematical model and showed that the infection rate and the growth rate of the tumor are the most important parameters for a successful treatment. Rihan et al. [88] investigated the effect of adoptive cellular immunotherapy and found out that only a combination of the treatment with IL-2 can be used to clear the tumor.

In summary, major contributions for clinical oncology have been made by the modeling community. However, although many models were designed and tested for clinical applications, the use in routine setting is sparse. One way to overcome this is to develop models for very specific applications and rigorously test the performance and the predictive power. Furthermore, the use of the available knowledge should be also part of the decision process. We envision a computational decision support system which is using clinical data, molecular data, publicly available data, as well as simulation results of mathematical models to reach a decision for therapeutic strategy.

Conclusion

In this review we presented an overview of mathematical models for translational oncology and clinical oncology beginning with carcinogenesis and proceeding to the different cancer treatments. By doing so we intended to highlight recent developments in the field and emphasize the power of this theoretical work. As demonstrated in a number of studies, mathematical modeling and computational simulation can provide valuable insights into the molecular mechanisms of cancer, can improve diagnosis and prognosis of the disease, and pinpoint novel therapeutic targets. As can be seen in Figure 1, it is often difficult to attribute the generation of new knowledge either to the modeling or to the experimental work. Regardless the origin, the insights obtained from such cycles of experiments and modeling can improve our understanding of the complexity of cancer progression and eventually be used to stop or at least slow down the processes of tumor initiation, evolution and resistance to therapies.

ACKNOWLEDGEMENTS

This work was supported by the Austria Science Fund (Projects Doktoratskolleg W11 Molecular Cell Biology and Oncology and SFB F21 Cell Proliferation and Cell Death in Tumors), the Tiroler Standortagentur (Bioinformatics Tyrol), and by the Austrian Research Promotion Agency (FFG), project Oncotyrol. We apologize to the authors of papers not cited in this review due to space constraints.

COMPETING INTERESTS

The authors declare that they have no competing interests.

AUTHORS' CONTRIBUTION

RG, ME, PC, HH, and ZT carried out literature search and wrote the manuscript. ZT conceived the study. All authors read and approved the final manuscript.

REFERENCES

1. Vogelstein B, Papadopoulos N, Velculescu VE, Zhou S, Diaz LA, Kinzler KW: Cancer genome landscapes. Science. 2013, 339: 1546-1558.

2. Pabinger S, Dander A, Fischer M, Snajder R, Sperk M, Efremova M, Krabichler B, Speicher MR, Zschocke J, Trajanoski Z: A survey of tools for variant analysis of next-generation genome sequencing data. Brief Bioinform. 2013

3. Knudson AG: Mutation and cancer: statistical study of retinoblastoma. Proc Natl Acad Sci USA. 1971, 68: 820-823.

4. Nowell PC: The clonal evolution of tumor cell populations. Science. 1976, 194: 23-28.

5. Swierniak A, Kimmel M, Smieja J: Mathematical modeling as a tool for planning anticancer therapy. Eur J Pharmacol. 2009, 625: 108-121.

6. Lowengrub JS, Frieboes HB, Jin F, Chuang Y-L, Li X, Macklin P, Wise SM, Cristini V: Nonlinear modelling of cancer: bridging the gap between cells and tumours. Nonlinearity. 2010, 23: R1-R9.

7. Byrne HM, Alarcon T, Owen MR, Webb SD, Maini PK: Modelling aspects of cancer dynamics: a review. Philos Transact A Math Phys Eng Sci. 2006, 364: 1563-1578.

8. Deisboeck TS, Wang Z, Macklin P, Cristini V: Multiscale cancer modeling. Annu Rev Biomed Eng. 2011, 13: 127-155.

9. Stransky B, de Souza SJ: Modeling tumor evolutionary dynamics. Front Physiol. 2012, 3: 480

10. Fisher JC, Hollomon JH: A hypothesis for the origin of cancer foci. Cancer. 1951, 4: 916-918.

11. Nordling CO: A new theory on cancer-inducing mechanism. Br J Cancer. 1953, 7: 68-72.

12. Armitage P, Doll R: The age distribution of cancer and a multi-stage theory of carcinogenesis. Br J Cancer. 1954, 8: 1-12.

13. Ashley DJ: The two "hit" and multiple "hit" theories of carcinogenesis. Br J Cancer. 1969, 23: 313-328.

14. Moolgavkar SH, Knudson AG: Mutation and cancer: a model for human carcinogenesis. J Natl Cancer Inst. 1981, 66: 1037-1052.

15. Luebeck EG, Moolgavkar SH: Multistage carcinogenesis and the incidence of colorectal cancer. Proc Natl Acad Sci U S A. 2002, 99: 15095-15100.

16. Gatenby RA, Vincent TL: An evolutionary model of carcinogenesis. Cancer Res. 2003, 63: 6212-6220.

17. Hanahan D, Weinberg RA: The hallmarks of cancer. Cell. 2000, 100: 57-70. 10.

18. Greenspan H: Models for the growth of a solid tumor by diffusion. Stud Appl Math. 1972, 52: 317-340.

19. McElwain DLS, Ponzo PJ: A model for the growth of a solid tumor with non-uniform oxygen consumption. Math Biosci. 1977, 35: 267-279.

20. Greenspan HP: On the growth and stability of cell cultures and solid tumors. J Theor Biol. 1976, 56: 229-242.

21. Byrne HM, Chaplain MAJ: Modelling the role of cell-cell adhesion in the growth and development of carcinomas. Math Comput Model. 1996, 24: 1-17.

22. Balding D, McElwain DL: A mathematical model of tumour-induced capillary growth. J Theor Biol. 1985, 114: 53-73.

23. Byrne HM, Chaplain MA: Mathematical models for tumour angiogenesis: numerical simulations and nonlinear wave solutions. Bull Math Biol. 1995, 57: 461-486.

24. Chaplain MA: Mathematical modelling of angiogenesis. J Neurooncol. 2000, 50: 37-51.

25. Chaplain MA, Stuart AM: A model mechanism for the chemotactic response of endothelial cells to tumour angiogenesis factor. IMA J Math Appl Med Biol. 1993, 10: 149-168.

26. Levine HA, Pamuk S, Sleeman BD, Nilsen-Hamilton M: Mathematical modeling of capillary formation and development in tumor angiogenesis: penetration into the stroma. Bull Math Biol. 2001, 63: 801-863.

27. Anderson AR, Chaplain MA: Continuous and discrete mathematical models of tumor-induced angiogenesis. Bull Math Biol. 1998, 60: 857-899.

28. Mantzaris NV, Webb S, Othmer HG: Mathematical modeling of tumor-induced angiogenesis. J Math Biol. 2004, 49: 111-187.

29. McDougall SR, Anderson ARA, Chaplain MAJ, Sherratt JA: Mathematical modelling of flow through vascular networks: implications for tumour-induced angiogenesis and chemotherapy strategies. Bull Math Biol. 2002, 64: 673-702.

30. Stéphanou A, McDougall SR, Anderson ARA, Chaplain MAJ: Mathematical modelling of the influence of blood rheological properties upon adaptative tumour-induced angiogenesis. Math Comput Model. 2006, 44: 96-123.

31. Stéphanou A, McDougall SR, Anderson ARA, Chaplain MAJ: Mathematical modelling of flow in 2D and 3D vascular networks: applications to anti-angiogenic and chemotherapeutic drug strategies. Math Comput Model. 2005, 41: 1137-1156.

32. D' Onofrio A, Gandolfi A: Tumour eradication by antiangiogenic therapy: analysis and extensions of the model by Hahnfeldt et al. (1999). Math Biosci. 2004, 191: 159-184.

33. Ledzewicz U, Schaettler H: Anti-angiogenic therapy in cancer treatment as an optimal control problem. SIAM J Control Optim. 2007, 46 (3): 1052-1079.

34. Hahnfeldt P, Panigrahy D, Folkman J, Hlatky L: Tumor development under angiogenic signaling: a dynamical theory of tumor growth, treatment response, and postvascular dormancy. Cancer Res. 1999, 59: 4770-4775.

35. Merlo LMF, Pepper JW, Reid BJ, Maley CC: Cancer as an evolutionary and ecological process. Nat Rev Cancer. 2006, 6: 924-935.

36. Greaves M, Maley CC: Clonal evolution in cancer. Nature. 2012, 481: 306-313.

37. Haeno H, Iwasa Y, Michor F: The evolution of two mutations during clonal expansion. Genetics. 2007, 177: 2209-2221.

38. Nowak MA, Michor F, Komarova NL, Iwasa Y: Evolutionary dynamics of tumor suppressor gene inactivation. Proc Natl Acad Sci U S A. 2004, 101: 10635-10638.

39. Gerstung M, Eriksson N, Lin J, Vogelstein B, Beerenwinkel N: The temporal order of genetic and pathway alterations in tumorigenesis. PLoS One. 2011, 6: e27136

40. Durrett R, Schmidt D, Schweinsberg J: A waiting time problem arising from the study of multi-stage carcinogenesis. Ann Appl Probab. 2009, 19: 676-718.

41. Attolini CS-O, Michor F: Evolutionary theory of cancer. Ann N Y Acad Sci. 2009, 1168: 23-51.

42. Beerenwinkel N, Antal T, Dingli D, Traulsen A, Kinzler KW, Velculescu VE, Vogelstein B, Nowak MA: Genetic progression and the waiting time to cancer. PLoS Comput Biol. 2007, 3: e225

43. Bozic I, Antal T, Ohtsuki H, Carter H, Kim D, Chen S, Karchin R, Kinzler KW, Vogelstein B, Nowak MA: Accumulation of driver and passenger mutations during tumor progression. Proc Natl Acad Sci U S A. 2010, 107: 18545-18550.

44. Quaranta V, Rejniak KA, Gerlee P, Anderson ARA: Invasion emerges from cancer cell adaptation to competitive microenvironments: quantitative predictions from multiscale mathematical models. Semin Cancer Biol. 2008, 18: 338-348.

45. Lee H-O, Silva AS, Concilio S, Li Y-S, Slifker M, Gatenby RA, Cheng JD: Evolution of tumor invasiveness: the adaptive tumor microenvironment landscape model. Cancer Res. 2011, 71: 6327-6337.

46. Gatenby RA, Gillies RJ: A microenvironmental model of carcinogenesis. Nat Rev Cancer. 2008, 8: 56-61.

47. Goldie JH, Coldman AJ: A mathematic model for relating the drug sensitivity of tumors to their spontaneous mutation rate. Cancer Treat Rep. 1979, 63: 1727-1733.

48. Michor F, Nowak MA, Iwasa Y: Evolution of resistance to cancer therapy. Curr Pharm Des. 2006, 12: 261-271.

49. Komarova N: Stochastic modeling of drug resistance in cancer. J Theor Biol. 2006, 239: 351-366.

50. Komarova NL, Wodarz D: Drug resistance in cancer: principles of emergence and prevention. Proc Natl Acad Sci U S A. 2005, 102: 9714-9719.

51. Basanta D, Gatenby RA, Anderson ARA: Exploiting evolution to treat drug resistance: combination therapy and the double bind. Mol Pharm. 2012, 9: 914-921.

52. Swierniak A, Smieja J: Analysis and optimization of drug resistant and phase-specific cancer chemotherapy models. Math Biosci Eng MBE. 2005, 2: 657-670.

53. Kimmel M, Axelrod DE: Mathematical models of gene amplification with applications to cellular drug resistance and tumorigenicity. Genetics. 1990, 125: 633-644.

54. Kimmel M, Swierniak A, Polanski A: Infinite-dimensional model of evolution of drug resistance of cancer cells. J Math Syst Estim Contr. 1998, 8 (1): 1-16

55. Smieja J, Swierniak A: Different models of chemotherapy taking into account drug resistance stemming from gene amplification. Int. J. Appl Math Comp Sci. 2003, 13.3: 297-306.

56. Harnevo LE, Agur Z: Drug resistance as a dynamic process in a model for multistep gene amplification under various levels of selection stringency. Cancer Chemother Pharmacol. 1992, 30: 469-476.

57. Foo J, Michor F: Evolution of resistance to targeted anti-cancer therapies during continuous and pulsed administration strategies. PLoS Comput Biol. 2009, 5: e1000557

58. Diaz LA, Williams RT, Wu J, Kinde I, Hecht JR, Berlin J, Allen B, Bozic I, Reiter JG, Nowak MA, Kinzler KW, Oliner KS, Vogelstein B: The molecular evolution of acquired resistance to targeted EGFR blockade in colorectal cancers. Nature. 2012, 486: 537-540.

59. Bozic I, Reiter JG, Allen B, Antal T, Chatterjee K, Shah P, Moon YS, Yaqubie A, Kelly N, Le DT, Lipson EJ, Chapman PB, Diaz LA, Vogelstein B, Nowak MA: Evolutionary dynamics of cancer in response to targeted combination therapy. Elife. 2013, 2: e00747

60. Sawyers C: Targeted cancer therapy. Nature. 2004, 432: 294-297. Fister KR, Panetta JC: Optimal control applied to cell-cycle-specific cancer chemotherapy. SIAM J Appl Math. 2000, 60: 1059-1072.

61. Byrne HM, Owen MR, Alarcon T, Murphy J, Maini PK: Modelling the response of vascu

62. lar tumours to chemotherapy: a multiscale approach. Math Models Methods Appl Sci. 2006, 16: 1219-1241.

63. De Pillis LG, Gu W, Radunskaya AE: Mixed immunotherapy and chemotherapy of tumors: modeling, applications and biological interpretations. J Theor Biol. 2006, 238: 841-862.

64. De Pillis L, Radunskaya A: A mathematical model of immune response to tumor invasion. Proc Second MIT Conf Comput Fluid Solid Mech KJ Bathe Ed Fluid Solid Mech. 2003, Comput: Solid

65. Jackson TL, Byrne HM: A mathematical model to study the effects of drug resistance and vasculature on the response of solid tumors to chemotherapy. Math Biosci. 2000, 164: 17-38.

66. Panetta JC, Adam J: A mathematical model of cycle-specific chemotherapy. Math Comput Model. 1995, 22: 67-82.

67. Powathil GG, Adamson DJA, Chaplain MAJ: Towards predicting the response of a solid tumour to chemotherapy and radiotherapy treatments: clinical insights from a computational model. PLoS Comput Biol. 2013, 9: e1003120

68. Powathil G, Kohandel M, Sivaloganathan S, Oza A, Milosevic M: Mathematical modeling of brain tumors: effects of radiotherapy and chemotherapy. Phys Med Biol. 2007, 52: 3291-3306.

69. Powathil GG, Gordon KE, Hill LA, Chaplain MAJ: Modelling the effects of cell-cycle heterogeneity on the response of a solid tumour to chemotherapy: biological insights from a hybrid multiscale cellular automaton model. J Theor Biol. 2012, 308: 1-19.

70. Cojocaru L, Agur Z: A theoretical analysis of interval drug dosing for cell-cycle-phase-specific drugs. Math Biosci. 1992, 109: 85-97.

71. Bozic I, Allen B, Nowak MA: Dynamics of targeted cancer therapy. Trends Mol Med. 2012, 18: 311-316.

72. Billy F, Ribba B, Saut O, Morre-Trouilhet H, Colin T, Bresch D, Boissel J-P, Grenier E, Flandrois J-P: A pharmacologically based multiscale mathematical model of angiogenesis and its

use in investigating the efficacy of a new cancer treatment strategy. J Theor Biol. 2009, 260: 545-562.

73. Kirschner DE, Jackson TL, Arciero JC: A mathematical model of tumor-immune evasion and siRNA treatment. Discrete Contin Dyn Syst - Ser B. 2003, 4: 39-58.

74. Dewanji A, Luebeck EG, Moolgavkar SH: A generalized Luria-Delbrück model. Math Biosci. 2005, 197: 140-152. Kronik N, Kogan Y, Vainstein V, Agur Z: Improving alloreactive CTL immunotherapy for malignant gliomas using a simulation model of their interactive dynamics. Cancer Immunol Immunother CII. 2008, 57: 425-439.

75. Nanda S, Moore H, Lenhart S: Optimal control of treatment in a mathematical model of chronic myelogenous leukemia. Math Biosci. 2007, 210: 143-156.

76. Wein LM, Wu JT, Kirn DH: Validation and analysis of a mathematical model of a replication-competent oncolytic virus for cancer treatment: implications for virus design and delivery. Cancer Res. 2003, 63: 1317-1324.

77. Mok W, Stylianopoulos T, Boucher Y, Jain RK: Mathematical modeling of herpes simplex virus distribution in solid tumors: implications for cancer gene therapy. Clin Cancer Res Off J Am Assoc Cancer Res. 2009, 15: 2352-2360.

78. Rockne R, Alvord EC, Rockhill JK, Swanson KR: A mathematical model for brain tumor response to radiation therapy. J Math Biol. 2008, 58: 561-578

79. Richard M, Kirkby KJ, Webb RP, Kirkby NF: A mathematical model of response of cells to radiation. Nucl Instruments Methods Phys Res Sect B Beam Interactions Mater Atoms. 2007, 255: 18-22.

80. Enderling H, Anderson ARA, Chaplain MAJ: A model of breast carcinogenesis and recurrence after radiotherapy. PAMM. 2007, 7: 1121701-1121702.

81. De Boer RJ, Hogeweg P, Dullens HF, De Weger RA, Den Otter W: Macrophage T lymphocyte interactions in the anti-tumor

immune response: a mathematical mode. J Immunol Baltim Md 1950. 1985, 134: 2748-2758.

82. Matzavinos A, Chaplain MAJ, Kuznetsov VA: Mathematical modelling of the spatio-temporal response of cytotoxic T-lymphocytes to a solid tumour. Math Med Biol J IMA. 2004, 21: 1-34.

83. Kirschner D, Panetta JC: Modeling immunotherapy of the tumor-immune interaction. J Math Biol. 1998, 37: 235-252.

84. De Pillis LG, Radunskaya AE, Wiseman CL: A validated mathematical model of cell-mediated immune response to tumor growth. Cancer Res. 2005, 65: 7950-7958.

85. Rentsch CA, Biot C, Gsponer JR, Bachmann A, Albert ML, Breban R: BCG-mediated bladder cancer immunotherapy: identifying determinants of treatment response using a calibrated mathematical model. PLoS One. 2013, 8: e56327-

86. Wei H-C: A numerical study of a mathematical model of pulsed immunotherapy for superficial bladder cancer. Jpn J Ind Appl Math. 2013, 30: 441-452.

87. Rihan FA, Safan M, Abdeen MA, Abdel Rahman D: Qualitative and computational analysis of a mathematical model for tumor-immune interactions. J Appl Math. 2012, Article ID 475720: 19

2

CHAPTER

Data Modeling Methods in Clinical Trials: Experiences from The Clinical Trial Methods in Neurodegenerative Diseases Project

Athanasios Anastasiou[1], Emmanuel Ifeachor[1] , John Zajicek[2]

[1]Signal Processing and Multimedia Communications Research Group, University of Plymouth, Drake Circus, Plymouth, UK. 2 Institute of Health Service Research (Peninsula College of Medicine and Dentistry.

OBJECTIVES

Clinical trials often generate large and diverse datasets. Data models are used to capture and organise the elements of the data in a meaningful way so that they can be stored and utilised by computer systems and support clinical decision making. This paper presents the data modeling considerations within the 'Clinical Trial Methods in Neurodegenerative Diseases' (CTMND) project funded by the NIHR [http://www.ctmnd.org].

The project adopts a holistic approach for the investigation of the suitability and efficiency of clinical observations in neurodegenerative diseases clinical studies. This ongoing research in novel clinical and surrogate outcome measures will be incorporated in an online data collection and analysis system to facilitate clinical trials and relevant research, taking into account, wherever possible, routinely collected NHS data.

This paper presents ongoing research in the project's data modeling aspects with the following objectives:

1. To review the current state of the art data models for capturing clinical information from the available literature.

2. To compare and contrast their features against the data management requirements of the project and outline the key factors that affected the adoption of a specific model for the CTMND project's information system.

METHODS

A set of key papers and past reviews were collected from the currently available literature detailing the characteristics of standard data models used in healthcare such as CDISC's ODM, Health Level 7 and others. The data models and associated approaches were compared and contrasted with each other by taking into account best practices and guidelines emerging from organizations such as the Object Management Group (OMG). Finally, having concluded in a specific modeling approach we were also able to look forward at the possibilities that a particular solution enables and propose a flexible way to model clinical trial data.

RESULTS

This review highlights a number of key data management and organization considerations that affect the adoption of a specific data model given the project specifications and resource constraints. The key factors were Current Resources, Interoperability (with current and future systems), Documentation and Reference Implementation availability.

CONCLUSIONS

Given the dynamic environment of clinical trials as well as the project's objectives to propose novel outcome measures, we comment on the suitability of the Dual Model approach for the efficient organization of clinical study data but more importantly for its flexibility in modeling novel outcomes with minimal software maintenance. According to this approach, a handful of elementary data structures (numbers, character sequences, lists, trees and others) are made available to a higher level model that is responsible for their ordering and semantics. Additionally we provide specific details regarding system implementation.

3

CHAPTER

Biostatistical and Medical Statistics Graduate Education

Michael B Brimacombe

Department of Biostatistics, KUMC, Kansas City, USA

ABSTRACT

The development of graduate education in biostatistics and medical statistics is discussed in the context of training within a medical center setting. The need for medical researchers to employ a wide variety of statistical designs in clinical, genetic, basic science and translational settings justifies the ongoing integration of biostatistical training into medical center educational settings and informs its content. The integration of large data issues are a challenge.

BIOSTATISTICAL AND MEDICAL STATISTICS GRADUATE EDUCATION

The quantitative education of graduate students in the health sciences is an important area of consideration in a modern internet based world. The onset of massive datasets and so-called Data Science and the related growth of computer science and engineering based programs in this area [1], has implied a need to carefully delineate and justify health-related statistical and biostatistical training, its core elements and how it may incorporate aspects of BigData approaches to the analysis of data structures in the health sciences. Such approaches typically reflect the massive nature of many health related databases and clinical data repositories where standard statistical methods may not easily apply. Even practical issues such as creating data architectures and ontologies that can be searched and subject to statistical analysis are challenging [1].

More generally, understanding how the concepts of randomness apply to the design and interpretation of clinical trials, observational medical studies and the improvement of clinical practice generally is of relevance to a wide audience of healthcare students and professionals [2]. Here we focus on graduate level training for students in the area of biostatistics in a medical center or school of public health environment, where the learning of statistical theory must be balanced with a wide variety of health related applications.

DEFINITION

Statistics and biostatistics are areas of applied mathematics that are required for the proper design and analysis of most experimental or observational data. They require an understanding of probability, related statistical models and theories of inferential probability. These areas are somewhat unique as their progenitors (Fisher [3], Pearson [4], and Jeffreys [5]) were mostly applied scientists who wrestled with the need to interpret real world experiments and data in the context of scientifically rooted mathematical or probability models, with applications including early population genetics, time series analysis, biometry and toxicology.

Biostatistics is a discipline with a long history and wide area of application, often termed biometrics in its early days, a word that has now taken on other meanings, it examines the application of statistical theory to biological problems of various types. With the onset of clinical trials and pharmaceutical studies, it has developed in the directions of clinical trial methodology, health outcomes research, survival analysis, longitudinal models and generalized linear models of various types [2, 6].

The role of probability in inference and (clinical) decision making is now well established [7]. The importance of incorporating randomly occurring variation when interpreting clinical results justifies the application of statistical techniques in a wide variety of medical and health related decision making. Elements of randomness also underlie most experimental settings and the interpretation of the many physiologic and biochemical measurements. At a minimum the understanding of p-values, confidence intervals, t-tests, ANOVA tables and basic statistical models such as linear or logistic regression, are an important aspect of the quantitative literacy that medical professionals, clinical researchers and basic scientists should all possess to interpret medical research findings [2]. The related area of Bayesian statistics with subjective risk and decision based clinical assessment is also a growing subject requiring appropriate integration into quantitative curriculums [8].

WHERE DOES IT LIVE

Historically biostatistical training has occurred in mathematics departments, with the hope that students can develop the ability to collaborate or consult with scientists. Over time this training has begun to migrate in some settings to medical centers and biostatistics departments in medical center settings, where faculty and the offered training exist in a medically oriented research setting. This results in a slightly less mathematically oriented curriculum, but a more focused set of priorities, often emphasizing collaboration with basic scientists and clinicians.

Schools of public health have also become home to biostatistical programs [9]. Here the focus is often on larger clinical trials and large healthcare database settings, different from the laboratory or clinical trials related studies that often predominated in medical centers. Biostatistics as a component of a medical center setting with or without a school of public health reflects a web of inter-related relationships and opportunities; supporting cancer center clinical and genetic research, nursing related health outcomes research, basic science research and clinical trials oriented research. This provides many opportunities for real world application as an essential component of biostatistics training. Often the responsibility for dealing with large scale data management falls to biostatisticians in addition to more traditional research efforts, though the growth of medical informatics is creating a need for informatics specialists who may or may not utilize statistical analysis in their work, focusing instead on Data Science and empirical models [10].

The overlap with medical or clinical settings may also draw biostatisticians into the world of training M.D.s, clinicians and related health professionals active in clinical medicine. In this setting, biostatistician groups or departments may offer certificates or degrees in aspects of clinical research for clinicians seeking to engage in research. This is an area where determining the degree of quantitative literacy M.D.s active in research should possess is open to further development [11]. Often these settings have a large online component to them and the challenge of teaching statistics online to medical students arises [12].

CHALLENGE: BIG DATA AND DATA SCIENCE

A challenge to biostatistics programs and all statistical programs is how to incorporate, interact with the phenomenon of BigData. Data science as it is being called is mostly the handling of massive datasets with multiple strata and thousands of variables. There is often limited statistical input apart from many different types of clustering algorithm or multiple association programs. Clinical data repositories and massive hospital data systems are becoming common and viewed as a potential tool for healthcare quality assessment, clinical trials and health outcomes research. Under the name of Informatics such computer science and engineering driven approaches are drawing the attention of the National Institutes of Health, creating massive clinical databases. However visualizing the data in such settings is a challenge, much less applying standard statistical methodology (standard errors and p-values) that have may have little or no meaning in very large sample sizes.

As this new science finds its home, perhaps on the engineering and computer science side of the ledger, it will be a challenge to biostatisticians to remain involved in the development of software and methodology in this area. This will impact support for training and the practical development and growth of biostatistical programs.

Much of this future is currently being decided [1] and often in the medical school or center setting where cost is a concern vis-a-vis output of research results.

TEACHING PHILOSOPHY & CURRICULUM

Biostatistics, at its core, is a mathematical subject, with its own set of core ideas, concepts and controversies. It typically differs from mathematical statistics training by incorporating more medically oriented statistical techniques and applications, and less theoretical probability theory. The teaching of a mathematical subject is by definition a challenge. Principles and mathematically justified procedures must be clearly and carefully defined and explained. Problems are often proof-based in advanced theory courses and require detailed applications in applied courses. Exposure to advanced computational skills and methods are also expected along the way. As retention is a goal, especially at the advanced levels, where ultimately a thesis must be produced, didactic teaching and mentoring is often emphasized. This may be at odds with the push to online in much of medical training.

The biostatistics curriculum in particular is a mixture of theory and application, reflecting the reality of modeling biological and medical phenomenon. This includes the analysis of real world datasets, which makes biostatistics and statistics somewhat unique in the mathematical world. The fitting of theorized mathematical models to data and the use of the resulting expected properties of these models for inference is the central challenge of much biostatistics. This requires exposure on the part of the student to consulting and collaboration, often with clinicians and basic scientists. This type of mentoring is a challenge but necessary to produce a quality biostatistician/researcher at the end of their studies.

The teaching of mathematics has a long and studied history. These tend to focus on basic concepts and mostly undergraduate education [13]. The philosophy of teaching statistics reflects similar considerations [14], and the evaluation of various approaches to the teaching of statistics is an ongoing effort [15, 16]. Given the wide variety of applications for which biostatisticians must train, if the student does not have a strong mathematical background, they may struggle with coursework and the writing of a thesis, but if they lack experience with health related applications, they may also face difficulties with the consulting aspect of the training process.

Given the cutting edge nature of much applied biostatistical work, there is ongoing discussion regarding the intellectual content of the biostatistics curriculum. This typically includes; modern statistical computing, frequentist methods, nonparametrics, likelihood and Bayesian approaches, mathematical statistics, design of experiments, linear models, survival analysis, longitudinal analysis, latent variable models, nonlinear models, categorical data analysis and clinical trials. See Table 1.

Table 1. List of typical core PhD, electives and future choices

Core Ph.D.	Electives	Future
Theoretical statistics	Advanced epidemiology	Visualization of large databases
Survival analysis	Analysis of healthcare data	Data algorithm development
Categorical analysis	Introduction to genomics	Computational platforms and structures
Longitudinal analysis	Aspects of U.S. medicare data	Large database inference
Structural equations models	U.S. Veterans Affairs data analysis	Programming big data
Multivariate analysis	Image analysis	Genetic function and structure
Bayesian analysis	Advanced programming	Analysis of restricted models

Such a mixture of theory, practice and applied modeling oriented courses allows the student to blend the designing of mathematical models and their underlying optimality properties with the fitting of these models to biomedical data. Interpreting the actual import of the fitted models is often a joint exercise with both biostatistician and clinician/researcher discussing the relevance and importance of the results. In the context of public health for example, the need to be fluent in various statistical methodologies and knowledgeable in applications to health policy, epidemiology and other public health areas is important.

The development of electives, primarily related to the application of statistical and informatic methods in related fields is important to broaden and fill out the education of future biostatistians. Epidemiology, disease processes, genomics, large data handling and investigation, informatics, health economics and outcomes research are all possible electives as are aspects of genetics. In reality, access to these courses may be limited by resources, agreements between school and departments and must be carefully organized. The teaching loads attached to the rather conservative listing given in Table 2 is a serious challenge in smaller departments.

Table 2. Areas and types of applications

Large data	Public health/health economics and policy	Medicine	Future
Genomics	Smoking cessation	Diabetes	Illness behavioral profiles
Brain imaging	Prevention	Neurological conditions	Health data mining
Medicare data	Utilization	Pallative care	Cost patterns identification
Clinical repository development	Health economics	Fetal and newborn care	Rare disorder identification

Give the polymath nature of many biostatistical positions and the mostly underappreciated ability of statisticians to modify the statistical design template for each applied setting; it is very useful for students to become fluent in the qualitative aspects of their thesis research. Students with knowledge of an applied area can more easily function as a collaborator and build a future career. The "generalist" label is not generally respected in research settings. Required and essential, defining of many biostatistical positions, but often not respected.

LEARNING CENTERS

It is worth considering the various learning formats available in a medical center setting in relation to biostatistics. Medical training has to a large extent moved to an online platform, with specific goals and a very parsed approach to the dissemination of knowledge. At the undergraduate level, the courses are very focused on aspects of anatomy, physiology, biochemistry etc. and the goal is to both succeed at the course level and the medical board exams. As such exposure to statistics or epidemiology tends to be in the form of brief three-week intensive courses with the learning geared to success on the exams. Research level biostatistics may become relevant in the last medical school year or at the resident/fellow stage.

In this context, biostatistical courses, often in standard fourteen week formats, are a separate entity, focused on M.S. and Ph.D. level training, often viewed as old-fashioned given the need to teach higher level mathematics at a pace which allows students to grasp, digest and apply theoretical concepts. Allied health, health policy and nursing typically also provide Ph.D. level training and as such will tend to have similar didactic teaching formats in the medical center context. The need to be aware of this diversity and integrate the different teaching cultures is a necessity in a medical center environment where the end product is well trained collaborative science, scientists and funded research.

ONLINE ISSUES

Much teaching in medical school and health related settings has migrated to online settings where the material presented to students can be standardized and presented in an easily updated format [17, 18]. While this may be appropriate for information and techniques relevant to medical training, the teaching of higher-level mathematical and statistical ideas in online formats is very new and remains an area of ongoing assessment [16, 19]. When applications are the core of the material, the online setting can be very useful, but if methods themselves are to be taught, including their theoretical justifications, the use of online settings remains an open issue. Much of the usefulness and relevance of online formats, especially in regard to retention, graduation rates and the quality of the graduates, remains a question for study [17, 18, 19]. While the technology is new and impressive, the ability of students to absorb mathematically related ideas from rather restrictive online settings seems to be successful for students who can learn independently, a path that becomes more difficult as the student moves to higher level courses [16].

The standardization of teaching imposed on much of the medical curriculum may not be a template for the presentation and learning of mathematical and statistical ideas. The development of online settings specifically tailored for these ideas in medical settings is very much a work in progress [12, 19]. Extending these into settings directly relevant to the statistical aspects of medical research is an ongoing challenge. Assessment and longer term follow-up will be required as online platforms become more prevalent.

HEALTH RESEARCH AND STATISTICAL IDEAS

The defining of new statistical ideas and their applications is a key aspect of Ph.D. training. In biostatistics, the development and investigation of specific types of models and their properties tends to support most research in the setting of graduate programs. For example categorical models, longitudinal models, survival models have been the subject of a very large number of dissertation projects over the past thirty years.

However, looking to the future, the new world of massive data, some of it clinical or genetic in nature, is certainly imposing and growing in importance as a challenge to biostatistical methodology, very little of which was developed for such large settings. Questions such as "Is the current level of training in this area appropriate?" "Can the world of informatics be left to non-statisticians?" seem very relevant.

Genomics and the search for genetic structures within large genomic databases have emerged as a component of training. Bioinformatics is often viewed as a separate entity, and much of it is not directly statistical in nature, as the issue of how to process such large datasets is a dominating consideration. Public health also requires the analysis of large healthcare related databases, both specifically and in relation to issues affecting the ongoing restructuring of the U.S. health system and is also a key area of potential research for biostatistics. BigData issues arise throughout here and many standard statistical methods perform poorly if analyses are to be conducted on millions of health care records.

In deciding what is a potentially important area of future research, it helps to consider where biostatisticians will fit in future research endeavors in both academia and industry. Are biostatisticians to form a bridge among the various applied disciplines, functioning as quantitative and design oriented collaborators with their own areas of application, or are they to function as technicians supporting clinicians and basic scientists including geneticists at a high level of application. Biostatisticians tend to have success as lead applied researchers in secondary data analysis of for example Veterans Affairs or Census based health outcomes research, but this requires the biostatistician be very knowledgeable in the content area. This is also true in public health settings. Professors looking to guide students in selecting topics relevant to the future of statistical analysis may consider these issues, especially in relation to the interests and abilities of the individual student. Areas of research that provide the most supportive environment for a research or applied statistical career should be identified and emphasized, a challenge as these change over time. This should be considered both internally to biostatistical research and in relation to overall health research related funding.

SUPPORT OVERVIEW

It is necessary to discuss support and type of support when taking on M.S. or in particular Ph.D. students for a four-to-five year period of training. The past may not be a useful guide to the present and future. Training grants as may become more relevant to the funding of students, rather than incorporating student support directly into research grants to individual investigators. Quantitative methods may require general training, but they may also come to be seen as essential to the basic or clinical sciences, requiring specific training outside of the standard biostatistical context.

Timelines are an issue as they affect and guide the level and length of support that can be given to each student in pursuit of the degree. Most programs have a maximum of seven years, but funding typically runs to a maximum of four or five years. Programs that develop students will have to plan for longer time frames as the definition and toolkit that defines biostatistics broadens and includes more coursework and consulting experience. Biostatistical students, once at a certain level of expertise, can function directly as biostatistical support on many applied projects and funding of biostatistical training as research assistant/consultant support to collaborative projects is a possibility. This is certainly true in medical center environments, which often provide many such opportunities, though sometimes have barriers of various sorts to optimal levels of collaboration [20].

SUMMARY

Development of an academic and intellectual setting where students can learn and further develop advanced biostatistical methods and applied applications, is the ongoing challenge of most biostatistical graduate programs, especially in the medical center environment. In these settings excellent opportunities abound for collaboration and exposure to cutting edge research. But much concern is focused on deteriorating funding levels and a lack of experience with data driven science. There is also the related issue of being available to train medical students and clinical researchers in a variety of statistical approaches. Online platforms are common in general medical education, however remain a challenge in relation to more mathematically oriented material. The final product of meeting and integrating these various challenges will be the development of the next generation of biostatistical scientists in many of the new scientific areas of health and medical research and the place of department of biostatistics in the medical center setting.

COMPETING INTERESTS

The author declares that he has no competing interests.

REFERENCES

1. West D: Big Data for Education: Data Mining, Data Analytics, and web Dashboards. 2012, Washington, D.C.: The Brookings Institution

2. Petrie A, Sabin C: Medical Statistics at a Glance. 2009, New York, NY: Wiley-Blackwell, 3

3. Kruskal W: The significance of Fisher: a review of R. A. Fisher. The life of a scientist. J Am Statist Assoc. 1980, 75 (1980): 1019-1030.

4. Pearson ES: Karl Pearson: An Appreciation of Some Aspects of his Life and Work. 1938, Cambridge, UK: Cambridge University Press

5. Jeffreys H: Theory of Probability. 1961, Oxford: Clarendon Press, 3

6. Zolman JF: Biostatistics: Experimental Design and Statistical Inference. 1993, New York: Oxford University Press

7. Banning M: A review of clinical decision making: models and current research. J Clin Nurs. 2007, 17 (2): 187-95. Epub 2007 Mar 1

8. Ashby D, Smith AFM: Evidence-based medicine as Bayesian decision-making. Statist Med. 2000, 19: 3291-3305. 10.1002/1097-0258(20001215)19:23<3291::AID-SIM627>3.0.CO;2-T.

9. Brownson RC, Kreuter MW, Arrington BA, True WR: Translating scientific discoveries into public health action: can schools of public health move us forward?. Public Health Rep. 2006, 121 (1): 97-103.

10. Cleveland WS: Data science: an action plan for expanding the technical areas of the field of statistics. Int Statist Rev. 2001, 69 (1): 21-26.

11. Reyna VF, Brainerd CJ: The importance of mathematics in health and human judgement: numeracy, risk communication and medical decision making. Learn Individ Differ. 2007, 17 (2): 147-159.

12. Bland JM: Teaching statistics to medical students using problem-based learning: the Australian experience. BMC Med Educ. 2004, 4: 31-10.1186/1472-6920-4-31.

13. Thurston WP: Mathematics education. Notices of the AMS. 1990, 37 (7): 844-850.

14. Snee RD: What's missing in statistical education?. Am Stat. 1993, 47 (2): 149-154.

15. Mills JD, Raju D: Teaching statistics online: a decade's review of the literature about what works. J Stat Educ. 2011, 19 (2): http://www.amstat.org/publications/jse/v19n2/mills.pdf.

16. Kreiner DS: A mastery-based approach to teaching statistics online. Int J Instr Media. 2006, 33: 73-79.

17. Wong G, Greenhalgh T, Pawson R: Internet-based medical education: a realist review of what works, for whom and in what circumstances. BMC Med Educ. 2010, 10: 12-10.1186/1472-6920-10-12.http://www.biomedcentral.com/1472-6920/10/12.

18. Skjødt B, Worm KJ: Does peer learning or higher levels of e-learning improve learning abilities? A randomized controlled trial. Med Educ Online. 2013, 18: 21877

19. Sedgwick P, Hall A: Teaching medical students and doctors how to communicate risk: combining the teaching of statistics with communication skills. BMJ. 2003, 327 (7417): 694-695. 10.1136/bmj.327.7417.694. doi: 10.1136/bmj.327.7417.694

20. Kon AA: The Clinical and Translational Science Award (CTSA) consortium and the translational research model. Am J Bioethics. 2008, 8 (3): 58-60.

4

CHAPTER

Assessment of Risk of Bias in Translational Science

Andre Barkhordarian[1] , Peter Pellionisz[2], Mona Dousti[1], Vivian Lam[1], Lauren Gleason[1], Mahsa Dousti[1], Josemar Moura[3] and Francesco Chiappelli[1,4]

[1]*Oral Biology & Medicine, School of Dentistry, UCLA, Evidence-Based Decisions Practice-Based Research Network, Los Angeles, USA.*

[2]*Pre-medical program, UCLA, Los Angeles, USA.*

[3]*School of Medicine, Universidade Federal de Minas Gerais, Belo Horizonte, Brazil.*

[4]*Evidence-Based Decisions Practice-Based Research Network, UCLA School of Dentistry, CHS 63-090, 10833 Le Conte Avenue, Los Angeles, CA 90095-1668, USA.*

ABSTRACT

Risk of bias in translational medicine may take one of three forms: A. a systematic error of methodology as it pertains to measurement or sampling (e.g., selection bias), B. a systematic defect of design that leads to estimates of experimental and control groups, and of effect sizes that substantially deviate from true values (e.g., information bias), and C. a systematic distortion of the analytical process, which results in a misrepresentation of the data with consequential errors of inference (e.g., inferential bias). Risk of bias can seriously adulterate the internal and the external validity of a clinical study, and, unless it is identified and systematically evaluated, can seriously hamper the process of comparative effectiveness and efficacy research and analysis for practice. The Cochrane Group and the Agency for Healthcare Research and Quality have independently developed instruments for assessing the meta-construct of risk of bias. The present article begins to discuss this dialectic.

BACKGROUND

As recently discussed in this journal [1], translational medicine is a rapidly evolving field. In its most recent conceptualization, it consists of two primary domains: translational research proper and translational effectiveness. This distinction arises from a cogent articulation of the fundamental construct of translational medicine in particular, and of translational health care in general.

The Institute of Medicine's Clinical Research Roundtable conceptualized the field as being composed by two fundamental "blocks": one translational "block" (T1) was defined as "...the transfer of new understandings of disease mechanisms gained in the laboratory into the development of new methods for diagnosis, therapy, and prevention and their first testing in humans...", and the second translational "block" (T2) was described as "...the translation of results from clinical studies into everyday clinical practice and health decision making..." [2]. These are clearly two distinct facets of one meta-construct, as outlined in Figure 1. As signaled by others, "...Referring to T1 and T2 by the same name—translational research—has become a source of some confusion. The 2 spheres are alike in name only. Their goals, settings, study designs, and investigators differ..." [3].

For the last five years at least, the Federal responsibilities for "block" T1 and T2 have been clearly delineated. The National Institutes of Health (NIH) predominantly concerns itself with translational research proper - the bench-to-bedside enterprise (T1); the Agency for Healthcare Research Quality (AHRQ) focuses on the result-translation enterprise (T2). Specifically: "...the ultimate goal [of AHRQ] is research translation—that is, making sure that findings from AHRQ research are widely disseminated and ready to be used in everyday health care decision-making..." [6]. The terminology of translational effectiveness has emerged as a means of distinguishing the T2 block from T1.

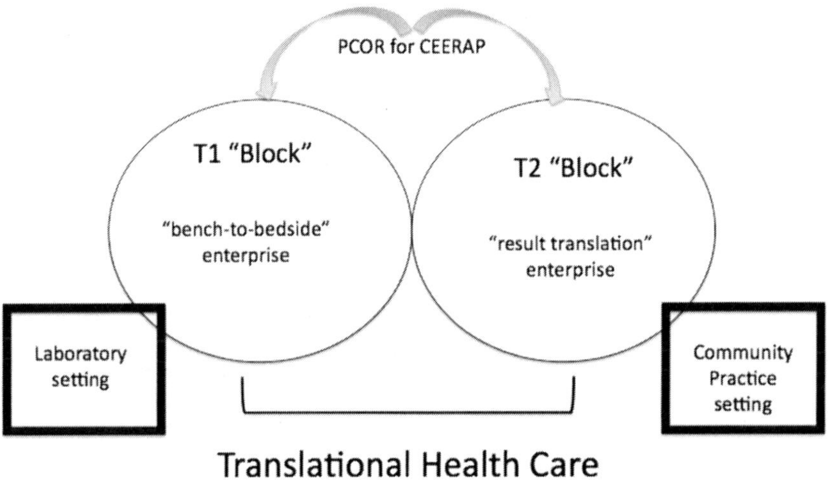

Figure 1. Schematic representation of the meta-construct of translational health care in general, and translational medicine in particular, which consists of two fundamental constructs: the T1 "block" (as per Institute of Medicine's Clinical Research Roundtable nomenclature), which represents the transfer of new understandings of disease mechanisms gained in the laboratory into the development of new methods for diagnosis, therapy, and prevention as well as their first testing in humans, and the T2 "block", which pertains to translation of results from clinical studies into everyday clinical practice and health decision making [**[3]**]. The two "blocks" are inextricably intertwined because they jointly strive toward patient-centered research outcomes (PCOR) through the process of comparative effectiveness and efficacy research/review and analysis for clinical practice (CEERAP). The domain of each construct is distinct, since the "block" T1 is set in the context of a laboratory infrastructure within a nurturing academic institution, whereas the setting of "block" T2 is typically community-based (e.g., patient-centered medical/dental home/neighborhoods [4]; "communities of practice" [5]).

Therefore, the bench-to-bedside enterprise pertains to translational research, and the result-translation enterprise describes translational effectiveness. The meta-construct of translational health care (viz., translational medicine) thus consists of these two fundamental constructs: translational research and translational effectiveness, which have distinct purposes, protocols and products, while both converging on the same goal of new and improved means of individualized patient-centered diagnostic and prognostic care.

It is important to note that the U.S. Patient Protection and Affordable Care Act (PPACA, 23 March 2010) has created an environment that facilitates the pursuit of translational health care because it emphasizes patient-centered outcomes research (PCOR). That is to say, it fosters the transaction between translational research (i.e., "block" T1) and translational effectiveness (i.e., "block" T2), and favors the establishment of communities of practice-research interaction. The latter, now recognized as practice-based research networks, incorporate three or more clinical practices in the community into a community of practices network coordinated by an academic center of research.

Practice-based research networks may be a third "block" (T3) in translational health care and they could be conceptualized as a stepping-stone, a go-between bench-to-bedside translational research and result-translation translational effectiveness [7]. Alternatively, practice-based research networks represent the practical entities where the transaction between translational research and translational effectiveness can most optimally be undertaken. It is within the context of the practice-based research network that the process of bench-to-bedside can best seamlessly proceed, and it is within the framework of the practice-based research network that the best evidence of results can be most efficiently translated into practice and be utilized in evidence-based clinical decision-making, viz. translational effectiveness.

TRANSLATIONAL EFFECTIVENESS

As noted, translational effectiveness represents the translation of the best available evidence in the clinical practice to ensure its utilization in clinical decisions. Translational effectiveness fosters evidence-based revisions of clinical practice guidelines. It also encourages effectiveness-focused, patient-centered and evidence-based clinical decision-making. Translational effectiveness rests not only on the expertise of the clinical staff and the empowerment of patients, caregivers and stakeholders, but also, and most importantly on the best available evidence [8].

The pursuit of the best available evidence is the foundation of translational effectiveness and more generally of translational medicine in evidence-based health care. The best available evidence is obtained through a systematic process driven by a research question/hypothesis that is articulated about clearly stated criteria that pertain to the patient (P), the interventions (I) under consideration (C), for the sought clinical outcome (O), within a given timeline (T) and clinical setting (S). PICOTS is tested on the appropriate bibliometric sample, with tools of measurements designed to establish the level (e.g., CONSORT) and the quality of the evidence. Statistical and meta-analytical inferences, often enhanced by analyses of clinical relevance [9], converge into the formulation of the consensus of the best available evidence. Its dissemination to all stakeholders is key to increase their health literacy in order to ensure their full participation in the utilization of the best available evidence in clinical decisions, viz., translational effectiveness.

To be clear, translational effectiveness – and, in the perspective discussed above, translational health care – is anchored on obtaining the best available evidence, which emerges from highest quality research. High quality of research is obtained when errors are minimized.

In an early conceptualization [10], errors in research were presented as those situations that threaten the internal and the external validity of a research study – that is, conditions that impede either the study's reproducibility, or its generalization. In point of fact, threats to internal and external validity [10] represent specific aspects of systematic errors (i.e., bias) in the research design, methodology and data analysis. Thence emerged a branch of science that seeks to understand, control and reduce risk of bias in research.

RISK OF BIAS AND THE BEST AVAILABLE EVIDENCE

It follows that the best available evidence comes from research with the fewest threats to internal and to external validity – that is to say, the fewest systematic errors: the lowest risk of bias. Quality of research, as defined in the field of research synthesis [11], has become synonymous with low bias and contained risk of bias [12, 13, 14, 15].

Several years ago, the Cochrane group embarked on a new strategy for assessing the quality of research studies by examining potential sources of bias. Certain original areas of potential bias in research were identified, which pertain to (a) the sampling and the sample allocation process, to measurement, and to other related sources of errors (reliability of testing), (b) design issues, including blinding, selection and drop-out, and design-specific caveats, and (c) analysis-related biases.

A Risk of Bias tool was created (Cochrane Risk of Bias), which covered six specific domains:

1. selection bias,
2. performance bias,
3. detection bias,
4. attrition bias,
5. reporting bias, and
6. other research protocol-related biases.

Assessments were made within each domain by one or more items specific for certain aspects of the domain. Each items was scored in two distinct steps:

1. the support for judgment was intended to provide a succinct free-text description of the domain being queried;
2. each item was scored high, low, or unclear risk of material bias (defined here as "...bias of sufficient magnitude to have a notable effect on the results or conclusions..." [16]).

It was advocated that assessments across items in the tool should be critically summarized for each outcome within each report. These critical summaries were to inform the investigator so that the primary meta-analysis could be performed either only on studies at low risk of bias, or for the studies stratified according to risk of bias [16]. This is a form of acceptable sampling analysis designed to yield increased homogeneity of meta-analytical outcomes [17]. Alternatively, the homogeneity of the meta-analysis can be further enhanced by means of the more direct quality-effects meta-analysis inferential model [18].

Clearly, one among the major drawbacks of the Cochrane Risk of Bias tool is the subjective nature of its assessment protocol. In an effort to correct for this inherent weakness of the instrument, the Cochrane group produced detailed criteria for making judgments about the risk of bias from each individual item [16]. Moreover, Cochrane recommended that judgments be made independently by at least two people, with any discrepancies resolved by discussion [16]. This approach to increase the reliability of measurement in research synthesis protocols is akin to that described by us [19, 20] and by AHRQ [21].

In an effort to aid clinicians and patients in making effective health care related decisions, AHRQ developed an alternative Risk of Bias instrument for enabling systematical evaluation of evidence reporting [22]. The AHRQ Risk of Bias instrument was created to monitor four primary domains:

1. risk of bias: design, methodology, analysis scoring – low, medium, high

2. consistency: extent of similarity in effect sizes across studies within a bibliome scoring – consistent, inconsistent, unknown

3. directness: unidirectional link between the interventions of interest and the sought outcome, as opposed to multiple links in a casual chain scoring – direct, indirect

4. precision: extent of certainty for estimate of effect with respect to the outcome scoring – precise, imprecise In addition, four secondary domains were identified:

a. Dose response association: pattern of a larger effect with greater exposure (Present/Not Present/Not Applicable or Not Tested)

b. Confounders: consideration of confounding variables (Present/Absent)

c. Strength of association: likelihood that the observed effect is large enough that it cannot have occurred solely as a result of bias from potential confounding factors (Strong/Weak)

d. Publication bias

The AHRQ Risk of Bias instrument is also designed to yield an overall grade of the estimated risk of bias in quality reporting:

- Strength of Evidence Grades (scored as high – moderate - low – insufficient)
- This global assessment, in addition to incorporating the assessments above, also rates:
- major benefit
- major harm
- jointly benefits and harms
- outcomes most relevant to patients, clinicians, and stakeholders

The AHRQ Risk of Bias instrument suffers from the same two major limitations as the Cochrane tool:

1. lack of formal psychometric validation as most other tools in the field [21], and
2. providing a subjective and not quantifiable assessment.

To begin the process of engaging in a systematic dialectic of the two instruments in terms of their respective construct and content validity, it is necessary to validate each for reliability and validity either by means of the classic psychometric theory or generalizability (G) theory, which allows the simultaneous estimation of multiple sources of measurement error variance (i.e., facets) while generalizing the main findings across the different study facets. G theory is particularly useful in clinical care analysis of this type, because it permits the assessment of the reliability of clinical assessment pro-tocols. The reliability and minimal detectable changes across varied combinations of these facets are then simply calculated [23]. However, it is recommended that G theory determination follow classic theory psychometric assessment.

Therefore, we have commenced a process of revision the AHRQ Risk of Bias instrument by rendering questions in primary domains quantifiable (scaled 1–4), which established the intra-rater reliability ($r = 0.94$, $p < 0.05$), and the criterion validity ($r = 0.96$, $p < 0.05$) for this instrument (Figure 2).

A similar revision of the Cochrane Risk of Bias tool may also yield promising validation data. G theory validation of both tools will follow. Together, these results will enable a critical and systematic dialectical comparison of the Cochrane and the AHRQ Risk of Bias measures.

DISCUSSION

The critical evaluation of the best available evidence is critical to patient-centered care, because biased research findings are fundamentally invalid and potentially harmful to the patient. Depending upon the tool of measurement, the validity of an instrument in a study is obtained by means of criterion validity through correlation coefficients. Criterion validity refers to the extent to which one measures or predicts the value of another measure or quality based on a previously well-established criterion. There are other domains of validity such as: construct validity and content validity that are rather more descriptive than quantitative. Reliability however is used to describe the consistency of a measure, the extent to which a measurement is repeatable. It is commonly assessed quantitatively by correlation coefficients. Inter-rater reliability is rendered as a Pearson correlation coefficient between two independent readers, and establishes equivalence of ratings

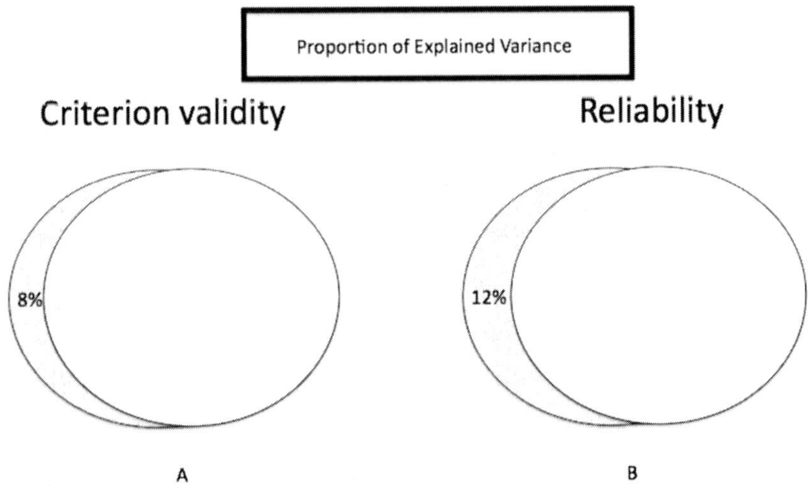

Figure 2. Proportion of shared variance in criterion validity (A) and inter-rater reliability (B) in the AHRQ Risk of Bias instrument revised as described. Two raters were trained and standardized [20] with the revised AHRQ Risk of Bias and with the R-Wong instrument, which has been previously validated [24]. Each rater independently produced ratings on a sample of research reports with both instruments on two separate occasions, 1–2 months apart. Pearson correlation coefficient was used to compute the respective associations. The figure shows Venn diagrams to illustrate the intersection between each two sets data used in the correlations. The overlap between the sets in each panel represents the proportion of shared variance for that correlation. The percent of unexplained variance is given in the insert of each panel.

produced by independent observers or readers. Intra-rater reliability is determined by repeated measurement performed by the same subject (rater/reader) at two different points in time to assess the correlation or strength of association of the two sets of scores.

To establish the reliability of research quality assessment tools it is necessary, as we previously noted [20]:

a) to train multiple readers in sharing a common view for the cognitive interpretation of each item. Readers must possess declarative knowledge a factual form of information known to be static in nature a certain depth of knowledge and understanding of the facts about which they are reviewing the literature. They must also have procedural knowledge known as imperative knowledge that can be directly applied to a task in this case a clear understanding of the fundamental concepts of research methodology, design, analysis and inference.

b) to train the readers to read and evaluate the quality of a set of papers independently and blindly. They must also be trained to self-monitor and self-assess their skills for the purpose of insuring quality control.

c) to refine the process until the inter-rater correlation coefficient and Cohen coefficient of agreement are about 0.9 (over 81% shared variance). This will establishes that the degree of attained agreement among well-trained readers is beyond chance.

d) to obtain independent and blind reading assessments from readers on reports under study.

e) to compute means and standard deviation of scores for each question across the reports, repeat process if the coefficient of variations are greater than 5% (i.e., less than 5% error among the readers across each questions).

The quantification provided by instruments validated in such a manner to assess the quality and the relative lack of bias in the research evidence allows for the analysis of the scores by means of the acceptable sampling protocol. Acceptance sampling is a statistical procedure that uses statistical sampling to determine whether a given lot, in this case evidence gathered from an identified set of published reports, should be accepted or rejected [12, 25]. Acceptable sampling of the best available evidence can be obtained by:

- convention: accept the top 10 percentile of papers based on the score of the quality of the evidence (e.g., low Risk of Bias);
- confidence interval (CI^{95}): accept the papers whose scores fall at of beyond the upper confidence limit at 95%, obtained with mean and variance of the scores of the entire bibliome;
- statistical analysis: accept the papers that sustain sequential repeated Friedman analysis.
- To be clear, the Friedman test is a non-parametric equivalent of the analysis of variance for factorial designs. The process requires the 4-E process outlined below:
- establishing a significant Friedman outcome, which indicates significant differences in scores among the individual reports being tested for quality;
- examining marginal means and standard deviations to identify inconsistencies, and to identify the uniformly strong reports across all the domains tested by the quality instrument
- excluding those reports that show quality weakness or bias
- executing the Friedman analysis again, and repeating the 4-E process as many times as necessary, in a statistical process akin to hierarchical regression, to eliminate the evidence reports that exhibit egregious weakness, based on the analysis of the marginal values, and to retain only the group of report that harbor homogeneously strong evidence.

Taken together, and considering the domain and the structure of both tools, expectations are that these analyses will confirm that these instruments are two related entities, each measuring distinct aspects of bias. We anticipate that future research will establish that both tools assess complementary sub-constructs of one and the same archetype meta-construct of research quality.

ACKNOWLEDGEMENT

The work was supported in part by Fulbright Specialist grant (FC). The authors thank the students and collaborators of the EBD Research Group for their constructive comments and criticisms leading to this work. The last author also thanks the students and faculty who participated in Advanced Evidence-Based Health Care at Universidade Federal de Minas Gerais, Belo Horizonte, Brazil (Fall 2012), where these thoughts were originally conceived.

COMPETING INTERESTS

The authors declare that they have no competing interests.

AUTHORS' CONTRIBUTIONS

This paper was planned by Dr. FC, and he is responsible for the initial drafting of the manuscript. AB provided the overall conception of the project, and crafting of the fundamental dialectics between the Cochrane and the AHRQ Risk of Bias instruments. Dr. JM did the initial exploratory work on the AHRQ Risk of Bias instrument, which was then substantially advanced and systematically analyzed by PP with the assistance of VL, LG, MoD and Dr. MaD. All authors contributed critical revisions of the manuscript for important intellectual content, and read and approved the final manuscript.

REFERENCES

1. Jiang F, Zhang J, Wang X, Shen X: Important steps to improve translation from medical research to health policy. J Trans Med. 2013, 11: 33-

2. Sung NS, Crowley WF, Genel M, Salber P, Sandy L, Sherwood LM, Johnson SB, Catanese V, Tilson H, Getz K, Larson EL, Scheinberg D, Reece EA, Slavkin H, Dobs A, Grebb J, Martinez

RA, Korn A, Rimoin D: Central challenges facing the national clinical research enterprise. JAMA. 2003, 289: 1278-1287

3. Woolf SH: The meaning of translational research and why it matters. JAMA. 2008, 299 (2): 211-213.

4. Chiappelli F: From translational research to translational effectiveness: the "patient-centered dental home" model. Dental Hypotheses. 2011, 2: 105-112.

5. Maida C: Building communities of practice in comparative effectiveness research. Comparative effectiveness and efficacy research and analysis for practice (CEERAP): applications for treatment options in health care. Edited by: Chiappelli F, Brant X, Cajulis C. 2012, Heidelberg: Springer–Verlag, Chapter 1

6. Agency for Healthcare Research and Quality: Budget estimates for appropriations committees, fiscal year (FY) 2008: performance budget submission for congressional justification. Performance budget overview. 2008, http://www.ahrq.gov/about/cj2008/cjweb08a.htm#Statement. Accessed 11 May 2013

7. Westfall JM, Mold J, Fagnan L: Practice-based research—"blue highways" on the NIH roadmap. JAMA. 2007, 297: 403-406.

8. Chiappelli F, Brant X, Cajulis C: Comparative effectiveness and efficacy research and analysis for practice (CEERAP) applications for treatment options in health care. 2012, Heidelberg: Springer–Verlag

9. Dousti M, Ramchandani MH, Chiappelli F: Evidence-based clinical significance in health care: toward an inferential analysis of clinical relevance. Dental Hypotheses. 2011, 2: 165-177.

10. Campbell D, Stanley J: Experimental and quasi-experimental designs for research. 1963, Chicago, IL: Rand-McNally

11. Littell JH, Corcoran J, Pillai V: Research synthesis reports and meta-analysis. 2008, New York, NY: Oxford Univeristy Press

12. Chiappelli F: The science of research synthesis: a manual of evidence-based research for the health sciences. 2008, Hauppauge NY: NovaScience Publisher, Inc

13. Higgins JPT, Green S: Cochrane handbook for systematic reviews of interventions version 5.0.1. 2008, Chichester, West Sussex, UK: John Wiley & Sons. The Cochrane collaboration

14. CRD: Systematic Reviews: CRD's guidance for undertaking reviews in health care. National Institute for Health Research (NIHR). 2009, University of York, UK: Center for reviews and dissemination

15. McDonald KM, Chang C, Schultz E: Closing the quality Gap: revisiting the state of the science. Summary report. 2013, U.S. Department of Health & Human Services. AHRQ, Rockville, MD: Summary report. AHRQ publication No. 12(13)-E017

16. Higgins JP, Altman DG, Gøtzsche PC, Jüni P, Moher D, Oxman AD, Savovic J, Schulz KF, Weeks L, Sterne JA, Cochrane Bias Methods Group; Cochrane Statistical Methods Group: The Cochrane Collaboration's tool for assessing risk of bias in randomised trials. British Med J. 2011, 343: d5928-

17. Bartolucci AA, Hillegas WB: Overview, strengths, and limitations of systematic reviews and meta-analyses. Understanding evidence-based practice: toward optimizing clinical outcomes. Edited by: Chiappelli F, Brant XMC, Oluwadara OO, Neagos N, Ramchandani MH. 2010, Heidelberg: Springer–Verlag, Chap 2**Google Scholar**

18. Jüni P, Altman DG, Egger M: Systematic reviews in health care: assessing the quality of controlled clinical trials. British Med J. 2001, 323 (7303): 42-46.

19. Chiappelli F, Arora R, Barkhordarian B, Ramchandani M: Evidence-based clinical research: toward a New conceptualization of the level and the quality of the evidence. Annals Ayurvedic Med. 2012, 1: 60-64.

20. Chiappelli F, Barkhordarian A, Arora R, Phi L, Giroux A, Uyeda M, Kung K, Ramchandani M: Reliability of quality

assessments in research synthesis: securing the highest quality bioinformation for HIT. Bioinformation. 2012, 8: 691-694.

21. Hartling L, Hamm M, Milne A, Vandermeer B, Santaguida PL, Ansari M, Tsertsvadze A, Hempel S, Shekelle P, Dryden DM: Validity and inter-rater reliability testing of quality assessment instruments. 2012, S. Department of Health & Human Services. AHRQ, Rockville, MD: AHRQ publication No. 12-EHC039-EF

22. Viswanathan M, Ansari MT, Berkman ND, Chang S, Hartling L, McPheeters LM, Santaguida PL, Shamliyan T, Singh K, Tsertsvadze A, Treadwell JR: Assessing the risk of bias of individual studies in systematic reviews of health care interventions. 2012, U.S. Department of Health & Human Services. AHRQ, Rockville, MD: AHRQ publication No. 12-EHC047-EF

23. Shavelson RJ, Webb NM: Generalizability theory: 1973–1980. Br J Math Stat Psychol. 1981, 34: 133-166. 10.1111/j.2044-8317.1981.tb00625.x.

24. Chiappelli F, Navarro AM, Moradi DR, Manfrini E, Prolo P: Evidence-based research in complementary and alternative medicine III: treatment of patients with Alzheimer's disease. Evidence-Based Comp Alter Med. 2006, 3: 411-424.

25. Montgomery C: Statistical quality control: a modern introduction. 2009, Chichester, West Sussex, UK: Johm Wiley & sons

5

CHAPTER

Genetic Algorithm and Ensemble Systems for Multi-biometric Cancellable Recognition

Canuto AMP[1], Pintro F[1] and Fairhurst MC[2]

[1] Department of Informatics and Applied Mathematics Federal University of RN, Brazil 2 School of Engineering and Digital Arts University of Kent, Canterbury, UK

ABSTRACT

Biometrics usually provides several advantages over traditional forms of identity authentication. However, there are some concerns about the security of personal biometric data, while these systems need to ensure their integrity and public acceptance. The idea of cancellable biometrics has been introduced to overcome these security concerns. In addition, an important way to increase security and performance in biometric systems is the multi-biometric approach, which combines different sources of biometric information. This paper investigates the benefits that optimized ensemble systems and cancellable transformation functions can provide to multibiometric authentication systems. The main aim of the work reported here is to provide more security and better performance in the multi-biometric authentication process. We use as examples two different biometric modalities (face and voice) separately and in the multi-modal context (multi-biometric). The datasets used in this analysis were TIMIT for voice and the AR Face dataset for Face. As a result of this analysis, we will observe that the use of cancellable transformations in the multi-biometric dataset increases the accuracy level for the ensemble systems.

Keywords: Ensemble systems; Cancellable Biometrics; Genetic Algorithms

INTRODUCTION

Biometrics have been extensively used in diverse identity authentication applications [1-5]. These systems use human physical characteristics in order to guarantee the veracity of a claimed identity of a given user. Using biometric s avoids problems found in more traditional identification scenarios, such as the vulnerabilities of passwords and PIN-based systems. Biometric traits provide a number of desirable properties with respect to their use in an authentication system, such as reliability, convenience and universality, but their principal advantage is in binding data or activity unequivocally to an individual person. Thus, biometricbased authentication systems have stimulated an evolution in the verification and identification of individuals [6].

An important concern in biometric-based systems is related to the security of biometric data, mainly when a biometric template is compromised, perhaps because it is lost or stolen, or through unauthorized copies. It is important to emphasis that biometric information is permanently related to a specific user and cannot be changed in the event of template compromise. Therefore, a fundamental requirement to promote future deployment of biometric-based authentication systems is the development of techniques that allow the use of biometric data without compromising system security. Cancellable biometrics has been proposed to address these security issues, since they apply functions (generally not invertible) on the original biometric data in order to obtain transformed or intentionally-distorted representations [7]. It is the transformed representations which are used by the authentication system. In the case of data compromise, a biometric template can then be replaced through the application of a new transformation function [7].

An important way to increase security and performance (identification accuracy) in biometrics systems is to adopt a multibiometric approach. This fuses multiple sources of biometric information to combine identity evidence (discriminating information) in order to enhance classification performance [8]. Multi-biometric systems can be configured in different ways: for example, multi-sensor, multi-algorithm, multi-instance, multi-sample, and multi-modal systems [8]. In this paper we will focus on two configurations, the multi-algorithm (different transformation functions) and the multi-modal (different biometric modalities) approaches. Using a multi-biometric recognition system is expected to improve accuracy and help to defeat spoofing attacks. On the other hand, using cancellable biometrics aims to increase the security of biometric data. The combination of these two elements, however, aims to achieve a win-win scenario of security, performance and privacy. However, the combination of template protection methods and multi-biometrics has not been fully explored in the literature. There are some studies, such as those reported in [9-14], but most of these are based on cryptosystems methods.

In this paper, we propose the use of the multi-biometric approach with cancellable biometric data. In order to achieve efficiency in the proposed configuration, we apply an optimized ensemble system as the main fusion structure to combine the different information sources. In an ensemble system, each input pattern is handled in a parallel way by different classification modules (ensemble components), which separately produce their estimates of the class label [15]. These individual results are then fused by a combination module, which is responsible for producing the overall ensemble decision

In previous work, [14,16], we applied ensemble systems to cancellable biometrics and achieved very promising results, demonstrating that the use of ensemble systems improves the accuracy of cancellable biometrics. However, we noticed that some cancellable transformations can degrade the accuracy level of ensemble systems. Therefore, in order to increase the effectiveness of the ensemble systems, a genetic algorithm is applied in three separate parts of the design of an ensemble system for biometric recognition, aiming to maximize the performance of these systems. The first genetic algorithm is used in the cancellable transformation (preprocessing phase), and its goal is to improve the efficiency of the discretization process of the cancellable transformation through the use of optimized discrimination intervals. The second GA selects features for the individual classifiers of the ensembles and aims to add diversity to these systems. Finally, the third GA tries to improve the performance of ensemble systems through the use of an optimized set of weights that are used along with the output of the individual classifiers to define the final output of the ensemble systems (weighted combination methods).

Therefore, in this paper, we will show that we can improve even further the performance of cancellable multi-biometric processing through the use of more efficient ensemble systems. We also contribute to a better performance in terms of accuracy and reliability in the identification of the individual, an aspect of increasing importance as systems are more widely applied. Therefore, we can state that the main contributions of this paper can be described as follows:

1. Use cancellable transformations in multi-algorithm fusion of the chosen multi-biometric approach;

2. Apply two different biometric modalities, face and voice, either using the same cancellable transformation (multi-modal fusion) or using different cancellable transformations (multi-modal and multi-algorithm fusion);

3. Use ensemble systems as the fusion approach for the multi-biometric recognition;

4. Optimize the recognition process, using genetic algorithms in the preprocessing (adaptation of a cancellable transformation and feature selection) and in the structure of the ensemble systems (set of weights to be used in the combination module).

This paper is divided into nine sections and structured as follows. A review of related research is presented in Section 2. Multibiometric template protection methods are described in Section 3, while Section 4 presents a detailed explanation of cancellable biometric data, focusing on the cancellable transformations used in this paper. In Section 5, we describe the main concepts of ensemble systems and the genetic algorithms are described in Section 6. The experimental work is presented in Section 7, while Section 8 presents and discusses the experimental results. Finally, in Section 9, some final observations about this work are presented.

RELATED WORK

There are many studies reported in the literature which use genetic algorithms in the biometric-based recognition process (either using the original or cancellable data). These studies usually present efficient ways of dealing with the main problems involved in biometric-based authentication systems, such as in [17-24].

For original biometric data, it is described by Parsi et al. in [22] a new approach which applies a feature selection method using GAs. This work is based on facial recognition where GAs are used to select the most significant features of the dataset, which are subsequently classified by a k-NN (k-Nearest Neighbour) classifier in an adaptive system, called Training Swap. In the proposed technique, the alternative fitness function swaps the GA test and training data in each generation and the resulting fitness is evaluated. According to the authors, when using this approach, the GA does not converge quickly for a local minimum and the rate of final recognition is reinforced. The presented results show a significant improvement in performance, testifying to the efficiency of GAs when used in attribute selection. Still in the context of original biometric data, the use of GAs in multi-sample biometric recognition is proposed by Tan et al. in [23], using two sets of minutiae extracted from two different fingerprints. According to the authors, this technique aims to solve the problems found in low-quality images of fingerprints that present disorder or significant occlusions and clutter of minutiae features. The experimental results show that the proposed approach can achieve good performance, even when a great number of poor quality fingerprints are used as input to the system.

For cancellable biometric data, in Jeong, et al. [21], for instance, a genetic algorithm is applied in the pre-processing phase of a multi-sample biometric system. It uses features of face images extracted through two techniques: PCA (Principal Component Analysis) and ICA (Independent Component Analysis). Then, the image samples are normalized and transformed by a weight matrix that is determined by means of a genetic algorithm. This weight matrix is formed by an optimized weight vector that minimizes the error rate, providing an adjustment in the attributes of the original dataset through a fitness evaluation. According to the authors, this process results in a considerably improved system performance. In the sequence, the two datasets (normalized and transformed) are combined by the random addition of normalized and transformed attributes. This combination provides an improvement in the level of precision achieved and also generates a non-invertible transformed dataset.

Unlike most of this reported work, in this paper we propose to use genetic algorithms in three different situations, in which the first two are in the pre-processing phase, as in [21,22,24]. In addition, we apply a GA in the recognition structure (ensemble system) in order to obtain the most effective recognition structure to be used in the multi-biometric cancellable recognition.

MULTI-BIOMETRIC RECOGNITION

There are many practical applications where the adoption of a single biometric modality is not able to meet all the required performance criteria. It is well known that the use of only one biometric modality tends to decrease the capability of biometricbased systems to have the needed requirements for an efficient system, in terms of performance (identification accuracy) and security (more difficult of being attacked). This problem may be more acute when working with cancellable data, where we have an increase in the complexity of the recognition process. Hence, solutions which involve the combination of different biometric sources (i.e. multi-biometric recognition) are of increasing interest. Multi-source fusion may occur in different phases of the recognition process: pre-processing (feature or sensor-level fusion), after the scores of the identification systems are produced (score-level) to the final phase, after a decision has been made (decision-level). In this paper, a score-level approach is considered, since this is the most natural choice when working with ensemble systems. Additionally, we can fuse the biometric data in several ways, such as:

- Multi-sensor: Only one biometric modality is used and the combination is made using different sources (sensors);
- Multi-algorithm: Only one biometric modality is used and we apply different recognition methods;
- Multi-sample: Only one biometric modality is used and we apply different pre-processing methods (feature extractors, different fingers or eye) of this biometric modality;
- Multi-modal: The combination of more than one biometric modality.

In this paper, we combine biometric data using multi-algorithm and multi-modal fusion approaches. The multi-biometric approach can be applied to either the original or the cancellable biometric data, and a number of attempts have been made to combine multibiometric recognition with cancellable biometrics, such as in [9-13]. However, most of these studies are based on cryptosystems template protection and using feature-level fusion.

CANCELLABLE BIOMETRIC DATA

The fact that biometric traits are unique and are permanently related to a user makes the security of biometric systems an important issue, since it is impossible to achieve its substitution or cancellation in the case of data compromise. This is one of the biggest problems in biometric-based systems. One of the solutions to this problem is the storage of a protected biometric model instead of the original biometric sample. In doing this, we eliminate any possibility of leakage of the original biometric trait [25]. In the literature, we can find many biometric template protection methods that, according to Jain et al. [7], can be divided into two types, which are: Biometric cryptosystems (some public information about the biometric templates is stored and a cryptographybased procedure is applied) and Feature transformations, or simply cancellable transformations, (a transformation function *(f)* is applied to the biometric template *(T)* and only the transformed template*(f(T))* is stored in the dataset).

According to the characteristics of the transformation function *f*, the feature transformation can be further divided into two classes: salting and non- invertible transformations. In the salting approach, the used transformation function *f* is invertible and, therefore, its security is based on a secret key or password [26]. Thus, if an intruder obtains access to the security key, the biometric data will be at risk. On the other hand, non-invertible transformations use one-way functions, making it computationally difficult or impossible to achieve an inversion of the transformed model, even having access to the security key. In our work reported here, we will focus on the use of non-invertible transformation functions. Hence, in the remainder of the present article, the terms transformation function or cancellable transformation will be taken as referring to the non-invertible case. We will use three cancellable transformations that will be presented in the next three subsections.

BIOHASHING

Biohashing uses a cancellable transformation that transforms the original biometric samples into a non-invertible number [27]. This technique has originally been used with biometric modalities such as fingerprint [27]. In this paper, we have applied this cancellable transformation to the face and voice biometric modalities. The original Biohashing procedure can be described as follows.

1. With the original biometric model $\Gamma \in R^n$, with n being the number of attributes of Γ, a set of pseudo-random vectors $\{p_i \in R^n \mid i = 1, ..., m\}$ is generated, where m is the number of vectors of dimension n and $m \leq n$;

2. The Gram-Schmidt algorithm is then applied in $\{p_i \in R^n \mid i = 1, ..., m\}$ to obtain m orthonormal vectors $\{o_i \in R^n \mid i = 1, ..., m\}$;

3. The inner product between the original biometric vector Γ and each pseudo- random *orthonormal vector* o_i is calculated, $\{(\Gamma \mid o_i) \mid i = 1, ..., m\}$, where $(o \mid o)$ indicates the inner product operation.

4. Finally, a binary discretization of the values obtained in the inner products is performed and we obtain an m-bit

Biohashing model, $\{b = b_i \mid i = 1, ..., m\}$, where: with τ being an empirically determined threshold.

$$b_i = \begin{cases} 0, if\langle \Gamma \mid o_i \rangle \leq \tau \\ 1, if\langle \Gamma \mid o_i \rangle > \tau \end{cases} \quad (1)$$

In this paper, we use an adaptation of this model, which was originally proposed by Pintro in [28]. This adaptation modifies step 4 of the standard Biohashing procedure (discretization function). It consists of two basic steps, which are: discretization of data into 4 values [0;0.33;0.66;1], instead of only 2 values [0;1], and the use of GAs to determine which are the optimal intervals for discretization. The purpose of using more discretization values is to enlarge the space of coding, enabling a better representation of the transformed dataset, without losing the characteristics of the Biohashing function. An initial investigation has led us to select 4 as the number of possible values for the discretization. Therefore the proposed discretization step is implemented as follows. First, a standard normalization is carried out on the result of step 3. Then, the normalized data is discretized according to the following intervals:

$$b_i = \begin{cases} 0, & if \quad 0 \leq \langle \Gamma \mid o_i \rangle < a \\ 0.33, & if \quad a \leq \langle \Gamma \mid o_i \rangle < b \\ 0.66, & if \quad b \leq \langle \Gamma \mid o_i \rangle < c \\ 1, & if \quad c \leq \langle \Gamma \mid o_i \rangle \leq 1 \end{cases} \quad (2)$$

The values for the discretization coefficients a, b and c of Eq. 2 are deter- mined by a genetic algorithm. The most important parameter in the Biohashing function is *m*, which represents the number of pseudo-random orthonormal vectors. This value must be determined empirically and corresponds to the number of attributes for each instance of the transformed dataset.

INTERPOLATION

This function generates a new biometric model based on the extraction of points of an interpolation process which is applied in the attributes of the original biometric model. The use of an interpolation-based method for obtaining cancellable biometric data was originally proposed by Pintro in [28] and, in this work, we adapt its use for face and voice modalities. It is a simple method and it adds the security level of a biometric system, since an inversion of the trans- formed function is difficult to achieve. This method then satisfies two main requirements for a cancellable transformation, efficiency and simplicity. The interpolation process is described as follows.

1. For each sample of the original biometric model $\Gamma \in R^n$, where n is the number of attributes of Γ, the interpolation polynomial of the attributes of the biometric model is applied to obtain a function *f(x)*. Therefore, we have a function *f(x)* for each biometric sample of the dataset. It is important to use a polynomial function with a significant degree g, usually given by the highest degree supported by the computational system, in order to have good approximation functions of the discretized data;

2. A vector of random numbers is generated $\delta \in R^d$ for all users. It consists of uniformly distributed pseudo random numbers, where d is the dimension of δ. The value of d is empirically defined and can have an impact on the behaviour of the model (usually $d = n$);

3. We then apply individually all created interpolation functions *f(x)* to the vector δ, generating the output the transformed dataset.

In the cases where the current random vector is corrupted or stolen, a new random vector can be used and we obtain a different transformed vector. Also, the interpolation model depends on variables such as the size *d* (step 2) of the random vector and the degree of the polynomial interpolator *g*.

BIO CONVOLVING

The BioConvolving function applies linear combinations of sub-parts of the original biometric template to create the protected template. The original biometric sequences are divided into *W* non-overlapping segments, based on a randomly selected transformation key *d*. Then, the transformed functions are obtained by performing a linear convolution between the resulting segments. This approach was originally proposed for use with a handwritten signature biometric [29] but here we apply it to face and voice data. A general description of BioConvolving is presented as follows.

1. Define the number of segments to divide the original biometric model (W).

2. Select randomly a number ($W-1$) of values d_j. The selected numbers have to be an integer between 1 and 99. In addition, these numbers must be ranked in an increasing order. The selected values are arranged in a vector $d = [d0, ..., dW]$, having kept $d_0 = 0$ and $d_W = 100$. The vector d represents the key of the adopted transformation.

3. Convert the values d_j into b_j based on the following function $b_j = round((\frac{d_j}{100})*n), j = 0, ..., W$, where n is the number of attributes and round represents the nearest integer,

4. Divide the original sequence $\Gamma \in R^n$, into W segments $\Gamma(q)$ of length $N_q = b_q - b_q - 1$ and which lies in the interval $[b_q - 1, b_q]$ of the attributes;

5. Apply the linear convolution of the functions $f(\Gamma(q))$, $q = 1..W$ to obtain the transformed function

$$f = \Gamma(1) * ... * \Gamma(W) \tag{3}$$

A transformed function is thus obtained through the linear convolutions of parts of the corresponding original functions Γ. Due to the convolution operation in step 3, the length of the transformed functions is equal to $K = n-W+1$, being therefore almost the same as the original data. Final signal normalization is then applied, oriented to obtain zero mean and unit standard deviation transformed functions. Different transformed results can be obtained from the same original functions, simply varying the size or the values of the parameter key *d*.

Ensemble Systems

As already noted, a natural way to combine different biometric sources is through the fusion of experts, an approach producing what are generally referred to as multi-classifier systems or ensemble systems [15]. Figure 1 illustrates the general structure of an ensemble system, which is composed of a set of c individual classifiers (ICs) which are organized in a parallel configuration. Therefore, unlabelled patterns $\{x_i \in R^d \,|i = 1, 2, ..., n\}$ are presented to all individual classifiers in a parallel way and a combination method combines their output to produce the overall output of the system $O = C\ omb(y_j\ ), \{y_j = (y_{j1}\ , ..., y_{jk} \,|j = 1, ..., c \text{ and } k = 1, ..., l\}$, where the number of individual classifiers is defined by c and l describes the number of labels in a dataset (Figure 1).

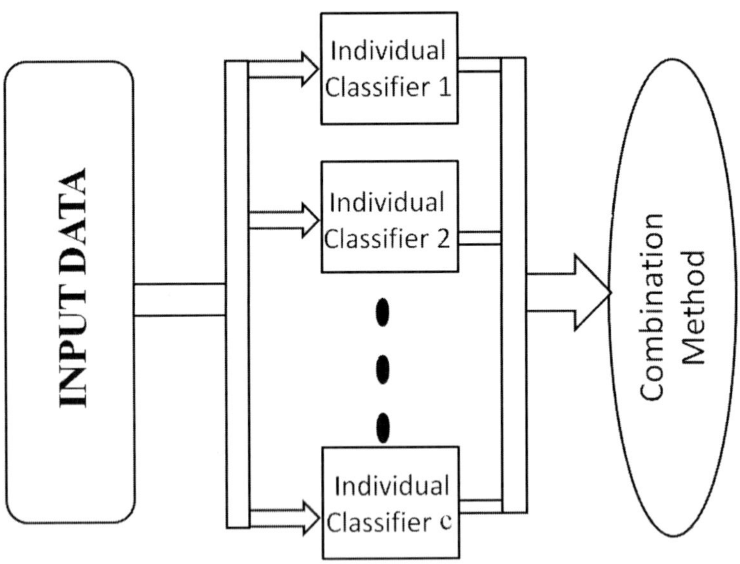

Figure 1: The general structure of an ensemble system

For ensemble systems, individual classifiers must offer complementary information about an input pattern and this complementary information tends to increase the effectiveness of the whole recognition process [15,30]. There- fore, it is important, when designing ensembles, to consider carefully individual components (classifiers) of an ensemble and its combination technique. With regard to the first of these, the ensemble size (number of individual classifiers) and composition (classification algorithms that comprise the ensemble systems) must be defined.

The design of an ensemble system can adopt of one two principal broad structures, designated respectively, heterogeneous or homogeneous structures. Different classification algorithms are selected as individual classifiers in the first case and only one classification algorithm is selected in the second case (for instance, ensembles of decision trees). When choosing the individual classifiers of an ensemble, the ensemble components must be different from each other, so that different, but complementary, information is generated, thereby improving the performance of the overall system. This characteristic is called ensemble diversity. Diversity in ensemble systems can be achieved when the individual classifiers are implemented under different circumstances, such as: parameter setting, classification type and datasets. In our empirical analysis, we use different classification types (heterogeneous structures) and datasets. In the case of different datasets, we apply feature selection methods which usually increases the diversity of the members of an ensemble.

Once the set of individual classifiers is created, an effective way of combining their estimates of the class label must be determined. Based on their functioning, one of the following three strategies is typically adopted: 1) Fusion: the combination module takes into consideration all the individual classifiers when defining the final output of the ensemble; 2) Selection: one individual classifier is selected and is used as a guide to provide the output of the system; and 3) Hybrid: we select from the strategies cited above. Basically, the idea is to use selection if and only if the best classifier is particularly effective in classifying the test pattern. Otherwise, fusion is used.

In this paper, we use four fusion-based combination methods in the ensemble systems, which are: Majority vote, sum, support vector machine (SVM) and k-nearest neighbor (k-NN) algorithms. We use traditional classification algorithms as the combination model, in which the combiner receives real numbers as input and provides the class label as output.

Experimental Work

In this paper, we analyse the benefits of using an optimized recognition structure for cancellable multi-biometric recognition. In order to do this, an empirical analysis is conducted. In this paper, we decided to use two biometric modalities, Face and Voice. The main reason for this choice is that these two modalities are the ones which have offered a high number of studies in the literature, such as in [31-34].

The general methodology of the empirical analysis is illustrated in Figure 2. In this methodology, we present a biometric template $X = x_1, x_2, ..., x_n$ where n represents the number of attributes of a biometric modality. This biometric template passes through three cancellable transformation modules (Biohashing, Interpolation and BioConvolving), producing three transformed datasets for each biometric modality (TF for face and TV for voice). It is important to observe that the Biohashing function uses a genetic algorithm to provide the best intervals for the discretization process. The transformed datasets are passed by a genetic algorithm for feature selection and they are then trained by individual classifiers. A genetic algorithm is then applied to define the best set of weights for the fusion approaches.

In this methodology, we apply a decision-level fusion approach that uses one of the four possible approaches (uni-modal and unialgorithm; uni-modal and multi-algorithm; multi-modal and uni-algorithm; and multi-modal and multi- algorithm). In the first approach, uni-modal and uni-algorithm, only information from one cancellable transformation of one specific biometric modality is taken into consideration. If we add one or more cancellable transformations, then we have the second approach, uni-modal and multi-algorithm. If we maintain one cancellable transformation and add one or more biometric modalities, we have the third approach, multi-modal and uni-algorithm. Finally, if we add one or more cancellable transformations and one or more biometric modalities, we have the last approach, multi-modal and multi-algorithm. Here, we will analyse all these four fusion approaches.

For convenience and clarity, Figure 2 shows only one possible combination (illustrated by means of the arrows linking individual classifiers and fusion modules), but in practice all the cancellable transformations are combined (Figure 2). Similarly, we present only the multi-biometric cancellable scenarios. However, for comparison purposes, the datasets with the original templates (original dataset) are considered in the empirical investigation and the genetic algorithm will also be applied to the original dataset.

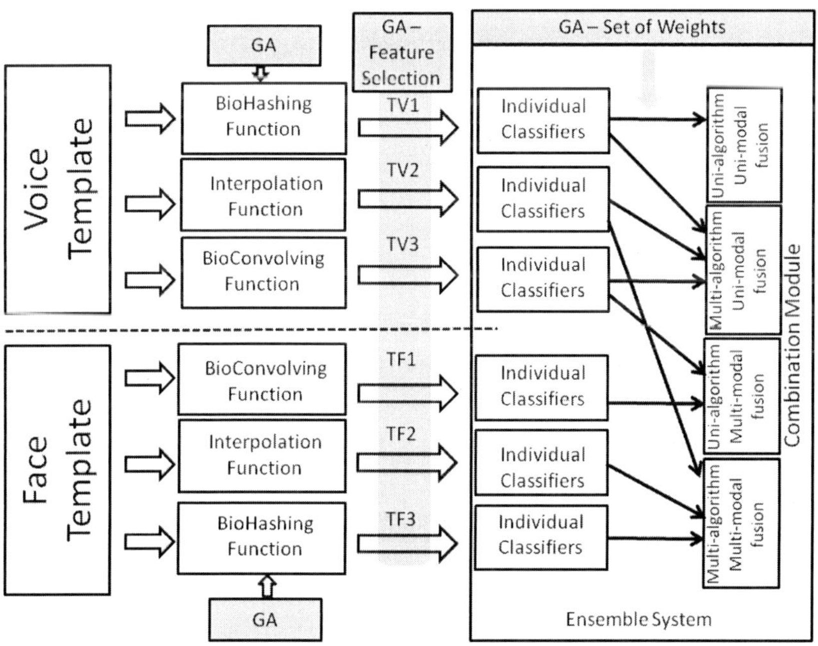

Figure 2: The general structure of the proposed methodology

Genetic Algorithms

The basic operating principle of genetic algorithms is to treat the possible solutions of a problem as individuals of a population, which will develop at each iteration or generation. In the context of ensemble systems, GAs has been widely used to optimize the structure of ensembles, including the features used by the individual classifiers. In this paper, we use GAs to improve the performance of the recognition process for cancellable multi-biometric systems. In order to do this, three genetic algorithms are used. The first is applied in the Biohashing method, the second to select features for the individual classifiers of the ensemble system and the third to define the optimal set of weights for the combination module of an ensemble system.

First, we apply a standard genetic algorithm to define the best intervals for discretization in the Biohashing cancellable transformation. The chromosomes are represented by a vector of real numbers that lie in the [0,1] interval and contain 3 values (one value for each coefficient of Equation 2). The initial population is randomly chosen. The population size is empirically defined as 250. In this case, we selected ten population sizes and we run the genetic algorithms using these sizes in a validation set. Then, the population size that obtained the best performance for both datasets over the validation set was selected. Finally, standard genetic operators (mutation and crossover) are used.

The second genetic algorithm is used to select attributes of the individual classifiers of an ensemble system. In this case, a binary chromosome is used to represent a possible solution. The size of the chromosome is $C * N$, where C represents the number of classifiers of the ensemble and N represents the number of attributes of the dataset. In this chromosome, the first N bits represent the feature subset for classifier C_1, followed by the N bits for classifier C_2, and so on. In each classifier, these bits represent the absence (0) or presence (1) of the corresponding attributes in the feature subset of the classifier. The initial population is formed by M individuals, with $M = 250$ for the experiments reported here. For the genetic operators, a standard one-point crossover and bit flipping mutation are used.

The choice of a fitness function is a problem when using an optimization technique in ensemble systems, since we can choose from filter-based approaches (independent of the learning algorithm) or wrapper-based approaches (a learning algorithm is used to guide the whole search). The filter-based approaches tend to have more flexibility, but with the drawback of low accuracy. The wrapper-based approaches are more accurate, but usually require a complex and time consuming process [35,36]. In this paper, for the first two genetic algorithms, we use a simplified wrapper-based approach in which we have chosen the average accuracy of two different learning algorithms (Naive Bayesian and k-NN) as the fitness function. The choice of these learning algorithms is because they are well-known simple methods, in terms of time consuming processing, and they have different classification criteria in their decision-making. This allows the fitness function to assess the possible solutions from two different points of view, increasing the ability to generalize.

For the third genetic algorithm, a set of optimal weights is defined. In ensemble systems, weights are associated with every example to denote the confidence (influence) of the individual classifiers in classifying the input pattern to a particular class. For this GA, we use a population of size 200, with each individual being represented by a vector of real numbers (in the [0,1] interval), representing the weights for each class of each individual classifier. The population is initialized assigning 1 to all weights of all individual classifiers. We then apply mutation and crossover as genetic operators and the stopping criterion is defined by the maximum number of iterations (varying from 400 and 1000, depending on the dataset used). Once again, we used a validation set to evaluate the performance of the genetic algorithms with different number of interactions. Then, for each dataset we selected the number of interaction that provided the best performance. As the fitness function, we use the accuracy level of the ensemble systems. Unlike the first two genetic algorithms, this GA is applied at the end of the recognition process and we can train all individual classifiers in advance since the possible solutions use the same trained individual classifiers. In this case, we can use the accuracy of the whole ensemble without incurring significant time overheads.

As we use an initial population composed of identical chromosomes (vectors of 1's), we apply the mutation operator with a variable rate. For the first iteration, the mutation rate is 20% and a reduction of 1% is applied every five iterations until it reaches 1% and it stabilizes. In addition, we apply the crossover operator only after the third iteration.

METHODS AND MATERIALS

In this investigation, we use three classification algorithms as individual classifiers, which are: *k*-NN (Nearest Neighbour), Naive Bayes and Multi-layer Perceptron Neural Networks (MLP). We selected these classification algorithms because they provide diversity in their classification criteria. In addition, in the decision-making process, the decisions of individual classifiers are combined by fusion-based functions to provide the final output of the ensemble systems. In this analysis, we use four methods, which are: Sum, majority voting, *k*-NN and SVM (Support Vector Machine). In addition, *k*-NN and SVM are considered trainable combination methods. In these cases, we generate a validation dataset for training these methods. All classification and optimization methods used in this study are coded in Matlab.

Three ensemble sizes are investigated here, with c = 3, 6 and 12 individual components. Additionally, we investigate several configurations for each ensemble size, including homogeneous and heterogeneous ones. As we aim to present the overall performance achieved by the ensemble systems, however, the values presented in this empirical analysis describe the accuracy averaged for all possible structures of the ensemble systems.

A standard k-fold cross validation method, with k = 7, was used in order to evaluate the classification systems. In order to compare the accuracy of the classification systems, the Wilcoxon signed-ranks test is used to evaluate the accuracy levels produced by the ensemble systems. We selected this test because it is a non-parametric test which is applied in order to compare two samples (related, matched or repeated measurements of a single sample) to evaluate the difference of their population mean rankings, whether statistically significant or not. This test can be used as an alternative to the student's t-test in cases where a population cannot be seen as normally distributed [37]. This test uses a degree of freedom (ρ), where $\rho = 0.05$ is used in this study.

Finally, for the multi-modal fusion approaches, we combined two biometric modalities (face and voice). In this combination, we performed two analyses. In the first, two thirds (2/3) of the individual classifiers use as input the face dataset and one third (1/3) used voice and, in the second analysis, the opposite proportions are chosen.

Datasets

The datasets used in our empirical investigation were the TIMIT dataset [38] for voice and The AR Face Database [39] for Face. The original and transformed datasets were composed of 100 different classes, with 7 instances per class, making a total of 700 instances for each dataset.

The voice dataset used in this investigation is extracted from the TIMIT database [38]. The procedure used to generate the original voice data used in this analysis consists of three main steps, which are: 1) Pre-processing: This step includes actions such as preemphasis, segmentation of data (frames), removal of silence and windowing of the voice data; 2) MFCC: In this step, MFCC (mel-cepstral coefficients) are extracted from each window (20ms duration extracted at a rate of 10 ms) of the signal [40]. In our work, we extract 12 coefficients; and 3) GMM-UBM: In using MFCC, we encounter input with variable size based on the length of the sample. Then, we apply the generative GMM-UBM (Gaussian Mixture model - Universal Background model) model in order to create feature vectors of fixed size to be used by any classification method. This procedure is similar to the one proposed by Kinnunen et al. [41]. Therefore, the attributes of the original voice dataset represent the mixtures of the Gaussian model provided by a GMM-UBM model. In this work, we use 30 mixtures and 12 MFCC coefficients, making a total of 360 attributes.

For the face images, features are extracted by the ICA method (independent component analysis) [42], which is a method for separating a multivariate signal into additive subcomponents by assuming that the subcomponents are non- Gaussian signals and that they are all statistically independent of each other. In this investigation, we use the 100 most relevant values for composing the original dataset. Therefore, the face dataset is composed of 100 attributes.

For the Biohashing dataset, we apply the procedure described in 4.1 and use a value of m equal to the number of attributes of the original datasets. In this case, the Biohashing datasets are composed of 360 and 100 attributes for voice and face, respectively.

In the interpolation process, Section 4.2, the highest degree of the polynomial interpolation allowed by the system was 6. Because of this, the original biometric traits are very large and a polynomial of degree 6 is not able to create a function of acceptable interpolation. Therefore, the original biometric samples are divided into I separate parts, with I = 10. The random vectors are also divided into I intervals (with 36 attributes for the random vector of voice and 20 attributes for face). Subsequently, for each subset of a biometric sample, an interpolation function is generated. After this, the transformed models M are created connecting the results of the interpolation function in all *I* intervals, making a total of 360 attributes for voice and 100 attributes for face.

In the BioConvolving function, we transform the biometric models into matrices, and these matrices, of 30 lines by 12 columns for voice and 10 lines by 10 columns for face, where each column is treated as a time sequence. The time sequences are divided into 2, $W = 2$, intervals, making the number of attributes equal to the original dataset, 360 for voice and 100 for face.

RESULTS AND DISCUSSION

In this paper, we will only analyse the performance of the cancellable biometric system. Although there are two more important criteria for cancellable biometric, diversity and non-invertibility, as we are not proposing new trans- formation functions, we will only analyse the effect, in terms of performance, of these transformation functions when using ensemble systems and applying ensemble systems.

These two criteria were investigated in the original paper of the transformation functions.

Additionally, it is important to emphasize that we have addressed in this paper a user biometric-based identification task. Therefore, when a biometric sample is provided, the classification systems output a class label which corresponds to a specific individual user. Alternatively, we could have implemented a verification task, as in [43-45]. However, identification is a U-class problem (where U is the number of enrolled users) and verification is, in effect, a two-class classification problem. In this case, from a classification point of view, identification is the more complex and time consuming task. In addition, as we want to analyse the benefits of wellestablished classification structures, we have chosen to focus on identification. Nonetheless, the proposed methodology can be easily adapted for verification tasks.

GENETIC ALGORITHMS

Aiming to demonstrate the benefits that genetic algorithms can bring to the development of more accurate biometric systems, this section presents the experimental results individually for all three genetic algorithms that are used. The first genetic algorithm is applied in the Biohashing function and the results are illustrated in Table 1, which shows the average accuracy of the individual classifiers when using the standard Biohashing and the adapted model proposed in this paper. These values represent the averaged results of all individual classifiers obtained in this experimental analysis. In addition, as we wish to observe the direct effect of the transformation functions, we considered only the individual classifiers.

Table 1: Accuracy level (%) and standard deviation of the individual classifiers with the standard and adapted Biohashing

FACE		VOICE	
Standard	**Adapted**	**Standard**	**Adapted**
76.24±4.24	78.37±4.69	75.53±5.66	80.5 ±2.77

In analysing Table 1, we can observe a substantial improvement in accuracy presented by the adapted model, reaching 5% points for voice dataset. Applying the statistical test shows that the improvements achieved with the adapted Biohashing are statistically significant in both cases. The use of the adapted Biohashing method helps to improve the accuracy of cancellable biometric systems. Therefore, henceforth, the Biohashing function used in this experimental work is the adapted one.

Table 2 presents the results of using GA to select features for the individual classifiers of an ensemble system, for the original datasets and all three transformed datasets (BioConvolving, Interpolation and Biohashing) using both biometric modalities. Once again, as the feature selection process has a direct impact in the accuracy of the individual classifiers, this table presents the results obtained by the individual classifiers. The NumAtt column represents the number of attributes of the corresponding dataset.

Table 2: Accuracy level (%) when selecting features for the individual classifiers

Datasets	FACE			
	Traditional		Feature Selection	
	NumAtt	Accuracy	NumAtt	Accuracy
Original	100	79.23±5.67	57	79.38±4.10
BioConvolving	100	79.07±4.65	55	79.12±3.65
Interpolation	100	78.65±5.03	61	78.75±4.00
Biohashing	100	78.12±5.64	74	78.37±4.69
VOICE				
Traditional			Feature Selection	
Datasets	NumAtt	Accuracy	NumAtt	Accuracy
Original	360	78.01±6.84	144	78.09±10.49
BioConvolving	360	78.27±5.12	168	79.45±3.62
Interpolation	360	75.17±5.10	173	75.96±8.32
Biohashing	360	79.68±4.23	147	80.50±2.77

As can be observed from Table 2, the use of genetic algorithms causes a significant reduction in the number of attributes (around 38% for the face dataset and 56% for voice). However, the accuracy of the individual classifiers using feature selection was slightly higher than the datasets without feature selection (complete dataset), for all analysed cases. We then apply the statistical test, on a two-by-two basis, to evaluate whether the observed improvement is statistically significant and this proved not to be statistically significant in any case. Nevertheless, it is important to emphasize that the reduced datasets decrease drastically the problem dimensionality (number of attributes) and offered a similar accuracy, when compared with the complete datasets. Therefore, hereafter, we will use the reduced datasets (with feature selection) in our analysis.

Table 3: Accuracy level (%) and standard deviation for the ensemble systems without and with a genetic algorithm to define the set of weights

	FACE		VOICE		FACE +VOICE	
	ES	ES+GA	ES	ES+GA	ES	ES+GA
Sum	84.29±5.29	90.38±4.96	87.02±5.38	93.89±4.98	94.25±3.64	96.86±2.15
MV	82.13±4.58	87.34±4.35	84.63±5.96	90.77±5.74	87.90±5.02	93.35±2.76
NB	81.66±4.55	86.15±3.87	81.3±40.88	86.94±4.09	86.18±6.73	90.67±3.92
k-NN	83.07±4.04	87.80±4.23	86.13±4.97	91.19±4.36	92.07±3.92	95.13±2.08
SVM	86.94±4.36	87.32±4.54	89.3±5.00	89.7±5.26	94.38±2.72	94.67±2.9

Next we will analyze the use of GAs in determining the set of weights to be used in the combination functions, and this result is shown in Table 3. This table reports the performance of the ensemble systems both with a uniform set of weights for all classifiers (standard ES) and when a GA has been applied to determine this set of weights (ES+GA). In this table, we illustrate the results of the ensemble systems for both biometric individually (face and voice) and for the combination of them (Face+voice). The shaded cells in Table 3 represent the highest accuracy achieved, for the ES and GA+ES cases, and for each dataset. In addition, the underlined numbers represent the cases where the improvement is statistically significant.

Table 3 shows that generally the use of GAs in determining the set of weights is an important tool in the development of more accurate ensemble systems, since it generates a significant increase in the accuracy achieved in all analysed cases. Also, by applying the statistical test, we can observe that the differences in accuracy delivered by the ES+GA ensemble systems are statistically significant for four combination methods (in voice, face and face+voice), rejecting the null hypothesis of equivalence. The only exception is when using SVM- based combination in which ES+GA ensemble provided higher accuracy than standard ensembles, but only marginally. We believe that the application of the GA improved the discriminability of the problem, decreasing the difficulty level of the classification process. Therefore, simple combination methods in the ensemble systems, such as the Sum and Voting approaches are then sufficient. Therefore, the difference in accuracy when moving from standard to ES+GA is high only for these simple combination methods.

In summary, we can observe that the genetic algorithm is an adaptable optimization technique since it can have positive effects on the performance of biometric systems when using at different stages of the recognition process.

CANCELLABLE DATA

This section reports the results of applying transformation functions (individually or combined), analysing the benefits of the different cancellable trans- formations when applied to the optimized ensemble systems. Tables 4 and 5 present the results obtained, individually and combined. These tables show the accuracy achieved and the standard deviation of the classification systems (individual classifiers-Ind, and ensemble systems combined with Sum, Majority Voting-VT, Naive Bayes-NB, k-NN and SVM). The results were obtained with homogeneous and heterogeneous structures, using 3, 6 and 12 individual classifiers. In order to provide a general perspective on the obtained results, the values presented in this section describe the accuracy averaged by all possible structures of the ensemble systems.

The shaded cells indicate the best results (the highest accuracy level for each line) attained by an ensemble system of the corresponding dataset, either original or transformed.

Individual Transformation Functions: Here, all individual classifiers of an ensemble system are trained individually for one cancellable transformation, either using one biometric modality (uni- algorithm uni-modal fusion) or combined datasets (unialgorithm multi-modal fusion). Table 4 presents the results of the classification systems for the biometric modalities Voice and Face individually, as well as the combined scenario.

The results in Table 4 illustrate, as expected, that the approach using a single cancellable transformation is not sufficient to provide an improvement in accuracy level of the ensemble systems. From these results, it can be seen that the use of cancellable transformation functions decreases the accuracy level achieved with the voice and face data in most of the analysed cases. In some cases, for the voice dataset, the use of cancellable transformation functions caused an improvement in the accuracy of the ensemble systems. Nevertheless, these improvements were not proved to be statistically significant. These results illustrate the need for approaches that involve more elaborate transformation functions in order to overcome the increase in complexity of the cancellable data.

In order to evaluate whether the improvement reached by the transformed datasets is statistically significant, we applied a statistical test (Wilcoxon signed-ranks test) comparing the best result (highest accuracy rate) with the second best result (second highest accuracy rate). In cases where the best result was a transformed dataset (except the original column), the statistical test always compared the best result with the original dataset. The statistically significant values are underlined. As a result of the statistical test, we can observe that the use of the transformed data cause a statistically significant decrease in only one case (voice dataset with ensembles combined by NB). This means that although there is a decrease in the accuracy, at least one cancellable transformation pro- vided accuracy rates similar to those delivered by the original dataset in most cases. On the other hand, the use of the transformed data causes a statistically significant increase in two cases (Biohashing for voice dataset with ensembles combined by

Sum and MV). In general, from a statistical point of view, the original dataset and the best cancellable transformation generate a similar accuracy rate.

Table 4: Accuracy level (%) and standard deviation of the classification systems when using the unialgorithm uni-modal fusion (Face and Voice) and the uni-algorithm multi-modal fusion (Face+Voice)

FACE				
	Original	**BioConvolving**	**Interpolation**	**Biohashing**
Ind	79.17±4.35	78.85 ±3.92	78.57 ±4.23	78.15 ±4.89
Sum	85.38 ±3.89	84.83 ±3.62	84.67 ±3.79	85.42 ±4.73
MV	84.23 ±5.00	83.95 ±4.61	83.82 ±4.63	84.33 ±5.72
NB	79.98 ±5.37	79.15 ±5.09	79.08 ±5.69	79.65 ±6.38
k-NN	82.33 ±5.09	81.52 ±4.88	81.35 ±4.86	81.82 ±6.05
SVM	83.18 ±5.76	82.05 ±6.03	82.87 ±4.56	83.085.63
VOICE				
	Original	**BioConvolving**	**Interpolation**	**Biohashing**
Ind	77.98 ±6.7	77.52 ±3.46	76.00 ±8.41	77.62 ±2.75
Sum	84.37 ±3.80	84.43 ±3.41	82.17 ±8.19	87.88 ±4.28
MV	84.43 ±3.68	84.03 ±3.40	82.10 ±7.55	87.60 ±3.27
NB	83.40 ±4.07	76.08 ±3.40	76.63 ±4.34	75.47 ±5.82
k-NN	84.70 ±3.39	80.85 ±3.76	79.72 ±8.59	84.77 ±4.19
SVM	87.83 ±3.09	83.00 ±3.79	83.05 ±8.22	86.98 ±3.04
FACE+VOICE				
	Original	**BioConvolving**	**Interpolation**	**Biohashing**
Ind	79.12±4.51	78.87 ±6.01	77.97 ±6.27	78.67 ±3.75
Sum	90.82 ±3.13	90.90 ±5.31	90.62 ±5.70	90.32 ±5.16
MV	90.28 ±3.63	90.30 ±5.75	90.17 ±5.80	89.67 ±5.11
NB	87.63 ±4.47	83.92 ±6.40	85.05 ±7.24	81.4 ±9.05
k-NN	89.45 ±3.99	87.48 ±6.12	87.72 ±6.37	87.1 ±5.72
SVM	91.45 ±3.79	88.83 ±6.43	90.15 ±5.88	88.88 ±4.66

Among the individual cancellable transformations, the interpolation function provides the highest accuracy for Face, while the Biohashing function achieves the highest accuracy level for voice and combined scenarios. This result shows that there are some differences in the different datasets and this may make a cancellable transformation viable for one specific application but not for another.

In analysing the effect of using a multi-biometric configuration (uni-algorithm multi-modal fusion), in comparison with the individual biometric modalities, we can see that in relation to the accuracy of the multi-biometric (combined) dataset, they provide the highest accuracy when analysing the ensemble systems. These results show that the use of ensemble systems applied to the multi- biometric dataset, along with ways to improve its effectiveness, have overcome the problems found in the individual modalities and have provided the highest accuracies achieved in this investigation.

COMBINED TRANSFORMATION FUNCTIONS

In this section, the results of the combination of the cancellable transformations are presented. As we have three cancellable transformations, the combination was investigated on a two-by-two basis (ConvBio for Convolution and Biohashing; ConvInt for Convolution and Interpolation; and BioInt for Biohashing and Interpolation) and the combination of all three functions (All three columns). Table 5 reports the accuracy and standard deviation of the classification systems in this combined scenario. For comparison purposes, the results of the ensemble systems using the original datasets are also provided in this table. Once again, the underlined numbers represent the highest accuracy level achieved for the ensemble systems, for each dataset.

Here, two different analyses are considered. The first compares the results of the ensemble systems with and without cancellable transformations. We see that the use of more than one cancellable transformation causes an improvement in the accuracy level in almost all cases. When combining all three cancellable transformations, for instance, this results in an improvement in all cases (ensemble systems), when compared with the original dataset.

Table 5: Accuracy level (%) and standard deviation: all three optimization techniques to select features for the ensemble systems

FACE					
	Original	**ConvBio**	**ConvInt**	**BioInt**	**All Three**
Ind	79.17 ±4.35	79.08 ±4.36	79.17 ±4.02	78.38 ±4.58	78.97 ±2.30
Sum	85.38 ±3.89	86.90 ±3.94	86.77 ±3.58	86.80 ±4.11	87.58 ±1.80
MV	84.23 ±5.00	85.10 ±4.70	85.07 ±4.46	85.02 ±4.92	85.78 ±2.58
NB	79.98 ±5.37	81.32 ±5.36	81.30 ±5.45	81.22 ±6.02	82.12 ±3.81
k-NN	82.33 ±2.09	83.43 ±5.33	83.30 ±4.81	83.38 ±5.19	84.32 ±3.06
SVM	83.18 ±5.76	84.43 ±5.47	84.48 ±5.02	84.67 ±4.91	85.25 ±3.15
VOICE					
	Original	**ConvBio**	**ConvInt**	**BioInt**	**All Three**
Ind	78.98 ±6.70	80.17 ±2.36	77.68 ±5.81	78.45 ±5.14	78.95 ±4.06
Sum	84.37 ±3.80	88.88 ±3.90	85.32 ±6.39	87.37 ±6.56	91.47 ±4.46
MV	84.43 ±3.68	87.87 ±2.98	84.42 ±5.59	86.92 ±5.44	90.25 ±4.17
NB	83.40 ±5.07	78.70 ±8.13	79.28 ±7.61	78.82 ±9.68	81.43 ±8.87
k-NN	84.70 ±4.39	86.87 ±3.90	83.97 ±6.21	85.63 ±6.22	89.25 ±4.89
SVM	87.83 ±4.09	88.72 ±2.99	86.50 ±5.42	88.38 ±4.96	90.78 ±3.84
FACE+VOICE					
	Original	**ConvBio**	**ConvInt**	**BioInt**	**All Three**
Ind	79.12 ±4.51	78.60 ±4.12	78.68 ±5.66	78.60 ±4.92	79.10 ±4.74
Sum	90.82 ±3.13	93.65 ±3.73	93.33 ±4.32	93.70 ±4.03	96.02 ±3.12
MV	90.28 ±3.63	92.23 ±3.58	92.05 ±4.29	92.58 ±3.81	94.52 ±3.30
NB	87.63 ±4.47	85.77 ±6.42	87.58 ±5.92	86.62 ±6.61	88.28 ±6.38
k-NN	89.45 ±3.99	90.90 ±4.34	90.93 ±4.78	91.08 ±4.32	93.28 ±3.88
SVM	91.45 ±3.79	92.32 ±3.66	92.80 ±4.26	93.15 ±3.27	94.52 ±3.12

We apply the same statistical test as used in the previous section, comparing the original dataset with the best transformed dataset (All Three dataset for all cases). The statistical test shows that the use of the transformed data causes no statistically significant decrease in performance. On the other hand, the use of the transformed data causes a statistically significant increase in almost all cases (14 out of 15 ensemble scenarios). In general, from a statistical point of view, the combination of all three cancellable transformations causes an increase in the accuracy rate of the ensemble systems.

In analyzing the use of more than one cancellable transformation, in comparison with one cancellable transformation, this brings about an improvement in the achievable accuracy in almost all cases. Once again, we emphasize the performance when combining all three cancellable transformations, which causes statistically significant improvements in all cases for the ensemble systems. The only exception is for ConvInt, which did not cause an improvement in accuracy.

An Analysis of the Combination Methods

Once we have carried out an investigation of the genetic algorithms and the cancellable data, we investigate the impact of a combination approach in the context of ensemble systems. From a general perspective, of the combination methods, the highest accuracy is achieved using the Sum method for most of the analyzed cases. However, in some cases, ensembles combined using SVM delivers the highest accuracy levels. Therefore, we can state that there is no "best" combination method from a general perspective. However, we can analyze the impact that the choice of combination method can have on the accuracy of the different ensemble structures over the different fusion approaches. In order to do this, Figure 3shows the accuracy achieved by ensembles combined by the Sum and the SVM methods, when varying the main parameters of an ensemble composition (ensemble structure and number of individual classifiers).

As can be observed from Figure 3, for the first fusion approach (uni-modal and uni-algorithm fusion), ensembles combined by the Sum method show the highest accuracy for the face dataset and ensembles combined by means of the SVM method produce the highest accuracy for the voice dataset. For the other fusion approaches, as the level of diversity increases (more than one dataset for the individual classifiers), we begin to observe a superiority, in terms of accuracy, of ensembles combined by the Sum method. For instance, when using three cancellable transformations in the second fusion approach (right graphic of the second line), we achieve the highest diversity level of this fusion approach and

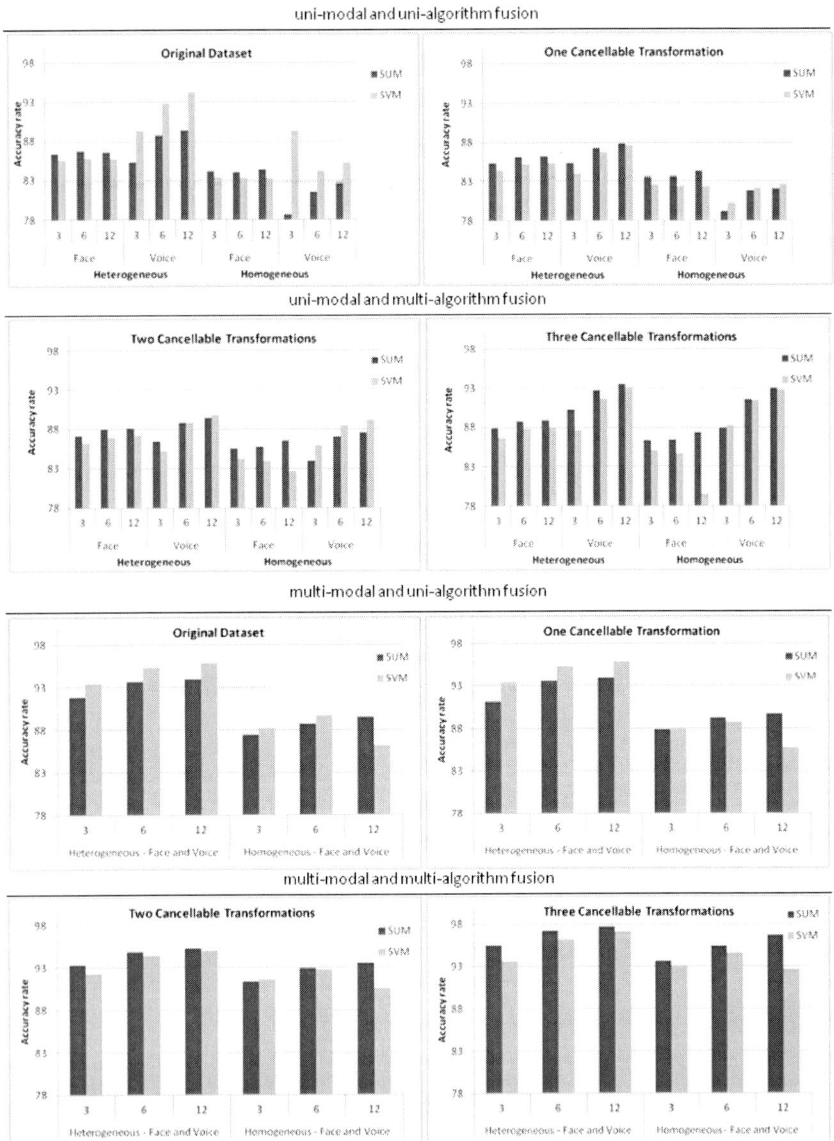

Figure 3: Accuracy rate of the ensemble systems combined with Sum and SVM for all four fusion approaches, varying the number of individual classifiers (3, 6 and 12) and ensemble structures (homogeneous and heterogeneous).

ensembles combined by Sum show the highest accuracy in 11 cases (out of 12), even in the voice dataset. The same scenario also happens in the fourth fusion approach with three cancellable transformations, in which ensembles combined by Sum show the highest accuracy in all 6 cases. These results show that when we have a low diversity level, we should use more elaborate and powerful combination modules in order to overcome the lack of diversity. In contrast, when the level of diversity increases, simple combination methods such as Sum, can be used with more satisfactory results (Figure 3).

In analyzing ensemble systems when varying the number of individual classifiers, performance usually increases when we increase the number of individual classifiers. However, this behavior is not observed very often when increasing the level of diversity of the ensemble systems, since the accuracy levels tend to stabilize or even decrease when increasing the number of individual classifiers. In relation to ensemble structures, the accuracy is usually higher for the heterogeneous structures than for the homogeneous structures. Once again, ensembles combined by SVM usually generate the highest accuracy levels in the homogeneous structures (low diversity level) while ensembles combined by Sum produce the highest accuracy levels in the heterogeneous structures (high diversity level).

FINAL REMARKS

This work has presented a new approach for the identification of multi- biometric cancellable identification, where genetic algorithms are applied in three different stages of the recognition process (cancellable transformation, feature selection and determination of the set of weights for the combination module) and ensemble systems are used as the recognition structure. We have used as examples two different biometric modalities (face and voice) separately and in a multi-modal context.

Through this analysis, an important conclusion which can be drawn is that the use of GAs in the search for more efficient and secure biometric systems has had a positive effect, since this increases the accuracy level of the ensemble systems in all three applications. In addition, this shows the flexibility of genetic algorithms, since their application is possible in different parts of a biometric recognition system, whether it is to optimize the set of weights in an ensemble system or to refine the processing of a cancellable transformation or even selecting features for the individual classifiers. Our approach means that we can implement a secure system while, at the same time, maintaining the highest accuracy level.

Another observation emerging from our work is that the combination of different cancellable transformation functions is more efficient than using individual transformation functions. We believe that this combination scenario compensates for the loss in performance attributable to the increased complexity associated with the individual transformation functions. The use of multi-modal fusion does cause an increase in the accuracy achievable by ensemble systems only when using one cancellable transformation. In this case, the diversity created by the use of two biometric modalities enhances the performance of the ensemble systems.

In general, we can conclude that the results of this study are very promising, showing numerous tools that can help the development of more efficient biometric systems, something increasingly important in today's society. The use of other cancellable transformations functions, as well as their application to other biometric modalities is the subject of ongoing research. Nevertheless, it is expected that this preliminary study can be beneficial to the development of biometric systems which are more generally viable in many current applications.

REFERENCES

1. Sae-Bae N, Ahmed K, Isbister K, Memon N (2012) Biometric-rich gestures: A novel approach to authentication on multi-touch devices. ACM CHI 12: 977-86.

2. Jung H, Lee EC, Kim D (2011) New finger biometric method using near infrared imaging. Sensors 11: 2319-33.

3. Arandjelovi´c O (2012) Color invariants under a non-linear photometric camera model and their application to face recognition from video. Pattern Recogn 45: 2499-509.

4. Lee JC (2012) A novel biometric system based on palm vein image. Pattern Recogn Let 33: 1520-8.

5. Komogortsev O, Karpov A, Price L, Aragon C (2012) Biometric authentication via oculomotor plant characteristics, in: Biometrics (ICB), 5th IAPR International Conference: 413-20.

6. Savvides M, Kumar BVKV, Khosla PK (2004) Cancelable biometric filters for face recognition. Pattern Recogn 3: 922-5.

7. Jain AK, Nandakumar K, Nagar A (2008) Biometric template security. EURASIP J Advances Signal Process 1: 1-17.

8. Ross AA, Nandakumar K, Jain AK (2006) Handbook of Multibiometrics, 1st Edition, International Series on Biometrics.

9. Cimato S, Gamassi M. Piuri V. Sassi R (2008) Privacy-aware biometrics: Design and implementation of a multimodal verification system. Computer Security Applications Conference 130-9.

10. Fu B, Yang S, Li J, Hu D (2009) Multibiometric cryptosystem: Model structure and performance analysis. Information Forensics Security IEEE Transactions 4: 867-82.

11. Kelkboom EJC, Zhou X, Breebaart J, Veldhuis RNJ, Busch C (2009) Multi-algorithm fusion with template protection. 3rd IEEE international conference on Biometrics: Theory, applications and systems IEEE Press: 222-9.

12. Sutcu Y, Li Q, Memon N (2007) Secure biometric templates from fingerprint-face features. Computer Vision and Pattern Recognition, IEEE Conference 1-6.

13. Nagar A, Nandakumar K, Jain A (2012) Multibiometric cryptosystems based on feature-level fusion. Information Forensics and Security, IEEE Transactions 7: 255-68.

14. Canuto AMP, Pintro F, Xavier JC (2013) Investigating fusion approaches in multibiometric cancellable recognition, Expert Systems with Applications 40: 1971-80.

15. Kuncheva LI (2004) Combining Pattern Classifiers: Methods and Algorithms. Wiley New York.

16. Canuto AMP, Fairhurst MC, Pintro F, Xavier JC, Neto AF, et al. (2011) Classifier ensembles and optimization techniques to improve the performance of cancellable fingerprint. Int J Hybrid Intell Syst 8: 143-54.

17. Feng YC, Yuen PC, Jain AK (2008) A hybrid approach for face template protection. Proc. SPIE Biometric Technology for Human Identification V.

18. Krishneswari K, Arumugam S (2012) Multimodal biometrics using feature fusion. J Comput Sci 6: 431-5.

19. Giot R, El-Abed M, Rosenberger C (2013) Fast computation of the performance evaluation of biometric systems: Application to multibiometrics. Future Gener Comput Sys 29: 788-99.

20. Altun AA, Kocer HE, Allahverdi N (2008) Genetic algorithm based feature selection level fusion using fingerprint and iris biometrics. Int J Pattern Recogn Artificial Intell 22: 585-600.

21. Jeong M, Choi JY, Kim J (2007) Using genetic algorithms to improve matching performance of changeable biometrics from combining PCA and ICA methods. Computer Vision and Pattern Recognition, IEEE Conference 1-5.

22. Parsi MSA, Doostmohammadi A (2012) Swap training: A genetic algorithm based feature selection method applied on face recognition system. World of Comput Sci Info Tech J 2: 125-30.

23. Tan X, Bhanu B (2006) Fingerprint matching by genetic algorithms. Pattern Recogn 39: 465-77.

24. Das A, Chakrabarty S, Pati S, Sahaji A (2012) Applying restrained genetic algorithm for attribute reduction using attribute dependency and discernibility matrix. Venugopal K, Patnaik L (Eds.) Wireless Networks Comput Intell 292: Springer Berlin Heidelberg 299-308.

25. Bolle CJ, Ratha RN (2002) Biometric perils and patches. Pattern Recogn 35: 2727-38.

26. Tilborg HCAV, Jajodia S (2011) Encyclopedia of Cryptography and Security. (2nd edition) Springer.

27. Teoh JBJ, Kuan YW, Lee S (2008) Cancellable biometrics and annotations on biohash. Pattern Recogn 41: 2034-44.

28. Ferna (2013) Ensemble of classifiers for the multi-biometric cancellable recognition, Ph.D. thesis, Federal University of Rio Grande do Norte.

29. Maiorana E, Martinez-Diaz M, Campisi P, Ortega-Garcia J, Neri A (2008) Template protection for hmm-based on-line signature authentication. IEEE Conference on Computer Vision and Pattern Recognition Workshops 1-6.

30. Canuto AMP, Abreu M, Oliveira L, Xavier JC, Santos A (2007) Investigating the influence of the choice of the ensemble members in accuracy and diversity of selection-based and fusion-based methods for ensembles. Patt Recogn Letters 28: 472-86.

31. Abdel-Hamid O, Mohamed A, Jiang H, Penn G (2012) Applying convolutional neural networks concepts to hybrid nn-hmm model for speech recognition. Acoustics, Speech and Signal Processing IEEE International Conference 4277-80.

32. Hinton G, Deng L, Yu D, Dahl G, Mohamed A, et al. (2012) Deep neural networks for acoustic modeling in speech recognition: The shared views of four research groups. Signal Processing Magazine IEEE 29: 82-97.

33. Liao S, Jain A (2011) Partial face recognition: An alignment free approach. Biometrics International Joint Conference 1-8.

34. Arandjelovi´c O, Cipolla R (2013) Achieving robust face recognition from video by combining a weak photometric model and a learnt generic face invariant. Pattern Recogn 46: 9-23.

35. Santana LEAS, Silva LMM, Canuto AMP (2011) Bio-inspired meta-heuristic as feature selector in ensemble systems: A comparative analysis. IEEE International Joint Conference on Neural Networks, IEEE Computer Society Washington: 1112-9.

36. Nascimento DSC, Canuto AMP , Silva LMM, Coelho ALV (2011) Combining different ways to generate diversity in bagging models: An evolutionary approach. International Joint Conference on Neural Networks 2235-42.

37. Demsar J (2006) Statistical comparisons of classifiers over multiple data sets. J of Machine Learning Res 7: 1-30.

38. Garofolo JS, Lamel LF, Fisher WM, Fiscus JG, Pallett DS, et al. (1993) TIMIT Acoustic-Phonetic Continuous Speech.

39. Martinez A, Benavente R (1998) The AR face database. CVC Tech Report: 24.

40. Davis S, Mermelstein P (1980) Comparison of parametric representations for monosyllabic word recognition in continuously spoken sentences. Acoustics, Speech and Signal Processing. IEEE Transactions on 28: 357-66.

41. Kinnunen T, Li H (2010) An overview of text-independent speaker recognition: From features to supervectors, Speech Communication 52: 12-40.

42. Bartlett M, Movellan JR, Sejnowski T (2002) Face recognition by independent component analysis. Neural Networks, IEEE Transactions 13: 1450-64.

43. Jain ARAK, Nandakumar K (2011) Introduction to Biometrics. Springer iSBN 978-0-387-77325-4.

44. Quinn G, Grother P (2012) The one-to-many multimodal fusion challenge. Biometrics IAPR International Conference 408-12.

45. Arandjelovic O (2014) A framework for improving the performance of verification algorithms with a low false positive rate requirement and limited training data. IEEE/IAPR International Joint Conference on Biometrics.

6
CHAPTER

Combining Epidemiologic and Biostatistical Tools to Enhance Variable Selection in HIV Cohort Analyses

Christopher Rentsch[1], Ionut Bebu[4], Jodie L. Guest[1,2,3], David Rimland[1,2], Brian K. Agan[4], Vincent Marconi[1,2,3]

[1]*Atlanta Veterans Affairs Medical Center, Decatur, Georgia, United States of America,*

[2]*Emory University School of Medicine, Atlanta, Georgia, United States of America,*

[3]*Rollins School of Public Health, Emory University, Atlanta, Georgia, United States of America,*

[4]*Infectious Disease Clinical Research Program, Uniformed Services University of the Health Sciences, Bethesda, Maryland, United States of America*

ABSTRACT

Background

Variable selection is an important step in building a multivariate regression model for which several methods and statistical packages are available. A comprehensive approach for variable selection in complex multivariate regression analyses within HIV cohorts is explored by utilizing both epidemiological and biostatistical procedures.

Methods

Three different methods for variable selection were illustrated in a study comparing survival time between subjects in the Department of Defense's National History Study and the Atlanta Veterans Affairs Medical Center's HIV Atlanta VA Cohort Study. The first two methods were stepwise selection procedures, based either on significance tests (Score test), or on information theory (Akaike Information Criterion), while the third method employed a Bayesian argument (Bayesian Model Averaging).

Results

All three methods resulted in a similar parsimonious survival model. Three of the covariates previously used in the multivariate model were not included in the final model suggested by the three approaches. When comparing the parsimonious model to the previously published model, there was evidence of less variance in the main survival estimates.

Conclusions

The variable selection approaches considered in this study allowed building a model based on significance tests, on an information criterion, and on averaging models using their posterior probabilities. A parsimonious model that balanced these three approaches was found to provide a better fit than the previously reported model.

INTRODUCTION

The methods commonly used in selecting variables for multivariate models can be overshadowed with objective statistical tests while others, in contrast, grant several subjective decisions to the researcher. There are risks associated with methods that rely too heavily on either objectivity or subjectivity. Most notably for the latter is the concept of researcher bias, which is a process in which the researcher influences the results of an analysis by forcing certain variables into or out of regression models typically based upon associations found in previous studies or logic determined by causal pathways [1]. For example, statistical tools, such as stepwise regression and collinearity diagnostics, could suggest a variable be dropped from further analysis in a multivariate model, but the researcher may decide to ignore the suggestion and force the variable into the model. Researcher bias has the ability to impact the accuracy and precision of conclusions output from data analyses.

Conversely, some variable selection processes allow for very little, if any, influence on which variables are kept in or dropped from multivariate analyses. Such processes include using statistical significance tests (e.g., Wald) in a stepwise fashion [2], [3], in which variables are selected and/or deleted from an analysis using a pre-specified significance level (p-value). In essence, the researcher inputs all variables of interest (which may already have some associated researcher bias) into a statistical software program, and runs a stepwise selection process. As a result, the computer program outputs a model that only includes variables that are statistically significant at the pre-specified significance level. There are many theoretical reasons why this approach may perform poorly in selecting potential confounders [4]–[10]. In this case, some subjective influence over which variables are selected may be preferred.

While some researchers may opt to utilize only one method in their analyses, there seems to be an underutilized complementary nature between objective statistics and subjective decisions when determining which multivariate model is the best representation of the data. It has been shown that there exists an inverse relationship between having too many or too few variables in a model; while the former results in high variance or uncertainty, the latter results in more bias [11], or equivalently, inflated Type II error versus inflated Type I error. Thus, a simplistic and parsimonious model that fits the data well is preferred.

In this investigation, data were made available by both the Department of Defense (DoD) and the Department of Veterans

Affairs (VA) in order to further examine a multivariate model (the "full" model) that has previously been published [12]. The goal of the present analysis was to compare time to all-cause mortality and clinical outcomes associated with HIV treatment and care between patients from the HIV Atlanta VA Cohort Study (HAVACS) and the US Military HIV Natural History Study (NHS) cohort, adjusted for possible confounders. Here we detail how using a mixture of commonly used hypothesis-testing statistics concurrently with information-theory approaches for model building can facilitate the detection of a preferred, parsimonious model. Alternatively, a Bayesian approach that combines several possible models is also described and compared to the other two approaches.

METHODS

Ethics Statement

The NHS cohort has been approved by the Institutional Review Board (IRB) centrally (Uniformed Services University of the Health Sciences, Bethesda, MD) and at each participating center (Walter Reed National Military Medical Center, Bethesda, MD; Naval Medical Center, Portsmouth, VA; San Antonio Military Medical Center, TX; Naval Medical Center, San Diego, CA; and Tripler Army Medical Center, Honolulu, HI). Written consent was obtained from each patient. The HAVACS cohort has been approved by Emory University's IRB and the Atlanta VA Medical Center Research and Development Committee. The HAVACS cohort does not require patients' written consent as it has an IRB-approved waiver of consent.

Study Participants

Data were collected from two cohorts: the HAVACS and the NHS. The NHS has enrolled over 5000 beneficiaries since 1986 into a prospective, multicenter observational study of HIV-infected active duty military personnel and other military beneficiaries living with HIV. The NHS cohort characteristics have been previously described [13]. The HAVACS includes all HIV-positive veterans seen for care at the Atlanta VA Medical Center since 1982 (n>3900). The cohort characteristics of HAVACS have been previously described [14]. Data are prospectively collected for both cohorts and are used for clinical care and research purposes.

Patients in both cohorts were eligible for inclusion in this analysis if they had an HIV diagnosis and began highly active antiretroviral therapy (HAART) treatment between January 1, 1996 and June 30, 2010. A total of 1199 NHS patients and 1065 HAVACS patients were followed from their recorded HAART initiation (HI) date through all-cause mortality or the date of last data entry. Separate internal analyses have determined that only 43 of the total >3900 HAVACS patients were in the NHS cohort, so the effect of any overlap between the patients examined in this analysis is negligible.

Variable Definitions

A HAART regimen was defined as the use of three or more antiretroviral medications, one of which has to be a protease inhibitor (PI), a non-nucleoside reverse transcriptase inhibitor (NNRTI), an integrase inhibitor, or an entry inhibitor. A participant's HI date was the date of the first HAART regimen that lasted greater than one month, utilizing an intention to treat format. Information regarding the participant's age at HI, sex, race, year of HIV diagnosis, time from HIV diagnosis to HI, viral load and CD4 count at HI (within three months prior to HAART start date), history of chronic hepatitis B and C co-infection, and previous AIDS-defining illness (ADI) excluding CD4<200, and previous ARV use (mono or dual NRTI) were also analyzed. There were no time-updated variables utilized in these analyses.

Statistical Analysis for Full Model

Potential covariates were selected based on previous literature regarding influences on survival of patients living with HIV in the presence of HAART [15]. Causal diagrams guided by literature were also drawn to ensure all selected variables would, in theory, reduce bias rather than induce bias in the analysis [10], [16]. The covariates were then screened using bivariate analyses and dropped from further inclusion in multivariate models if their crude association's p-value with the outcomes were greater than 0.5. Using an epidemiological modeling approach [16], [17], all the remaining variables and their interactions with the study's exposure were combined in a multivariate model (the "global" model) and assessed for collinearity. Using the concept of hierarchically well-formulated models [16], the interaction terms were first assessed for elimination from the model using a likelihood ratio test for significance. The non-interaction, confounding terms were then assessed utilizing the change-in-estimate approach [4]–[7], [9], [10]. This approach is similar to a backwards selection procedure, and a variable was kept in the multivariate model if its exclusion resulted in an "important" change to the main exposure variable's coefficient estimate. A 10% change cut-off was deemed "important" in this analysis. Covariates that remained after these procedures were utilized throughout all analyses.

Kaplan-Meier curves and Cox proportional hazards models were fitted to investigate time from HI to all-cause mortality by cohort. Specific to survival analysis, the proportional hazards (PH) assumptions were gauged for each covariate utilizing a consensus of three different approaches: graphical, goodness of fit, and extended Cox modeling [17], [18]. All covariates of interest satisfied the PH assumption. Thus, we can assume that the model including all remaining covariates (the previously published "full" model), or any subset of covariates, fit the data [19].

Statistical Analysis for Parsimonious Model

The Score test [20] is an hypothesis-testing statistic that is similar to commonly used likelihood ratio tests and Wald tests. All three are equivalent in large samples [21]. The Score statistic is less computational (requiring only evaluations under the null), and can be used as the basis for eliminating or including variables in such models. It is important to note that only nested models can be compared under this approach.

The Akaike Information Criterion (AIC) provides a practical and versatile way to identify a parsimonious model from a set of competing final models, by adding a penalty term proportional to the number of parameters in the model. This penalty term guards against overfitting. The AIC procedure yields an objective mathematical tool to determine parsimony in model construction and is free of subjective judgments [22]. Based on a penalized likelihood, the AIC allows comparison of non-nested models as well. Its benefits have been extensively described, particularly in the context of ecological and genetic study designs[23]–[28]; however, AIC procedures are applicable to other research topics, such as survival of patients living with HIV [29]. The AIC value was manipulated into two other related statistics; Akaike weights (w_i) and evidence ratios (ER) [30]. An Akaike weight is found by taking the proportion of the exponentiated AIC differences between model *i* and the model with the smallest AIC value to the sum of all these differences in all *K* subset models:

$$w_i = \frac{\exp(-(AIC_i - \min(AIC))/2)}{\sum_{k=1}^{K} \exp(-(AIC_i - \min(AIC))/2)} \quad \textbf{(1)}$$

The resulting value indicates the probability that the chosen *i* model is the best to represent that data among the whole set of *K* candidate models (those that were used when calculating the denominator in equation 1 above).

Evidence ratios are a small extension to Akaike weights – it directly compares the weights of two models *i* and *j*:

$$ER = \frac{w_j}{w_i} \quad \textbf{(2)}$$

The yielded value depicts the likelihood that model *j* is better or worse than model *i* to best represent the data given the two models selected.

An important remark regarding the previous approaches is that they are two-step procedures: first select a model (variable selection), and second perform statistical tests given (conditional on) the selected model being correct. This approach underestimates the variability in the data, by ignoring the uncertainty in the selected models. Moreover, in practice, two models can fit the data equally well but provide different estimated effect sizes[31]. Bayesian model averaging addresses these issues in a Bayesian context. Several models are considered, and the posterior distribution of the quantity of interest is the average of the posterior distributions under each model considered, weighted by their posterior model probabilities [32]. More specifically, given the data D, the posterior distribution of the parameter of interest β is given by

$$P(\beta|D) = \sum_{i=1}^{K} P(\beta|M_i, D) \bullet P(M_i|D) \quad (3)$$

Where $M_1,\ldots M_K$ are the models considered, and $P(M_i/D)$ is the posterior probability of the model M_i given the data.

In a survival data context, several Cox models $M_1,\ldots M_K$ are fitted, and β is the hazard ratio of interest [33]. The best K models in terms of the Bayesian information criterion (BIC) are selected using an efficient leaps and bound algorithm [34], and the posterior hazard ratio is estimated. One can also estimate a conditional posterior hazard ratio (HR), conditional on that particular covariate be included in all K models considered. The conditional HRs for each variable are obtained after averaging the posterior HRs only for the models containing that particular variable, and therefore are more likely to have nonzero HRs, while the unconditional HRs are obtained by averaging over all top K selected models. The result is that unconditional HRs are expected to be closer to zero than conditional HRs. We emphasize the conditional approach to Bayesian model averaging because it strikes a balance between an unconditional approach and stepwise selection – it averages over the posterior models that include the particular variable, allowing for the other variables to be included or not in the model.

Analyses were conducted with SAS 9.2 (SAS, Cary, NC, USA) and R (R Development Core Team (2008). R: A language and environment for statistical computing. R Foundation for Statistical Computing, Vienna, Austria). SAS and R code can be found as Figure S1.

RESULTS

Hypothesis-Testing Approach

Twelve covariates were initially selected from the databases to be included in the modeling process. These potential confounders were selected due to their influences on the survival of patients living with

HIV in the presence of ARV therapy [35]. After bivariate analyses, one variable, year of HIV diagnosis, was dropped. The global model was constructed to include the 11 remaining covariates and their interactions with the main exposure variable, which denotes the cohort of each patient. After collinearity assessments and backwards elimination processes, all interaction terms were dropped from the list of potential covariates. The change-in-estimate procedure detected subset models; however, none of these models performed better than a model including all remaining covariates with regards to the precision of the exposure's effect. Thus, the full model included only 12 covariates, one of which was the main exposure.

Information-Theory Approach

Instead of halting the variable selection process, Score tests and AIC comparisons were then implemented on the full model to determine if a better fitting and more parsimonious model existed. All 12 variables were cumulatively added to a multivariate model in two fashions: by the largest incremental change in AIC value and by the largest incremental change in Score statistic. Both of these statistics detected the existence of a parsimonious model; in fact, the same parsimonious model was found using both methods to add covariates to the model (Figure 1).

Akaike weights and ERs were computed for each subset model and found that a parsimonious model that did not include race, time from HIV diagnosis to HI, and previous ADI was 10.9 times more likely than the full model to be the best model to represent the data, given the chosen set of subset models. The Score tests similarly suggested that this parsimonious model was the best model.

The full model controlling for all 12 covariates concluded that patients in NHS were 57% less likely to die during follow-up compared to patients in HAVACS (HR 0.43, 95% CI 0.27, 0.70; p=0.0005). However, the parsimonious model that dropped race,

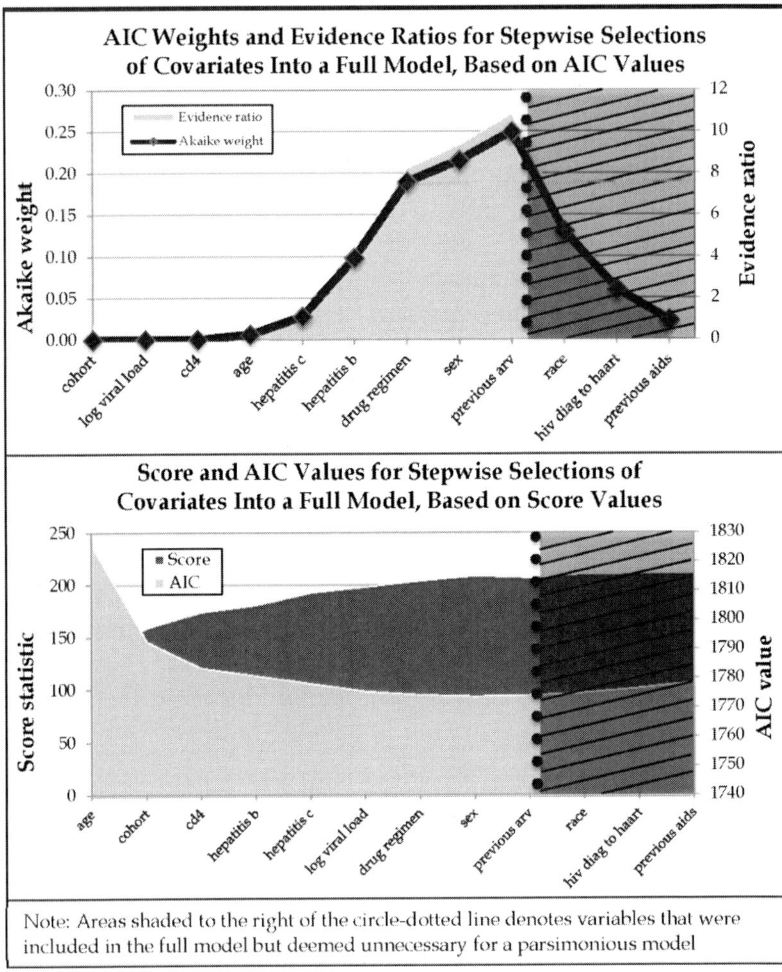

Note: Areas shaded to the right of the circle-dotted line denotes variables that were included in the full model but deemed unnecessary for a parsimonious model

Figure 1. Comparing Subset Models to a Full Model in Order to Detect a Potential Parsimonious Model. Top panel title: AIC Weights and Evidence Ratios for Stepwise Selections of Covariates Into a Full Model, Based on AIC Values. Bottom panel title: Score and AIC Values for Stepwise Selections of Covariates Into a Full Model, Based on Score Values. Note: Areas shaded to the right of the circle-dotted line denotes variables that were included in the full model but deemed unnecessary for a parsimonious model.

previous ADI, and time from HIV diagnosis to HI, concluded that NHS patients were 58% less likely to die during follow-up compared to patients in HAVACS (HR 0.42, 95% CI 0.27, 0.65; p=0.0001). The minimal change in the main effect estimate between the models can be attributed to the lack of information the three variables (race, previous ADI, and time from HIV diagnosis to HI) brought to the full model. In fact, after exploring the distributions of these three variables, there was evidence for a lack of racial diversity in the HAVACS cohort (78.8% were African-American/Black), a lack of previous ADI events in the NHS cohort (3.4%), and there were similar time periods between HIV diagnosis and HI in the entire sample (median: 4.7 months in the NHS; 5.0 months in the HAVACS, p=0.6774).

Bayesian Model Averaging Approach

The model with the highest approximate posterior probability was a model including cohort, age, CD4, and hepatitis C. This model represented only 11.3% of the total posterior probability, while the top five models had a cumulative posterior probability of 42.2%, indicating a moderately high model uncertainty. Figure 2 depicts the top 44 models (columns) in terms of their posterior probability that were used for model averaging (K=44). Variables (rows) positively correlated with the outcome appear in black, while those negatively correlated with the outcome appear in grey. Column width for each column (model) is proportional to the posterior probability of that model.

Table 1 also presents the posterior hazard ratios and the conditional hazard ratios, conditional on the corresponding variable being included in the model. The posterior probability is the probability that the corresponding variable is correlated with the outcome. There is close agreement between the AIC-based variable selection approach and the Bayesian model averaging. The variables race, time from HIV diagnosis to HI, and previous ADI were dropped from the parsimonious model and similarly had low posterior probabilities (4.3%, 3.2%, and 3.4%, respectively). The only discrepancy is the variable initial HAART regimen, which was not dropped in the AIC approach, but has a zero posterior probability under the Bayesian

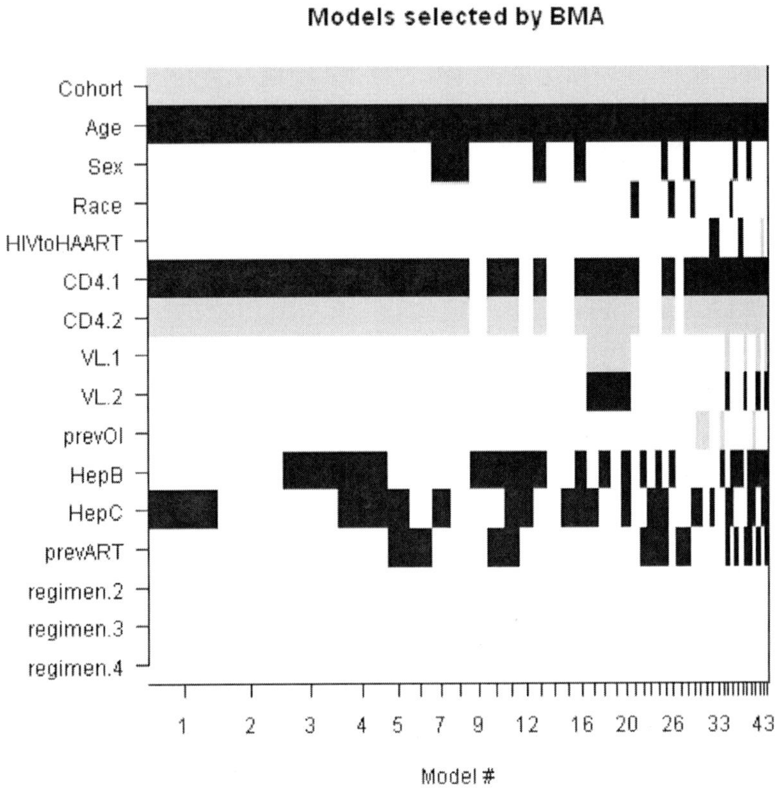

Figure 2. Models Considered by Bayesian Model Averaging, in Order of Posterior Probability. Variables Positively (Negatively) Associated With Outcome are in Grey (Black).

approach. It is of note that within the AIC approach, the difference in AIC values for a model including initial HAART regimen and one without the variable was merely 0.46 (1773.57 vs. 1774.04, respectively). Regarding the selected variables, a general remark is that the confidence intervals in the parsimonious model are usually tighter, due to decreased uncertainty introduced by the excluded variables. The effects of hepatitis B and C and previous ARV use appear more impactful in the AIC-based approach relative to the Bayesian approach (HR 1.86, 1.63, and 1.33 versus HR 1.33, 1.24, and 1.08, respectively). Interestingly, the two approaches give very similar results conditional on the variables being included in the model. Thus, the biostatistical tools used in these analyses detected problematic variables and removed them to form a better fitting model that collinearity tests alone could not identify. Otherwise, the conclusions that the full model suggests are similar to those of the parsimonious model, thus confirming the AIC's detection of a model that results in minimal information loss.

Table 1. Comparison of All-Cause Mortality Cox Regression Models Between NHS and HAVACS Patients Based on Three Approaches: Hypothesis-Testing, Information-Theory, And Bayesian Model Averaging, 1996 – 2010, n=1,727.

	Hypothesis-testing		Information-theory		Bayesian model averaging				
	"Full" model		"Parsimonious" model			Posterior		Conditional posterior	
Covariate	HR	95% CI	HR	95% CI	Selected (%)	HR	95% CI	HR	95% CI
Cohort, NHS vs. HAVACS	**0.43**	**0.27, 0.70**	**0.42**	**0.27, 0.65**	**100.0%**	**0.39**	**0.25, 0.61**	**0.38**	**0.25, 0.61**
Demographics									
Age at HAART initiation	**1.06**	**1.04, 1.08**	**1.06**	**1.04, 1.08**	**100.0%**	**1.06**	**1.04, 1.08**	**1.06**	**1.04, 1.08**
Sex, female vs. male	2.64	0.64, 10.80	2.50	0.63, 10.66	14.1%	1.14	0.50, 2.64	2.60	0.64, 10.59
Race, AA vs. other	1.20	0.80, 1.79	–		4.3%	1.00	0.91, 1.11	1.16	0.79, 1.74
Medical history (prior to HAART initiation)									
HIV diagnosis to HAART initiation	1.00	0.99, 1.01	–		3.2%	1.00	1.00, 1.00	1.00	0.99, 1.01
Viral load at HAART initiation, log copies/mL					9.8%				
<2.60	0.46	0.19, 1.15	0.47	0.19, 1.15		0.93	0.55, 1.57	0.46	0.08, 2.87
2.60–3.99	1.46	0.91, 2.33	1.46	0.91, 2.33		1.04	1.01, 1.36	1.48	0.27, 8.25
≥4.00	ref		ref			ref		ref	
CD4 at HAART initiation, cells/mL					85.0%				
<200	1.28	0.79, 2.07	1.30	0.82, 2.06		1.36	0.84, 2.20	1.43	0.45, 4.60
200–349	0.60	0.34, 1.03	0.61	0.35, 1.05		0.69	0.38, 1.24	0.64	0.19, 2.26
≥350	ref		ref			ref		ref	
Previous AIDS-defining illness[a]	0.95	0.62, 1.43	–		3.4%	1.00	0.92, 1.08	0.92	0.61, 1.39
Chronic hepatitis B co-infection	**1.89**	**1.10, 3.25**	**1.86**	**1.09, 3.20**	44.5%	1.33	0.65, 2.73	1.90	1.10, 3.26
Hepatitis C co-infection	**1.60**	**1.08, 2.38**	**1.63**	**1.12, 2.39**	49.0%	1.24	0.75, 2.06	1.55	1.06, 3.26
Previous antiretroviral use	1.40	0.95, 2.07	1.33	0.93, 1.92	23.6%	1.08	0.78, 1.49	1.38	0.96, 1.98
Initial HAART regimen					0.0%				
Non-nucleoside reverse transcriptase inhibitor	ref		ref						
Boosted protease inhibitor	**1.78**	**1.10, 2.86**	**1.74**	**1.08, 2.81**					
Unboosted protease inhibitor	1.28	0.86, 1.90	1.29	0.87, 1.91					
Other	0.72	0.25, 2.01	0.71	0.25, 1.99					

Abbreviations: AA - African -American/Black ; AIDS - acquired immune deficiency syndrome; CD4 - cluster of differentiation 4; CI - confidence interval; HAART - Highly Active Antiretroviral Therapy; HAVACS - HIV Atlanta VA Cohort Study; HR - hazard ratio; NHS - US Military HIV Natural History Study; ref - referent group.
Notes: Bold hazard ratios and 95% confidence intervals are significant at the $P<0.05$ level.
[a]1993 definition, exclusive of CD4<200.

DISCUSSION

The AIC has been reported to be a better tool in the field of model selection than traditional hypothesis-testing [22], [28]. In certain instances, stepwise variable selection based on hypothesis-testing may lead to different final models, depending on the order the variables are considered (e.g., forward, backward). The information-theoretic approach utilized by the AIC statistic often yields consistent results and does not depend on the order of which variables are selected [19], [28], [36]. In this example, an information-theoretic approach was balanced with a limited use of hypothesis-testing, which resulted in a parsimonious model that was nearly 11 times more likely than the full model to be the best choice. The utilization of AIC values or Score tests resulted in the same parsimonious model, which suggests that any additional exploration for a better-fitting model to only traditional hypothesis-testing may result in less variance in its estimates. The variables dropped from the full model to create the parsimonious model were chosen to be included in the initial multivariate analyses due to their cited influences on the survival of patients living with HIV while on HAART; nevertheless, due to the unique characteristics of the cohorts used in this analysis, they did not necessarily need to be controlled for in a model. Furthermore, the excluded variables were already being controlled for indirectly; in particular, previous AIDS diagnosis was partly captured by the CD4 count at HAART initiation variable (i.e., AIDS is usually associated with lower CD4).

Stepwise methods, such as the AIC approach used in this analysis, are two-stage procedures. First, a model that shows evidence of fit is selected, and then, conditional on this model being correct, one estimates the hazard ratios associated with the variables selected, and significance tests are performed. The Bayesian approach provides an alternative paradigm in which several models are considered at the same time, and the posterior parameters are simply weighted averages of the estimates from each model, with weights given by the posterior probability of each model given the data. One benefit of this approach is that it provides a coherent framework for distinguishing between lack of power to detect a significant effect, and a lack of correlation between the covariate and the outcome [33].

These analyses emphasize that while no single model is perfect, some are more useful than others. Similarly, these analyses suggest that only using the common hypothesis-testing methods could result in a model including variables that introduce excessive variance in the estimates. The goal is to have an expansive and rich "toolbox" of methods than can guide a researcher to a more useful model. When multiple approaches lead to the same or similar results, the conclusion is considerably strengthened and ultimately variance is diminished. The statistical tools used in this analysis are also applicable to other regression-type models. Further research should be employed on alternative datasets and data types to explore situations in which this multiple-approach method does not result in the same or similar final models as well as models aiming to make accurate predictions of an outcome.

CONCLUSIONS

Given the advent of methodological developments and the availability of statistical software, exploring several options for variable selection may prove beneficial when building complex multivariate models. Our analyses demonstrated such an amalgamation that resulted in a better-fitting, parsimonious multivariate model than what would have been reported by utilizing only one approach. We propose the usage of the same or similar robust, multi-approach methodology in an attempt to detect a preferred parsimonious model in other analyses.

AUTHOR CONTRIBUTIONS

Conceived and designed the experiments: CR VM. Performed the experiments: CR IB. Analyzed the data: CR IB. Contributed reagents/materials/analysis tools: DR BA. Wrote the paper: CR IB JG DR BA VM.

REFERENCES

1. Johnson RB (1997) Examining the validity structure of qualitative research. Educat 118: 282–292.

2. SAS Institute Inc (2012) SAS Guide for Personal Computers. Cary, NC: SAS Institute Inc.

3. Greenland S (1989) Modeling and Variable Selection in Epidemiologic Analysis. Am J Public Health 79: 340–349. doi: 10.2105/ajph.79.3.340

4. Breslow N, Day N (1980) Statistical Methods in Cancer Research. I: The Analysis of Case-Control Studies. Lyon: IARC.

5. Dales LG, Ury HK (1978) An Improper Use of Statistical Significance Testing in Studying Covariables. Int J Epidemiol 7: 373–375.

6. Greenland S, Neutra R (1980) Control of Confounding in the Assessment of Medical Technology. Int J Epidemiol 9: 361–367.

7. Miettinen OS (1976) Stratification by a Multivariate Confounder Score. Am J Epidemiol 104: 609–620.

8. Robins JM, Greenland S (1986) The Role of Model Selection in Causal Inference From Nonexperimental Data. Am J Epidemiol 123: 392–402.

9. Rothman KJ (1977) Epidemiologic Methods in Clinical Trials. Cancer 39: 1771–1775.

10. Rothman KJ, Greenland S, Lash TL (2008) Modern Epidemiology. Philadelphia, PA: Lippincott Williams & Wilkins.

11. Burnham KP, Anderson DR (2001) Kullback-Leibler information as a basis for strong inference in ecologic studies. Wildl Res 28: 111–119.

12. 12.Guest JL, Weintrob AC, Rimland D, Rentsch C, Bradley WP, et al. (2013) A Comparison of HAART Outcomes between the US Military HIV Natural History Study (NHS) and HIV Atlanta Veterans Affairs Cohort Study (HAVACS). PLoS ONE 8: e62273.

13. Sweeney S, Obure CD, Maier CB, Greener R, Dehne K, et al. (2012) Costs and efficiency of integrating HIV/AIDS services with other health services: a systematic review of evidence and experience. Sex Transm Infect 88: 85–99.

14. Weintrob AC, Grandits GA, Agan BK, Ganesan A, Landrum ML, et al. (2009) Virologic Response Differences Between African Americans and European Americans Initiating Highly Active Antiretroviral Therapy With Equal Access to Care. J Acquir Immune Defic Syndr 52: 574–580.

15. Anderson K, Guest J, Rimland D (2004) Hepatitis C Virus Coinfection Increases Mortality in HIV-Infected Patients in the Highly Active Antiretroviral Therapy Era: Data from the HIV Atlanta VA Cohort Study. Clin Infect Dis 39: 1507–1513. doi: 10.1086/425360

16. Kleinbaum DG, Klein M (2010) Logistic Regression: A Self-Learning Text. New York, NY: Springer.

17. Kleinbaum DG, Klein M (2005) Survival Analysis: A Self-Learning Text. New York, NY: Springer.

18. Therneau TM, Grambsch PM (2000) Modeling Survival Data: Extending the Cox Model: Springer-Verlag.

19. Anderson DR, Burnham KP, Thompson WL (2000) Null Hypothesis Testing: Problems, Prevalence, and an Alternative. J Wildl Manag 64: 912–923.

20. Kleinbaum DG, Kupper LL, Chambless LE (1982) Logistic regression analysis of epidemiologic data: theory and practice. Commun Stat - Theory and Methods 11: 485–547.

21. .Lehmann E (2009) Elements of Large Sample Theory: Springer.

22. Akaike H (1974) A new look at the statistical model identification. IEEE Transact Autom Contr 19: 716–723.

23. Anderson DR, Burnham KP, White G (1994) AIC Model Selection in Overdispersed Capture-Recapture Data. Ecol 75: 1780–1793.

24. Bozdogan H (1987) Model selection and Akaike's information criterion (AIC): the general theory and its analytical extensions. Psychometrika 52: 345–370.

25. Burnham KP, Anderson DR, Huyvaert KP (2011) AIC model selection and multimodel inference in behavioral ecology: some background, observations, and comparisons. Behav Ecol Sociobiol 65: 23–35.

26. Huggins RM (1991) Some practical aspects of a conditional likelihood approach to capture experiments. Biometrics 47: 725–732.

27. Lebreton J-D, Burnham KP, Clobert J, Anderson DR (1992) Modeling Survival and Testing Biological Hypotheses Using Marked Animals: A Unified Approach with Case Studies. Ecol Monogr 62: 67–118.

28. Posada D, Buckley TR (2004) Model selection and model averaging in phylogenetics: advantages of akaike information criterion and bayesian approaches over likelihood ratio tests. Syst Biol 53: 793–808.

29. .May M, Royston P, Egger M, Justice AC, Sterne JA (2004) Development and validation of a prognostic model for survival time data: application to prognosis of HIV positive patients treated with antiretroviral therapy. Stat Med 23: 2375–2398.

30. Wagenmakers E-J, Farrell S (2004) AIC model selection using Akaike weights. Psychonom Bull Rev 11: 192–196

31. Regal RR, Hook EB (1991) The Effects of Model Selection on Confidence Intervals for the Size of a Closed Population. Stat Med 10: 717–721.

32. Hoeting JA, Madigan D, Raftery AE, Volinsky CT (1999) Bayesian Model Averaging: A Tutorial. Statist Sci 14: 382–417.

33. Volinsky CT, Madigan D, Raftery AE, Kronmal RA (1997) Bayesian Model Averaging in Proportional Hazard Models: Assessing the Risk of a Stroke. Appl Statistics 46: 433–448.

34. Furnival GM, Wilson RW (1974) Regressions by Leaps and Bounds. Technometrics 16: 499–511.

35. Marconi VC, Grandits GA, Weintrob AC, Chun H, Landrum ML, et al. (2010) Outcomes of highly active antiretroviral therapy in the context of universal access to healthcare: the U.S. Military HIV Natural History Study. AIDS Res Ther 7: 14.

36. 36.Burnham KP, Anderson DR (2002) Model selection and multimodel inference: a practical information-theoretic approach. New York, NY: Springer-Verlag New York, Inc.

7

CHAPTER

Computational Approaches for Predicting Biomedical Research Collaborations

Qing Zhang[1¤], Hong Yu[1,2]

[1]*Department of Quantitative Health Sciences, University of Massachusetts Medical School, Worcester, Massachusetts, United States of America,*

[2] *VA Central Massachusetts, Leeds, Massachusetts, United States of America*

ABSTRACT

Biomedical research is increasingly collaborative, and successful collaborations often produce high impact work. Computational approaches can be developed for automatically predicting biomedical research collaborations. Previous works of collaboration prediction mainly explored the topological structures of research collaboration networks, leaving out rich semantic information from the publications themselves. In this paper, we propose supervised machine learning approaches to predict research collaborations in the biomedical field. We explored both the semantic features extracted from author research interest profile and the author network topological features. We found that the most informative semantic features for author collaborations are related to research interest, including similarity of out-citing citations, similarity of abstracts. Of the four supervised machine learning models (naïve Bayes, naïve Bayes multinomial, SVMs, and logistic regression), the best performing model is logistic regression with an ROC ranging from 0.766 to 0.980 on different datasets. To our knowledge we are the first to study in depth how research interest and productivities can be used for collaboration prediction. Our approach is computationally efficient, scalable and yet simple to implement. The datasets of this study are available at

INTRODUCTION

Millions of researchers contribute to biomedical research, collectively publishing tens of millions of research papers. These research papers interlink researchers into a complex co-authorship network. Biomedical research is a fast-growing interdisciplinary field that frequently requires high degree of collaboration. It has been found that the average number of collaborators in the biomedical field is twice that in physics and more than four times that in mathematics [1]. Such collaborations span basic, translational, and clinical research. Successful collaborations often yielded high impact work [2]–[5] such as the Gene Ontology[6].

The importance of scientific collaboration has motivated the development of researcher profile platforms, most of which focus on facilitating institutional collaborations. Such platforms, including the Harvard Catalyst Profile [7], SciVal Experts [8], and ProQuest Pivot [9], integrate research and collaboration information—including publication history, co-authorship connections, research topics, and funding information—making it easier to find potential collaborators. In addition, semantic Web resources, including VIVO [10], have been developed to provide a general scheme to describe researcher profiles so that the profiles can be embedded in particular applications. Online communities, including BiomedExperts [11], allow users to upload their personal profiles and help them make new connections. Few systems, however, have the functionality of recommending collaborators automatically. Such services, on the other hand, may be important for researchers, especially junior researchers, whose work depends upon successful collaborations. Automatically recommending collaborators may offer an attractive alternative to traditional ways of finding a collaborator, such as socializing at a scientific conference or being introduced by a mutual colleague.

We formulate research collaboration prediction as a link prediction problem in the context of a co-authorship network. Since joint publication is one of the most effective representations of collaboration, a co-authorship indicates a collaborative relation. Our goal is illustrated in Figure 1, where author *s* has collaborated with authors *a*, *c*, and *e* and we would like to know the probability that *s* will collaborate with *b*, *f*, and *d*.

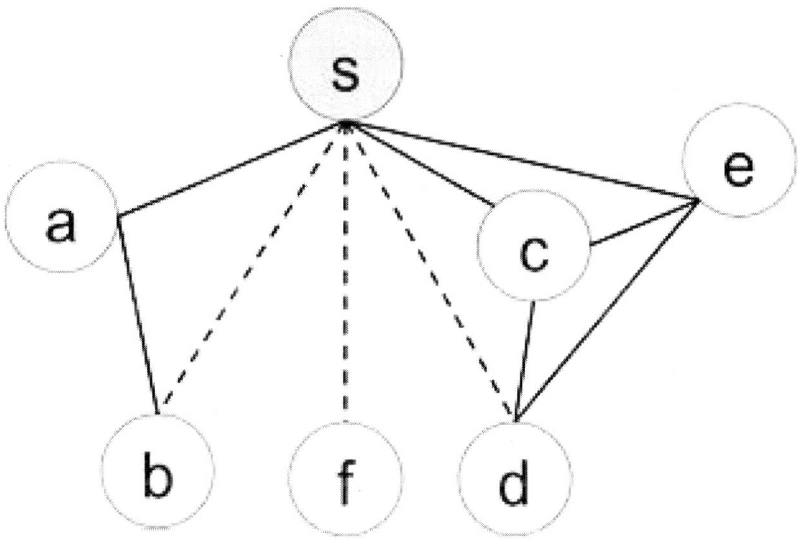

Figure 1. An illustration of automatic research collaboration recommendation. The graph shows a co-authorship network in which the nodes are authors and the links represent co-authorship. The solid lines represent existing co-authorships. Our study is to build a computational model to predict whether author *s* will collaborate with authors *b*, *f*, and *d* based on their existing research and collaborations.

Link prediction has been studied in social networks. Liben-Nowell and Kleinberg [12] used various topological features for link prediction. For example, two researchers are more likely to collaborate with each other when they have common collaborators.

Al Hasan, et al. [13]compared different machine learning models and learning features for predicting author collaboration. They found that support vector machines (SVMs) performed the best and shortest distance (i.e., the minimum number of edges that separate two authors) is a top topological feature. In addition, they explored node attributes (e.g., author's productivity and the research similarity between two authors) as additional features and concluded that they are top features for the prediction. Backstrom and Leskovec [14] explored a supervised random walk model and found it outperformed decision tree and logistic regression models in predicting new friends in Facebook. The aforementioned work provides important understanding of link predictions problem formulation. However most of the work mainly explored network topological structures. On the other hand, the rich semantic information (research work and collaboration activities), well documented by their publications, have been explored little.

In this paper we report the development and evaluation of Automatic Research Collaboration Recommendation (ARCR) system to predict new author collaborations. ARCR was built on supervised machine learning models. Our contributions are: We explored rich learning features, which were derived from the semantic content of an author's research profile. Our supervised machine learning models and learning features are computationally efficient, making them applicable to the big data challenge of scientific collaboration recommendation. In addition, we evaluated our approaches on various datasets reflecting data sparseness, a common problem in the real world. Finally, we provided in-depth analysis of important features including research interest and mutual collaborators that contribute to biomedical collaborations.

BACKGROUND

Author collaboration prediction can be considered as a case of modeling evolving networks. Significant amount of theoretical work is based on network structures and their evolution. Early work modeled the network as random graph, where the establishment of a connection follows Poisson distribution [15]. Later the scale-free model was proposed, in which the probability of a new node connecting with a given node is proportional to the degree of the node [16]. This phenomenon, which is also called preferential attachment, has been observed in many evolving networks, including social networks [1], [17], World Wide Web [18], and the protein-protein interaction network [19]. Additional findings, including "first-mover-advantage" [20] and "the-fit-get-richer" [21], have enriched further the scale-free model.

"Small world" is another important characteristic in various networks [22], [23]. A social network, including a co-authorship network, consists of both structured (close neighbors) and random contacts and one can navigate from one node to another with very few steps. Newman[17] found that only five to six steps are needed to navigate from one randomly chosen scientist to another in a community. In addition, social networks appear assortative, meaning that nodes tend to connect to other nodes with similar characteristics (e.g., the degree [24]).

In computer science, author collaboration prediction is often formulated as a link prediction problem. Early work focuses on topology-based prediction that utilizes network structure, including the connectivity and similarity of neighbor nodes. As stated earlier in this paper, Liben-Nowell and Kleinberg [12] comprehensively evaluated a collection of topological predictors, including number of common co-author and random walk, for the link prediction in co-authorship network of physics field. The work is one of the foundations of many later studies[13], [14], including ours.

Much work in link prediction explored supervised machine learning models and different learning features. As stated earlier, Al Hasan et al. [13] explored naïve Bayes and SVMs. They explored topological features (e.g., the number of common co-authors) and simple semantic features (e.g., the overlap of the keywords of two author's publication profiles). Sun et al [25] studied topological features in the heterogeneous networks consisting both co-authorship and citation relations to predict co-authorship in the DBLP data sets. Backstrom and Leskovec [14] applied supervised machine learning to predict the strength of a connection. The predicted weight is subsequently used to guide the random walk. The stationary probability of landing on a particular node is considered as the chance of a connection from the starting node. Wang et al [26] modeled the local topological structure by Markov Random Field to infer the co-occurrence probability of two nodes, and subsequently integrated with other topological and semantic features for link prediction.

Co-authorship networks have been widely studied. For example, Newman [17] compared the co-authorship network in biomedicine with that in physics and observed differences. He made several observations. In the biomedical domain, it is less common that two researchers collaborate when they have a mutual collaborator than in physics. The networks are scale free: the network structure is dominated by many "little" people with few collaborators, instead of a few people with many collaborators. He also observed that two researchers are more likely to collaborate if they have had a strong history of collaborations, either between themselves or with others) [27].

Several studies showed that co-authorship networks in the biomedical domain exhibit different characteristics than network in other domains. Newman [1] showed that biomedical research has the highest degree of collaboration, in comparison with the physics and mathematics domains. Huang, et al. [28] observed that the collaboration pattern and its evolution in the computer science domain are more similar to the mathematics domain than to biology. Ding[29] found that, in the information retrieval field, productive authors tend to collaborate with and cite researchers who have the same research interests.

Factors that lead to successful collaborations have also been studied, including various social and environmental factors: leadership, geographical proximity, and the personalities of the team members. For example, one study concluded that a leader in a research field typically plays an important "broker" role to bridge people from different disciplines [5]. Physical proximity between first and last author was found to be positively related to the impact of collaboration, measured by the citation received [30]. They concluded that close geographical distance is important for the outcome of the collaboration. International collaborations, however, are found to be a positive factor for the impact of a work. As shown in [31], the average number of citations increases with the number of affiliated countries. Certain characteristics of team members, such as openness and flexibility, also contribute to the success of the collaboration [5], [32].

Our work is closely related to the work of Al Hasan, et al. [13]. However, unlike their approach which mainly explored topological features, we explored rich semantic features derived from the author's research profile, including publication history similarity, citation similarity, and common co-authors, and we show that these semantic features significantly improve the research collaboration predictions.

MATERIALS AND METHODS

We formulate research collaboration prediction as a classification task and therefore explore supervised learning approaches. In the following we first describe the supervised machine learning models we used and then the feature set.

Supervised Machine Learning Models

We explored four supervised machine learning models: naïve Bayes, naïve Bayes multinomial, Support Vector Machines (SVMs), and logistic regression, which are all commonly used for classification tasks. A naïve Bayes classifier is a probabilistic classifier based on Bayes' theorem with the naïve assumption that the features are independent from each other, given the instance label [33]. The naïve Bayes multinomial model assumes the conditional probability of the feature, given a class, follows a multinomial distribution [34]. SVMs are based on the concept of maximum margin decision planes that define generalizable decision boundaries for classification and regression. An SVM constructs a hyperplane to maximize the margin between the data points and the hyperplane, often after mapping the data points to a higher-dimensional space in which they are linearly separable or close to it [35]. We explore an SVM model with the widely-used linear kernel for its efficiency. Logistic regression estimates discrete or continuous value parameters to predict discrete category values. The probabilities that describe the possible class of a single instance are trained as a function of explanatory variables, using a logistic function[33]. These four classifiers are not only the well-studied models in a variety of classification tasks [36], but also widely available in open source software communities. In addition we used K-nearest neighbor model (KNN) as it particularly learns non-linear decision boundaries and is easy to interpret [36], [37]. We use data mining software Weka [38] to build and evaluate naïve Bayes, naïve Bayes multinomial and logistic regression models, LIBSVM [39] for SVM, and the python machine learning package Scikit[40] for KNN.

Features

There are many reasons why two researchers collaborate, e.g., geographically close proximity (e.g., within or outside institutes) [30], proximity in the network (e.g., two researchers who have colleagues in common are more likely to collaborate) [12], and proximity in research (two researchers with the same goal in research may collaborate). Topological proximity has long been studied and considered as a factor of establishing connection in social networks. Semantic features, on the other hand, integrate specific domain knowledge of the nodes and have not yet been fully explored, which are the major contributions of this paper. In the following we will first describe the topological features, and then the semantic features.

CO-AUTHORSHIP NETWORK CONNECTIVITY.

Newman [1] observed that two scientists with a common collaborator are more likely to co-author a paper than two scientists who have no common collaborator. We therefore explored this feature called *numCommonCoauthor* of authors *x* and *y*, which is defined as $numCommonCoauthor(x,y) = |\Gamma(x) \cap \Gamma(y)|$ where $\Gamma(.)$ is the set of coauthors, and the feature value is number of co-authors two researchers have in common.

coAuthorJaccard and *Adamic* are two extensions of the common coauthor feature, both of which have been studied by Liben-Nowell et al [12]. *coauthorJaccard* is the number of co-authors two researchers have in common normalized by the total number of their unique co-authors. *Adamic* was first introduced by Adamic et al in [41] to measure the similarity of two web pages. The idea is that two web pages are more similar if they have common web pages that link both. Web pages that are exclusive to the two web pages are weighted more than those that also link to other web pages. *Adamic* was explored for link prediction [12], [13], although its contribution to link prediction remain inconsistent among different studies. While Liben-Nowell and Kleinberg [12] found that *Adamic* was one of the most valuable features, Hasan et al [13] did not report any performance improvement. Here we adopted *Adamic* to measure the similarity of two researchers by their common neighbors. For authors x and y,

$$Adamic(x,y) = \sum_{z \in \Gamma(x) \cap \Gamma(y)} \frac{1}{\log|\Gamma(z)|}$$

where z is the common neighbor (co-author) of *x* and *y*. The larger the value, the more similar *x* and *y* are. The higher number of the common co-authors is, the higher the *Adamic* value is. Each common co-author is also weighted by their exclusiveness to authors *x* and *y*. The less inclusive a common co-author is, the higher its *Adamic* value. Assuming that researcher z is the only common neighbor of *x* and *y* and that z has no other connections other than *x* and *y*(or *x* and *y* are the only co-authors of z), the *Adamic* value of *x* and *y* is 1/log(2). On other hand if z has 3 connections in addition to *x* and *y*, the value becomes 1/log(5). Therefore *x* and *y* are more similar in the former case.

A feature commonly used for describing the small-world characteristics in a network is clustering coefficient [27], which we designated the feature as *sumClusteringCoef.* It is the sum of each researcher's clustering coefficient, a measure of the probability that a researcher's collaborators have collaborations among themselves. The higher the clustering coefficient the closer the nodes in the network are connected.

We also included the feature *sumCoauthor*, which is the sum of each researcher's average number of unique co-authors per year. *SumCoauthor* represents how active a researcher is in collaboration with others, which is defined as $sumCoauthor(x,y) = avgCoauthor(x) + avgCoauthor(y)$

where *avgCoauthor(.)* is the average number of unique co-author per year.

RESEARCH PROFILE SIMILARITY.

It was reported that the keyword overlap from two author's publication history was more effective than topological features [13]. We therefore explored research profile similarity as additional features. To do so, we first built a research profile for every author. Specifically the research profile of an author comprises of three components of all his/her publications: abstracts, the assigned Medical Subject Headings (MeSH) terms, and the citations. We speculate that these components represent the author's research interests: abstract is the summary of an article by the author(s); MeSH terms represent main topics of the article; and out-citing citations (other articles cited by the article) show the relevant background information of the article while in-citing citations (other articles that cite the article in question) represent the recognition of the work by peers.

We used the classical vector space model (TF*IDF weighted) to build the research profile. Assuming that the publication collection of author s by a certain year is D, the TF-IDF for term$t$ in D is calculated by

$$tfidf(t,D) = idf(t,D) * \sum_{d \in D} tf(t,d)$$

where $idf(t, D)$ is the inverse document frequency of term t which is calculated from the entire MEDLINE database and $tf(t,d)$ is the term frequency of term t in collection D. Using the aforementioned formula, we built three vector space models to represent abstracts, in-citing and out-citing citations, respectively. We did not compute the MeSH TF-IDF vector due to our preliminary study from which we found that the TF-IDF representation for MeSH terms did not improve the performance. Instead, we included all unique MeSH terms in the collection to represent an author's MeSH profile.

We then derive learning features from two authors' research profiles. Specifically we define features *simText*, *simOutcite*, and *simIncite* as the cosine similarity of two researchers' abstract profiles, out-citing citation profiles, and in-citing citation profiles, respectively. Concretely,

$$simText(x,y) = \frac{abstract(x) \circ abstract(y)}{|abstract(x)||abstract(y)|}$$

where *abstract(.)* is the TF-IDF term vector of the author's publication history. Similarly

$$simOutcite(x,y) = \frac{outcite(x) \circ outcite(y)}{|outcite(x)||outcite(y)|}$$

And

$$simIncite(x,y) = \frac{incite(x) \circ incite(y)}{|incite(x)||incite(y)|}$$

where *outcite(.)* is the TF-IDF term vector of the author's out-citing citations from the publication history, while *incite(.)* is the TF-IDF term vector of the author's in-citing citations of the publication history. We also define *simMeSH* as the Jaccard coefficient of the two researchers' MeSH profiles. Concretely,

$$simMeSH(x,y) = \frac{|MeSH(x) \cap MeSH(y)|}{|MeSH(x) \cup MeSH(y)|}$$

Where *MeSH(.)* is the MeSH terms of author's publication history.

Collective Productivity.

The total number of publications of an author was explored in [13] and was shown effectiveness for predicting author collaborations. Here we use the average number of publications per year to measure productivity and *sumPub* as the sum of two researchers' average publications. Formally it is defined as $sumPub(x,y) = avgPub(x) + avgPub(y)$ where *avgPub(.)* is average publication per year. In addition, similar to age effect [42] we attempted to increase the weight of recent year productivity and defined an author's *recency* as the sum of the inversed publication time distances to the present. This metrics will weigh-in most recent activity. The *recency* of author *x* is defined as

$$recency(x) = \sum_{i \in papers(x)} 1/t_i$$

where *papers(x)* is the publications of the author x, and t_i is the distance between publication year of paper *i* and the *present* year. The *sumRecency* is thus the sum of two researcher's *recency* scores.

Seniority.

The relations between two researchers include junior–senior relations (e.g., student and advisor) and collegial relations, which may be important for research collaborations. We define an author's *seniority* as the average number of times that the author has been a senior author, which is approximated by the corresponding author in this study. The *seniority* of author *x* is defined as

$$seniority(x) = \frac{1}{|papers(x)|} \sum_{i \in papers(x)} I(x)$$

where *I(x)* is the indicator function; it equals one if x is the corresponding author of the particular publication, and is zero otherwise. For example, assume an author had 5 publications and was the corresponding author on 2 of them, thus the author's seniority is 2/5. The feature *diffSeniority* is thus defined as the seniority difference between two researchers.Table 1 shows the formal definitions of features we explored.

Baselines

The first baseline model, called *PreferentialAttachment,* is based on the Barabasi-Albert scale-free model[16]. As described in the background section, preferential attachment is a well-studied network growth pattern. The more existing links a node has, the higher the chance a new node will link to it. We implemented this baseline based on Liben-Nowell and Kleinberg's description [12]. Specifically $score(x,y) = |\Gamma(x)||\Gamma(y)|$, where $\Gamma(.)$ represents the set of neighboring nodes. For each pair of nodes *x* and *y* in a testing set, we computed the corresponding *score(x,y)*. The higher the score, the larger the chance that the two nodes *x* and *y* will connect (or collaborate).

Table 1. Feature definition.

Category	Feature	Definition
Connectivity	*numCommonCoauthor*	$\lvert\Gamma(x)\cap\Gamma(y)\rvert$ $\Gamma(.)$ is the set of the researcher's co-authors (neighbors in the network)
	coauthorJaccard	$\frac{\lvert\Gamma(x)\cap\Gamma(y)\rvert}{\lvert\Gamma(x)\cup\Gamma(y)\rvert}$
	Adamic	$\sum_{z\in\Gamma(x)\cap\Gamma(y)}\frac{1}{\log\lvert\Gamma(z)\rvert}$ The idea is that two nodes are more similar if they share a lot of neighbors that mainly connect to these two nodes.
	sumClusteringCoef	Sum of both researchers' clustering coefficients
	sumCoauthor	avgCoauthor(x) + avgCoauthor(y) avgCoauthor(.) is the researcher's average number of unique co-authors per year.
Research profile similarity	*simText*	$\frac{abstract(x)\cdot abstract(y)}{\lvert abstract(x)\rvert\lvert abstract(y)\rvert}$ Cosine similarity of two researcher's publication history, measured by abstract TF-IDF term vectors
	simOutcite	$\frac{outcite(x)\cdot outcite(y)}{\lvert outcite(x)\rvert\lvert outcite(y)\rvert}$ Cosine similarity of two researchers' out-citing citations' TFIDF term vectors
	simIncite	$\frac{incite(x)\cdot incite(y)}{\lvert incite(x)\rvert\lvert incite(y)\rvert}$ Cosine similarity of two researchers' in-citing citations' TF-IDF term vectors
	simMeSH	$\frac{\lvert MeSH(x)\cap MeSH(y)\rvert}{\lvert MeSH(x)\cup MeSH(y)\rvert}$ *MeSH(.)* is the MeSH term set of the researcher's publication history
Collective productivity	*sumPub*	$avgPub(x)+avgPub(y)$ *avgPub(.)* is the researcher's average number of publications per year
	sumRecency	*recency(x)+recency(y)* and $recency(x)=\sum_{i\in papers(x)} 1/t_i$ t_i is the time difference between the publication date of paper *i* to the present, and *Paper* is the publications of author *x*.
Seniority	*diffSeniority*	*seniority(x)-seniority(y)* seniority(.) is the average number of times a researchers has been a senior author

We also used *JaccardBaseline*, which describes the importance of the common co-author in the author pair, as the third baseline model as it has demonstrated strong performance in previous research [18]. Its definition is the same as for the feature *coauthorJaccard*.

Data

We used the citation/co-authorship network database CiteGraph [43] as the data source. The database comprises of 1.6 million full-text articles, a joint set of the Elsevier database (1899–2011) and the MEDLINE database. Each article entry includes the title, author(s), abstract, full text, year of publication, and the MeSH terms, as well as the in-cites and out-cites. We disambiguated author names and built a co-authorship network.

Figure 2 shows the collaboration frequency distribution in the CiteGraph dataset. As shown in the figure, an 80.5% majority of researcher pairs collaborate only once, while less than 20% collaborate two or more times. The highest number of collaborations for the same researcher pair is 159, spanning 12 years. The percentage, y, of researcher pairs that collaborate x times follows the power law distribution $\log y = -3.59 * \log x + 0.885$, where x refers to the number of collaborations, with statistical significance ($p<0.05$, t-test) for the linear regression.

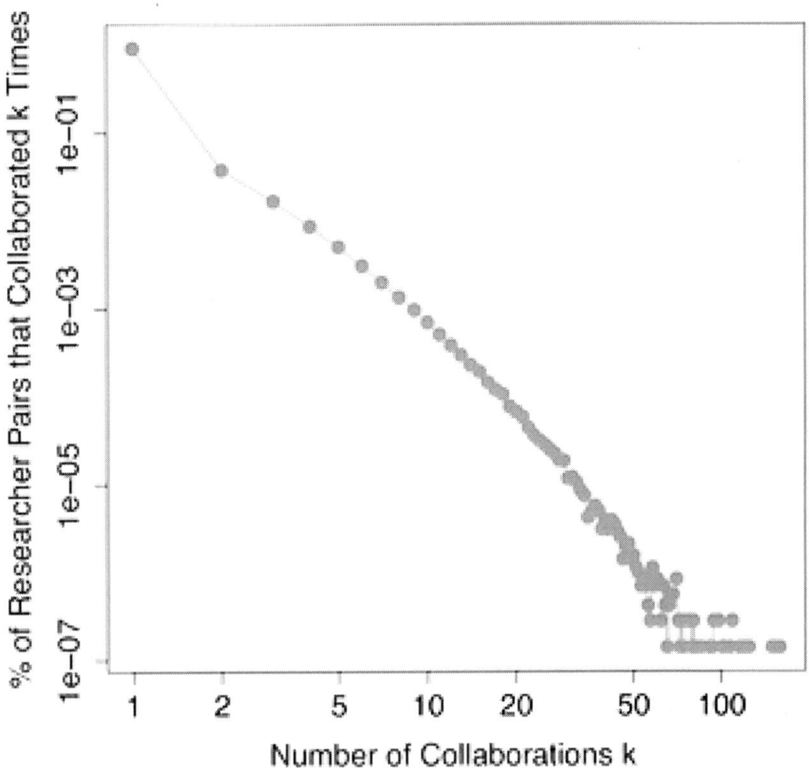

Figure 2. Collaboration frequency distribution for the CiteGraph dataset. It is a power law distribution $\log(y) = -3.59 * \log(x) + 0.885$, where y refers to the percentage of researcher pairs that collaborate x times, with x referring to the number of collaborations.

Training Dataset

We used CiteGraph for both the training and testing data. We selected equal numbers of positive and negative instances for training and testing as such makes results more comparable to previous work [13]. The positive training instances are author pairs whose first collaborations took place in 2007 or 2008. The negative training instances are author pairs who did not collaborate before 2009. We randomly selected 10,000 positive and 10,000 negative author pairs and extracted each pair's features, and the sampling method is similar with the static graph sampling algorithm proposed in [44]. Since article information, including the abstract, was not available for some authors, we filtered out these pairs, resulting total of 5361 positive instances and 5361 negative instances. The combined group of 10,722 author pairs was used as the training set.

Testing Datasets

We created two sets of testing data. The first set of data, *RandomPairCategory*, was created from a random selection of publications from 2009 and 2010 using the same sampling approach as training set. The positive instances were those in which the author pair first collaborated in 2009 or 2010, while the negative instances were author pairs who never collaborated before 2011. We randomly identified a total of 10,000 positive and 10,000 negative author pairs. Of these, we found that 4726 positive and 4726 negative author pairs had complete features. These 9,452 author pairs were used as the testing set. Note that the selection method of *RandomPairCategory* was utilized for the training data; therefore, the two datasets represent the same distribution.

The second testing dataset, *IndividualAuthorCategory*, was selected based on the collaboration network topology. We randomly selected four authors (target authors) with multiple publications (we set a minimum of 10) in 2009 and 2010. For each author, we built a sub-graph comprising three hops of a breadth-first traversal of the collaboration network established prior to 2011. We thus not only built a sub-graph, but also created the testing set with authors who are close topologically. The positive instances are collaborations established by authors (in the sub-graph) who collaborated with the target author during 2009 and 2010 and the negative instances are those (in the sub-graph) who did not collaborate with the target author before the end of 2010. The statistics of each sub-graph are shown in Table 2. When constructing the testing set for each author, we used all the positive instances and randomly sampled 200 negative instances for each author.

Table 2. *IndividualAuthorCategory* testing sets.

Author	Number of Publications	Sub-Graph Size	Positives	Negatives Sampled
Jeroen Bax	28	69,487	31	200
Mathew Farrer	10	66,876	13	200
Filippo Marte	59	418	11	200
Christodoulos Stefanadis	30	33,869	16	200

The *IndividualAuthorCategory* evaluation dataset complements the *RandomPairCategory*dataset because the former consists of author pairs who tend to be more similar in research while the latter represents a broader selection of potential collaborators.

We calculate precision (TP/(TP + FP)), recall (TP/(TP + FN)), the receiver operating characteristic—or ROC, the area under the curve of the true positive rate (TPR) over the false positive rate (FPR)—sensitivity (the same as recall), specificity (TN/(FP+TN)), and accuracy ((TP+TN)/ALL), where TP, FP, TN, FN and ALL stand for number of true positives, false positives, true negatives, false negatives, and number of total instances respectively. F1 score is defined as the harmonic mean of recall and precision, specifically 2*recall*precision/(recall+precision). In addition we use log loss[33] to measure the prediction cost of logistic regression model. It is defined as

$$J = \sum_{i=1}^{m} y_t \log y_p + (1 - y_t) \log (1 - y_p)$$

where $y_t \in \{0,1\}$ is class label, and $y_p = P(y_t = 1)$ is the predicted probability of being positive.

Feature and Research Profile Analysis

We analyzed the importance of features using information gain and feature value distributions of true positive (TP), false positive (FP), true negative (TN), and false negative (FN) predictions. We also studied how features' contributions evolve over time, as the authors presumably become more senior.

RESULTS

10-fold Cross Validation on the Training Set

Table 3 shows the 10-fold cross-validation results on the training dataset. The logistic regression and SVM demonstrated the best performance, with a 0.878 ROC and 0.797 F1 for logistic regression and 0.878 ROC and 0.780 F1 for SVM. The naïve Bayes model performs the second best, with an ROC of 0.838. The naïve Bayes multinomial performed the worst among the models. Logistic regression as well as SVM outperformed the naïve Bayes and naïve Bayes multinomial models with statistical significance ($p<0.05$, t-test).

Table 3. 10-fold cross-validation on the training set.

Model	ROC	Precision	Recall	F1	Accuracy
Naive Bayes	0.838	0.798	0.708	0.684	0.708
Naïve Bayes Multinomial	0.659	0.795	0.655	0.609	0.655
Logistic Regression	**0.878**	**0.803**	**0.797**	**0.796**	**0.797**
SVM	0.878	0.855	0.718	0.780	0.798
KNN (N=51)	**0.858**	**0.868**	**0.636**	**0.734**	**0.769**

Testing Set 1

Table 4 shows the results of models that were trained on the entire training dataset and then tested on the *RandomPairCategory* testing set, which was created by randomly selecting author pairs published during 2009 and 2010. Consistent with the cross-validation results, the logistic regression and SVM outperformed the other models, yielding an ROC of 0.871 and an F1 of 0.789 for logistic regression and 0.871 ROC and 0.769 F1 for SVM. The topology baseline models *PreferentialAttachment* and *JaccardBaseline* yielded ROC values of 0.4583 and 0.278, respectively. All the supervised machine-learning models outperformed the baseline systems. Logistic regression outperformed the naïve Bayes and naïve Bayes multinomial models with statistical significance ($p<0.05$, t-test).

Table 4. *RandomPairCategory* evaluation results.

Model	ROC	Precision	Recall	F1	Accuracy
Naïve Bayes	0.819	0.786	0.694	0.667	0.694
Naïve Bayes Multinomial	0.626	0.790	0.644	0.592	0.644
Logistic Regression	**0.871**	**0.794**	**0.789**	**0.788**	**0.789**
SVM	**0.871**	**0.842**	**0.708**	**0.769**	**0.787**
KNN (n = 51)	0.850	0.854	0.632	0.726	0.762
PreferentialAttachment	0.584	0.574	0.567	0.556	0.567
JaccardBaseline	0.639	0.789	0.639	0.585	0.639

Testing Set 2

We evaluated the top-performing supervised machine-learning model, logistic regression, on the *IndividualAuthorCategory* testing set, and the results are shown in Table 5. Our model yielded ROC ranging from 0.766 to 0.980, while the best ROC for the baseline models was 0.634 for the prediction for author Jeroen Bax for the *PreferentialAttachment* model; the*JaccardBaseline* model performed best for predicting collaborators of Mathew Farrer, with an ROC of 0.917. The performance differences between ARCR and the baselines are both statistically significant ($p<0.05$, t-test).

Table 5. *IndividualAuthorCategory* evaluation results.

Author	ARCR ROC	Pref. Attach.* ROC	JaccardBaseline ROC
Jeroen Bax	0.917	0.634	0.620
Mathew Farrer	0.980	0.537	0.917
Filippo Marte	0.800	0.302	0.455
Christodoulos Stefanadis	0.766	0.548	0.313
Macro Average	0.866'	0.505	0.576

*Pref. Attach stands for *PreferentialAttachment*.

Inter- vs. Intra-discipline Collaboration

We further examined inter- and intra-disciplinary collaboration predictions separately. Although*simMeSH* can be used as the discipline measure, we assume that the abstract has more detailed information than keywords. We therefore split the training data using different values of *simText* as our threshold in order to approximate inter-discipline and intra-discipline collaboration. The training set and the *RandomPairCateory* testing set were divided into inter-/intra-disciplinary training/testing sets using the threshold. We varied the threshold from*simText* values of 0.01 to 0.30 with 15 evenly distributed data points. For example, when the*simText* threshold was set to 0.01, author-pair instances with *simText* values less than 0.01 were categorized as inter-disciplinary whereas the author-pair instances with *simText* values greater than 0.01 were categorized as intra-disciplinary. For each threshold value, we trained inter-and intra-disciplinary learning models using their respective training sets and then tested them on the corresponding inter /intra-disciplinary testing sets. Since there was very little data when *simText* is larger than 0.3, we did not explore larger thresholds. Overall the inter-disciplinary collaboration resulted in ROC and F1 ranging from 0.75–0.86 and 0.66–0.77 respectively across different thresholds. The intra-disciplinary prediction achieved ROC 0.78–0.87 and F1 0.61–0.77. As shown in Figure 3, when *simText* <0.19, the intra-disciplinary model yielded a better performance according to F1. When *simText* was over 0.19, the inter-disciplinary model outperformed the intra-disciplinary model. The inter-disciplinary collaboration in general under-performed the intra-disciplinary one, suggesting it is more difficult to predict former and there might be other potentially important factors that influence the inter-disciplinary collaboration. Although there is no absolute *simText* value to divide the inter-/intra-diciplinary collaboration, as a reference our preliminary study shows that *simText* 0.1 represent distant topic (research interest) pair such as *diabetes* and *gene regulation*, while more related topic pair *brain* and *Alzheimer* has *simText* 0.3.

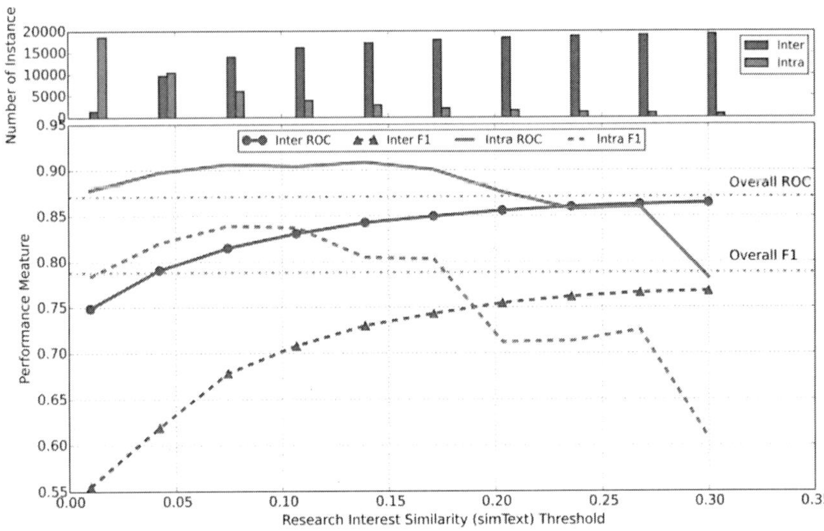

Figure 3. Intra and inter-disciplinary collaboration prediction performance by ROC and F1 measurement. Training set and *RandomPairCateory* test set were divided by the threshold into inter- (<threshold) and intra-disciplinary (>threshold) training/test sets. For each threshold, we trained inter- and intra-disciplinary models and tested them on the corresponding inter-/intra-disciplinary testing sets. The histogram on the top is the number of instances (training+testing) of inter- and intra-disciplinary subset according to the threshold cutoff. The ROC and F1 of overall data are also denoted as the two dotted horizontal lines.

Feature Ranking

To identify the features' contributions, we ranked them using information gain [45]. As shown inTable 6, the research interest features *simOutcite* and *simText* are the top-ranked features, both with information gain greater than 0.2. The features *coauthor Jaccard*, *Adamic*, and*numCommonCoauthor* are the next top ranked, based on the common co-author count. The next features are *simMeSH* and *simIncite*, which also represent research interest. In contrast, the contributions of *sum Clustering Coef* and *sumPub* are considerably smaller and *diffSeniority*shows no contribution.

Table 6. Training set feature ranking, by information gain.

Rank	Feature	Information Gain
1	*simOutcite*	0.265
2	*simText*	0.202
3	*coauthorJaccard*	0.173
4	*Adamic*	0.173
5	*numCommonCoauthor*	0.173
6	*simMeSH*	0.145
7	*simIncite*	0.101
8	*sumCoauthor*	0.055
9	*sumRecency*	0.024
10	*sumPub*	0.022
11	*sumClusteringCoef*	0.002
12	*diffSeniority*	0

In order to analyze error patterns across different datasets, we calculated sensitivity and specificity for the logistic regression model evaluation on all the testing sets. As shown inTable 7, the *RandomPairCategory* testing set has lower sensitivity than the*IndividualAuthorCategory* testing set, while the former has higher specificity than the latter.

Table 7. Sensitivity and specificity for all testing sets by logistic regression model.

Testing Set		Sensitivity	Specificity
RandomPairCategory		0.718	0.859
IndividualAuthor Category	Jeroen Bax	0.968	0.345
	Mathew Farrer	1.000	0.125
	Filippo Marte	0.818	0.460
	Christodoulos Stefanadis	0.813	0.352
	Macro Average	0.900	0.321

In our study we found that research interest features are an important feature category (Table 6). In contrast, such features were not studied extensively in other work. We therefore further analyzed their characteristics, such as their relation with author seniority. As shown in Figure 4, the research profile similarity features *simText, simIncite,* and *simOutcite* all increase as author seniority increases. Our results suggested that young researchers are more likely to collaborate with those whose research interests differ while senior or experienced researchers tended to collaborate with those whose research interests are close to them. In addition, the number of author pairs decreases as the authors get more senior, indicating fewer collaborations as the researchers become more senior. We did not show the data in which the authors have over 15 years of research because the data was very sparse.

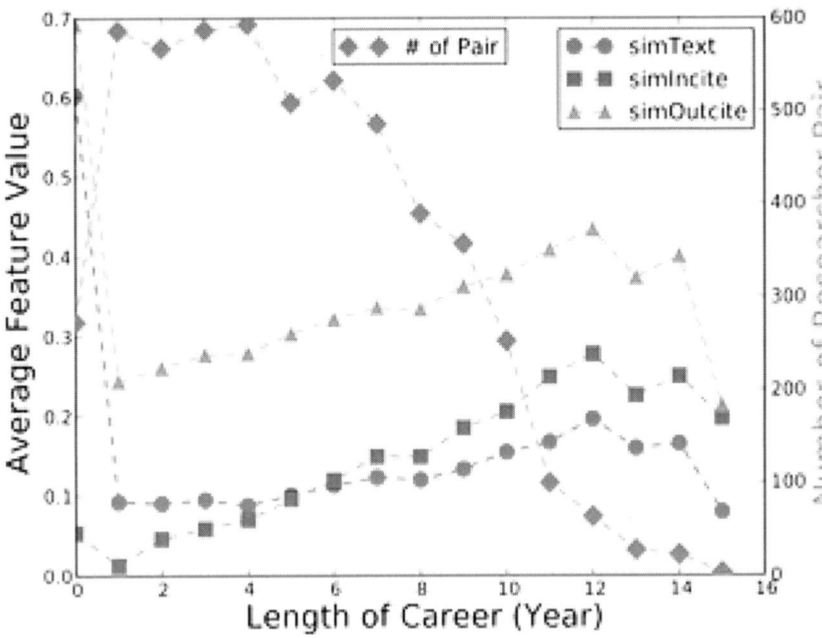

Figure 4. Research interest similarities over researcher career span. In the early stages of a researcher's career, collaborators with less research similarity are found but collaboration between two experienced researchers shows greater research interest similarity.

DISCUSSION

Models

The evaluation results for both the 10-fold cross-validation and the testing data (on the*RandomPairCategory* testing set) show that the logistic regression and SVM models are two best performing supervised machine learning models (logistic regression yielded an F1 score of 0.796 for 10-fold cross-validation and a score of 0.788 for testing while SVM produced 0.780 and 0.769 respectively, as shown in Tables 3 and 4). *IndividualAuthorCategory* is a more challenging evaluation data set as we tried to predict collaborators for individual researchers from the candidates that were collected from their close neighbors in the network. ARCR outperformed all the baselines with statistical significance (Table 5), which further shows that our model has the ability to recommend collaborators for the researcher. KNN model, which learns a non-linear decision boundary, did not perform as well as SVM and Logistic Regression as it only had an F1 score of 0.734 for the cross-validation on the training dataset and 0.726 on the *RandomPairCategory* testing set. This suggests that a linear decision boundary might be preferred.

In contrast, neither the naïve Bayes nor the naïve Bayes multinomial model performed well: an F1 score of 0.684 for 10-fold cross-validation and a score of 0.667 for the *RandomPairCategory*test set with the naïve Bayes model and an F1 score of 0.609 for 10-fold cross validation and 0.592 for the *RandomPairCategory* test set with the naïve Bayes multinomial model. The performance differences between logistic regression and the naïve Bayes and naïve Bayes multinomial models are both statistically significant ($p<0.05$, t-test). A possible reason for this under-performance is that both models assume conditional independence, which might not hold in our study. For example, *coauthorJaccard* and *numCommonCoauthor* are related, since they both depend on the number of common co-authors.

Feature Analysis

Table 6 shows that the most important feature for collaboration prediction, according to information gain, is the similarity of out-citing citations, which represents an author's knowledge background. True positive instances tend to have a larger *simOutcite* value than negative instances (mean *simOutcite* is 0.305 for *RandomPairCategory* and 0.462*Individual Author Category* positive instances while it is 0.159 and 0.264 for negative instances in the two categories respectively), suggesting that common background knowledge increases the chance for collaboration. As for the feature *simOutcite*, collaborating pairs have a higher*simText* score than non-collaborating pairs do. An author's publication history represents the author's research area and *simText* shows the similarity of two researchers' fields. Our results also show that research field overlap is positively related to potential collaborations.

MeSH terms can be considered the topics of a biomedical article, with the feature *simMeSH* a measure of research interest similarity. Therefore it is not surprising that *simMeSH* contributes to the classification. Keyword overlap was explored in [13] and was a top-ranking feature. In contrast to that study and [14] that did not explore text as features, we found that the feature*simMeSH* ranks below *simText* in information gain. We speculate that although MeSH terms represent an article's semantic content, they are not as robust as the bag of words formulation of *simText* for the task of author collaboration classification, because MeSH terms may not be considered as fine grained as word features in the abstract.

Our results also show that neighborhood structure plays an important role in predicting collaboration. The features *numCommonCoauthor*, *coauthorJaccard*, and *Adamic* all have large information gain. Note that [12] did not find *Adamic* is a useful feature. Positive instances tend to have larger number of common co-authors than negative instances, as for the*IndividualAuthorCategory* testing dataset, where researchers are topologically close (mean*numCommonCoauthor* is 1.0) but negative pairs still tend not to have common collaborators (the mean is closed to 0). Our results suggest that the strength of social ties is important for establishing collaboration. This conclusion is consistent with our hypothesis and previous findings, which show that common neighbors are a very effective predictor in social networks[12], [13].

Features that are related to researcher activity level, such as *sumCoauthor*, *sumRecency*, and*sumPub*, are ranked lower than *simOutcite*, *simText*, *coauthorJaccard*, *Adamic*,*numCommonCoauthor*, *simMeSH*, and *simIncite*, as measured by information gain, suggesting that two researchers' specific activities do not have to be closely related to establish a new collaboration. In contrast, the sum of co-authors was found to be among top features in [13], but it is not clear if this was influenced by the normalization by year, as carried out in our study. Consistent with previous findings, the clustering coefficient, which describes the transitivity of a collaboration, is not an effective feature [13]. It is also interesting to note that difference in seniority between collaborators, described by *diffSeniority*, has no impact on establishing a new collaboration in our approach.

Furthermore, we trained classifiers using every single feature individually and analyzed the performance as shown in Figure 5. 1) Research interest features *simText*, *simMesh* and*simOutcite* (Figure 5 panels *a*, *b* and *d*) have large ROC areas, showing that they are informative for the classification. *simIncite* (Figure 5*c*) however is not as large as other features in this category with 0.56 ROC only. 2) Common co-author based features (Figure 5panels *f*, *k* and *l*) exhibit distinct patterns and are essentially equivalent features as they have large correlation coefficients among each other. For example *Adamic* and*numCommonCoauthor* have a correlation coefficient of 0.96. This suggests that we can use*numCommonCoauthor* as a feature and remove *Adamic*. The ROC curve for them is a straight line due to the fact that most of the author pairs (especially negative instances) don't have any common coauthors, and only 1/3 of the positive instances have non-zero common co-authors. 3) Other features such as *sumCoauthor* (Figure 5*f*) is also effective for classification with 0.67 ROC. Activity feature *sumRecency* (Figure 5*i*) has 0.60 ROC, and so does *sumPub* (Figure 5*e*). *sumClusteringCoef* and *diffSeniority* (Figure 5 panels *h*, *j*) show only 0.53 and 0.54 ROC respectively The individual ROC is consistent with information gain analysis, which also shows that the research interest features are most informative, followed by common neighbor based features.

There are inconsistency between the single feature logistic regression and information gain, and it is due to the fact that these two ranking mechanisms address feature contribution from slightly different perspectives. Information gain is the entropy difference of before and after splitting the data set by a specific value of this particular feature, and the entropy itself measures the level of impurity of the dataset. Single feature logistic regression, on the

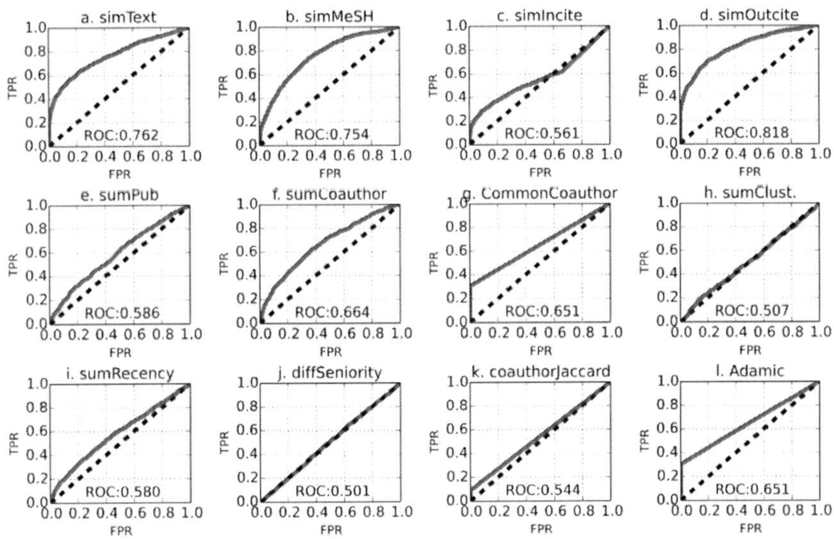

Figure 5. ROC for logistic regression classifiers trained by single feature. 1) Research interest features *sim Text*, *sim Mesh* and *sim Outcite* (panels a, b and d) have large ROC areas, showing that they are informative for the classification. *simIncite*(panel c) however is not as large as other features in this category with 0.56 ROC only. 2) The ROC curves for common co-author based features (panels f, k and l) are a straight lines due to the fact that most of the author pairs (especially negative instances) don't have any common coauthors, and only 1/3 of the positive instances have non-zero common co-authors. 3) Other features such as *sumCoauthor* (panel f) is also effective for classification with 0.67 ROC. Activity feature *sumRecency* (panel i) has 0.60 ROC, and so does *sumPub* (panel e). *sumClusteringCoef* and *diffSeniority*(panels h, j) show only 0.53 and 0.54 ROC respectively. The individual ROC is consistent with information gain analysis, which also shows that the research interest features are most informative, followed by common neighbor based features.

other hand, is essentially fitting the data by the particular feature. *simMeSH and sumCoauthor* is ranked lower than connectivity features (*numCommonCoauthor, coauthorJaccard* and *Adamic*) by information gain but higher than them by single feature logistic regression. The reason is that the above connectivity features have skewed distribution (almost all the negative instances don't have any common coauthors, and only 1/3 of the positive instances have non-zero common co-authors). Therefore it is easier to split the data set into two by value zero to yield high information gain. On the other hand *simMeSH* and *sumCoauthor* better fit the overall data due to their less skewed distributions.

In summary, previous work in author collaboration prediction mainly explored topological features. Our results, in contrast, show that in addition to topological features, semantic features are important. For example, we found that research interest is important for establishing a new collaboration. Specifically, research profile similarity features such as*simOutcite* and *simText*, as shown in Table 6, are the most important features–surpassing any of the topological features–for the classification. Tables 4 and 5 show that the supervised machine learning models that incorporate research similarity features significantly outperformed the baseline systems, which were built upon widely used topological features (*PreferentialAttachment, JaccardBaseline*). Possible interpretation is that knowing the other's work is a form of shared experience and the foundation of trust between two researchers. Their common knowledge, represented by the research similarity features, plays an important role for building collaboration.

As discussed earlier, although seniority plays a limited role in a collaboration, Figure 4 shows that when in their early career stage, researchers are more likely to collaborate with those whose research interests differ from theirs, suggesting that junior faculty are more open to collaborations. In contrast, collaborations between two senior researchers exhibit a higher degree of research interest similarity, suggesting that established researchers are more comfortable in their own fields and are less likely to initiate collaborations.

Error Analysis

In order to determine if our data size or features are sufficient, we analyzed the learning curve for the logistic regression model. The training set was split into two sets: training (66% of total instances) and validation set, and log loss is used for the error metric for the curve. As shown in Figure 6 the training error and validation error converges by the time the dataset reaches the size of 1000 author pairs. Therefore the training set size (5361 positive instances and 5361 negative instances) is sufficient for the task.

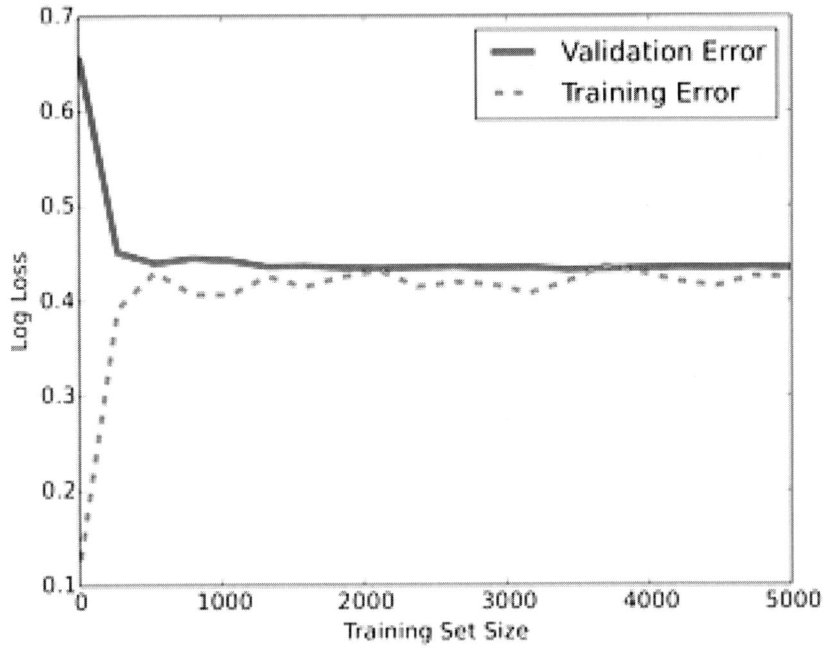

Figure 6. Learning curve for logistic regression with log loss metric. The training error and validation error converges by the time the dataset reaches the size of 1000 author pairs. Therefore the training set size (5361 positive instances and 5361 negative instances) is sufficient for the task.

We also manually analyzed the prediction errors. We found that authors' publication history is important as many of our semantic features are derived from authors' research profile. If an author has few publications and few co-authors in the past, there is little information we can derive for features such as research interest, network topology, and productivity (or activity) level and therefore will not be able to predict accurately his/her future collaborators.

We found that the data incompleteness is one of the most important reasons for false negatives. The network that we used in this study is a sub-graph of MEDLINE publications only and therefore provides an incomplete picture of the publication history of certain authors. For example, Flaumenhaft R (author of PMID 12837380) has only one publication prior to 2009 with only one co-author. His/her pairing with Laurence RG (author of PMID 18715793) has a *simText* value of 0.010 and a *simOutcite* value of 0.143 (the average value for each feature in the positive training data was 0.134 and 0.325, respectively), although Laurence RG is more prolific in our network with 12 publications and 35 co-authors. In fact, by searching the larger database the MEDLINE we found that Flaumenhaft R has been publishing almost every year from 2003 to present and has many common co-authors with Laurence RG; this information was missing entirely in our network, which was built using the joint MEDLINE and Elsevier data only. As a result, our models predicted Flaumenhaft R was unlikely to collaborate with Laurence RG, which is therefore a false negative. On the other hand, false positive errors can arise due to the fact that these author pairs have features very much like those in the positive training data. These authors, however, might never have had a chance to actually know each other, leading to a false positive.

We also found that the noises in author name disambiguation contribute errors for both false positives and false negatives. Data sparseness arises when one author is mapped to two unique IDs by the author name disambiguation database we used. For example Guida M (author of PMID 17113552) has two IDs. There are only five publications assigned to the ID that we happened to use in our network, while there are 94 publications under the other ID. We are also aware that it is possible for an author to share the same ID with another, unrelated author; this can also cause a disambiguation error and the information from the unrelated author will be wrongly attributed to the original author. However, we did not actually find any such cases in our test sets.

Recall we have built two different testing data sets, and our analyses of true positive, false positive, true negative and false negative of the three testing data sets show interesting results (Table 7). In the *RandomPairCategory* dataset (i.e, positive and negative author pair data were randomly selected) our classification has low sensitivity (0.718) and high specificity (0.859) while *IndividualAuthorCategory* yielded the opposite (0.900 sensitivity and 0.321 specificity). The high specificity of *RandomPairCategory* is due to the fact that the negative instances are "very negative" as they were constructed by the random combination of two authors; therefore, they tend to share few research interests and even fewer common friends. In contrast, the negative instances of *IndividualAuthorCategory* testing set were from the sub-graph of the author, so they do have similar research interests and have a higher chance of sharing a common collaborator. The sensitivity advantage of *IndividualAuthorCategory* can be understood in a similar way, as the positive instances, which were sampled from the sub-graph of the author, are "very positive" and share research interests and common collaborators, which increases the likelihood of the classifiers to classify them as positive.

Limitations

There are several limitations to this study. First, we did not explore learning features of broad social factors, including institutional policies like the status of an IRB application or institution-specific restrictions, because it is difficult to obtain these data. Second, our data are incomplete and contain missing information. We used a sub-graph of the MEDLINE co-author network and therefore the author publication histories may not be complete, as we described in the error analysis. Missing publications indicates missing the important research interest information. It also takes time for an article to accumulate citations, so *simIncite* may be biased to have more citations for older works than for recent ones. Finally, our training and testing period time cutoff is ad-hoc, and we define a negative instance pair as authors who did not collaborate by the time of the training or testing period, which might not be true in reality for every pairs.

Future Work

We identify the following directions for future research. First, we would like to incorporate all the available MEDLINE records to minimize the challenges of missing data. Secondly, we would like to explore additional learning features including the funding status, the collaboration strength, and the impact of an article. Thirdly, it is important to analyze in depth the research collaboration network and its topological characteristics. For example, interdisciplinary collaboration may involve a sub-graph (inter-group collaboration) that may exhibit different characteristics from the overall graph. Finally we may explore other machine learning models, including collaborative filtering.

CONCLUSIONS

In this study we applied and evaluated four established supervised machine-learning models, namely naïve Bayes, naïve Bayes multinomial, SVMs, and logistic regression, and explored rich learning features for automatic research collaboration prediction. We found supervised machine learning models can predict research collaboration with a high performance with an ROC ranging from 0.766 to 0.980 on different datasets, and logistic regression and SVMs performed the best. In addition, we identified three key factors for establishing new collaboration: research interest, common collaborators, and research productivity. Our research is important as it not only produces an important tool for automatic author collaboration prediction, but also contributes significantly to the science of evolving network modeling.

ACKNOWLEDGMENTS

The authors would like to thank Ricky J. Sethi for the comments and Rebecca Kinney for the proofreading.

AUTHOR CONTRIBUTIONS

Conceived and designed the experiments: QZ. Performed the experiments: QZ. Analyzed the data: QZ. Contributed reagents/materials/analysis tools: QZ. Wrote the paper: QZ HY.

REFERENCES

1. Newman ME (2004) Coauthorship networks and patterns of scientific collaboration. Proc Natl Acad Sci U S A 101: 5200.

2. Luo J, Flynn JM, Solnick RE, Ecklund EH, Matthews KRW (2011) International stem cell collaboration: how disparate policies between the United States and the United Kingdom impact research. PLoS ONE 6: e17684

3. Jones BF, Wuchty S, Uzzi B (2008) Multi-university research teams: shifting impact, geography, and stratification in science. Science 322: 1259–1262.

4. Okeke IN, Wain J (2008) Post-genomic challenges for collaborative research in infectious diseases. Nat Rev Micro 6: 858–864

5. Gray B (2008) Enhancing transdisciplinary research through collaborative leadership. Am J Prev Med 35: S124–S132.

6. Ashburner M, Ball CA, Blake JA, Botstein D, Butler H, et al. (2000) Gene Ontology: tool for the unification of biology. Nat Genet 25: 25–29.

7. Harvard Catalyst. Available: http://catalyst.harvard.edu/. Accessed 27 November 2012.

8. Vardell E, Feddern-Bekcan T, Moore M (2011) SciVal Experts: a collaborative tool. Med Ref Serv Q 30: 283–294.

9. COS Pivot: the next generation of funding and research expertise—connected. Available: http://www.refworks-cos.com/pivot/. Accessed 27 November 2012.

10. The VIVO Project. Available: http://vivoweb.org. Accessed 3 February 2012.

11. Elsevier Inc. BiomedExperts – Your scientific professional network. Available:http://www.biomedexperts.com. Accessed 3 February 2012.

12. Liben-Nowell D, Kleinberg J (2003) The link prediction problem for social networks. Proceedings of the Twelfth International Conference on Information and Knowledge Management. CIKM '03. New York, NY, USA: ACM. pp. 556–559.

13. Al Hasan M, Chaoji V, Salem S, Zaki M (2006) Link prediction using supervised learning. SDM'06: Workshop on Link Analysis, Counter-terrorism and Security.

14. Backstrom L, Leskovec J (2011) Supervised random walks: predicting and recommending links in social networks. Proceedings of the fourth ACM international conference on Web search and data mining pp 635–644.

15. Erdös P, Rényi A (1959) On random graphs I. Publ Math Debr 6: 290–297.

16. Barabási AL, Albert R (1999) Emergence of scaling in random networks. science 286: 509–512.

17. Newman MEJ (2001) The structure of scientific collaboration networks. Proc Natl Acad Sci 98: 404–409.

18. Adamic LA, Huberman BA (2000) Power-law distribution of the world wide web. Science 287: 2115–2115.

19. Barabási A-L, Oltvai ZN (2004) Network biology: understanding the cell's functional organization. Nat Rev Genet 5: 101–113.

20. Newman MEJ (2009) The first-mover advantage in scientific publication. EPL Europhys Lett 86: 68001.

21. Bianconi G, Barabási A-L (2001) Bose-Einstein condensation in complex networks. Phys Rev Lett 86: 5632.

22. Watts DJ, Strogatz SH (1998) Collective dynamics of "small-world"networks. nature 393: 440–442.

23. Kleinberg JM (2000) others (2000) Navigation in a small world. Nature 406: 845–845.

24. Newman MEJ (2003) Mixing patterns in networks. Phys Rev E 67: 026126.

25. Sun Y, Barber R, Gupta M, Aggarwal CC, Han J (2011) Co-author relationship prediction in heterogeneous bibliographic networks. Advances in Social Networks Analysis and Mining (ASONAM), 2011 International Conference on. pp. 121–128.

26. Wang C, Satuluri V, Parthasarathy S (2007) Local probabilistic models for link prediction. Data Mining, 2007. ICDM 2007. Seventh IEEE International Conference on pp 322–331.

27. Newman ME (2001) Clustering and preferential attachment in growing networks. Phys Rev E 64: 025102.

28. Huang J, Zhuang Z, Li J, Giles CL (2008) Collaboration over time: characterizing and modeling network evolution. Proceedings of the international conference on Web search and web data mining pp 107–116.

29. Ding Y (2011) Scientific collaboration and endorsement: network analysis of coauthorship and citation networks. J Informetr 5: 187–203

30. Lee K, Brownstein JS, Mills RG, Kohane IS (2010) Does collocation inform the impact of collaboration? PloS One 5: e14279.

31. Pan RK, Kaski K, Fortunato S (2012) World citation and collaboration networks: uncovering the role of geography in science. Sci Rep 2

32. Choi BC, Pak AW (2007) Multidisciplinarity, interdisciplinarity, and transdisciplinarity in health research, services, education and policy: 2. Promotors, barriers, and strategies of enhancement. Clin Invest Med 30: E224–E232.

33. Hastie T, Tibshirani R, Friedman JJH (2001) The elements of statistical learning. Springer New York doi: 10.1007/978-0-387-21606-5

34. McCallum A, Nigam K (1998) A comparison of event models for naive bayes text classification. AAAI-98 Workshop on Learning for Text Categorization

35. Manning CD, Raghavan P, Schütze H (2008) Introduction to information retrieval. Cambridge University Press Cambridge p319.

36. Caruana R, Niculescu-Mizil A (2006) An empirical comparison of supervised learning algorithms. Proceedings of the 23rd international conference on Machine learning pp 161–168.

37. Huang J, Lu J, Ling CX (2003) Comparing naive Bayes, decision trees, and SVM with AUC and accuracy. Data Mining, 2003. ICDM 2003. Third IEEE International Conference on pp 553–556.

38. Weka3: Data Mining Software In Java. Available:http://www.cs.waikato.ac.nz/ml/weka/. Accessed March 2013.

39. LIBSVM. Available: http://www.csie.ntu.edu.tw/~cjlin/libsvm/. Accessed November 2013.

40. Scikit. Available: http://scikit-learn.org/stable/. Accessed November 2013.

41. Adamic LA, Adar E (2003) Friends and neighbors on the web. Soc Netw 25: 211–230.

42. Dorogovtsev SN, Mendes JFF (2001) Effect of the accelerating growth of communications networks on their structure. Phys Rev E 63: 025101.

43. Zhang Q, Yu H (2013) CiteGraph: A Citation Network System for MEDLINE Articles and Analysis. Studies in Health Technology and Informatics Vol. 192 pp 832–836

44. Ahmed NK, Neville J, Kompella R (2012) Network sampling: from static to streaming graphs. ArXiv Prepr ArXiv12113412

45. Yang Y, Pedersen JO (1997) A comparative study on feature selection in text categorization. ICML Vol. 97 pp 412–420.

8

CHAPTER

The Attitude, Knowledge and Management Response to Fever Experiences

Ilker Etikan

Department of Biostatistics, Nicosia-TRNC Near East University, Cyprus

ABSTRACT

Background: The most common symptoms experienced by individuals is "fever". It can be managed with the use of antipyretics or without the use of antipyretics. The leading cause of fever symptoms are infectious diseases. The attitude, knowledge and management of fever were studied.

Results: In this study, the overall participants are 100 persons, 14 health care workers, 20 children and 66 students. We evaluated among the participants the students have the highest frequency of not considering fever as an important physiological response and mechanism of defense against infections, which has led to poor knowledge and management of fever. It is shown that the highest usage of antipyretic among the participants is "paracetamol". Among the parents interviewed, it is discovered that most parents becomes afraid when the symptom begins in their children.

Conclusion: Fever (high body temperature) is sign/symptoms not actually a disease. Our study has shown that there is high rate of fear among parents when their children experience fever. Fever can be managed at home without the use of medication but it becomes complicated, individual can seek for medical attention.

Keywords: Fever; Medication; Antipyretic; Pediatric; Health worker; Students

INTRODUCTION

Fever is a condition when an individual has a temperature above normal that is 38ºC and above. It is the most symptom that keeps one alert to the change in the body system. Fever symptom gives the awareness that a foreign body has invaded the internal body environment, which causes a change to body homeostasis by increasing the body temperature are making the internal body environment uncomfortable for the foreign invaders. In some cases, fever can be managed at home without medication that is; nurses/caregiver can use a wet sponged/towel to rub the forehead and body without the person being hospitalized [1]. But if the fever persists and also causes pain in other areas like headache, backache, dizziness, then one should seek for medical attention. It can be treated by medications. The medications used for fever is called "antipyretics".

Sometimes fever can be fatal if left untreated and it rises up to 41ºC. It causes damaged to the brain.

It is important that people check their temperature at home with a thermometer especially for children, in case they sense any unusual feeling of sickness or fatigue or sleepiness, depression, because fever can be a sign for so many medical/conditions. In children, the common infectious diseases that leads to fever are; flu, diphteria, pneumonia, chicken pox [2-5].

Fever is stated by people to be a disease or illness. But it is an important part of the body's defense to fight against infectious disease agents such as bacteria and viruses. It is not an "infectious disease" as people think.

This study is designed to evaluate the understanding of Fever among health workers, students on campus and among parents. And to describe the attitude, knowledge and management of fever among the participants in the respect to ages, sex, work status.

MATERIALS AND METHODS

The research was carried out in Near East University, North Cyprus and in the school hospital of Near East University [6]. There were 100 persons that participated in the research carried out. 66 students based on sex and marital status, 14 health care workers based on sex and marital status, pediatric based on sex.

The research was carried out among the participants in Near East university campus both in the dormitory and in Near East Hospital. The mothers in the hospital were interviewed to provide their experiences with their children having fever.

The method used to carry out this study was an interview with the answering of the questionnaire form by every participant. The questionnaire form contains 20 questions with direct options for both students and health worker. While 21 questions for pediatric. At questionnaire administration, an explanation was given on how to fill the form to the participants [7-10].

Statistically, the data was analyzed. The frequency table was used to analyze the frequency percentage of values of the group variables. Cross tab was used, comparing two variables among the group participant.

I. The two variables analyzed in the "student group" were sex and 20 question variables.

II. The two variables analyzed in the pediatric group were sex and 21 question variables

III. The variables analyzed in the health workers were sex, marital status and the 20 question.

Chi-square was used for differences between groups of categorical variables.

RESULTS

The total number of participant who were studied are 100. The study has shown the rate of people's response to fever.

The research was conducted among 20 mothers to know their understanding and their child's experience with fever [11]. The attitude, knowledge and the management towards their child feverish condition were observed.. Both male and female children were observed. It has shown in this statistics there is a higher rate of mother becoming afraid when their child experiences this symptom (Figure 1).

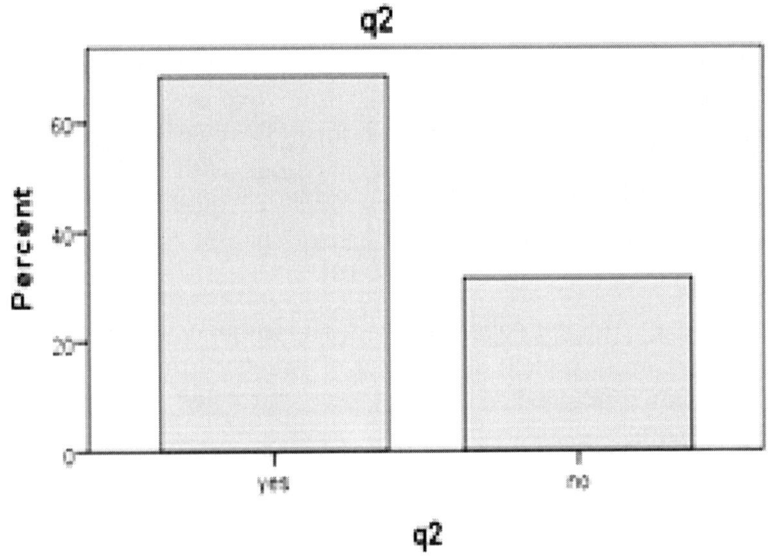

Figure 1: This is showing statistically, the rate of fear in mothers when their children have fever.

70% of mother believes that fever is harmful to the body. The most occurrences of infectious diseases among the children observed was "flu", and it is known that infectious diseases trigger the body temperature of becoming high. It was also observed that the most used antipyretic drug is paracetamol, and the high frequency of mothers treat their children with recommendation from doctors rather than self recommendation. This condition in children has brought about fear in mothers.

The research was carried out on the health workers in the hospital. Most of the health workers strongly agree that fever is the body defense mechanism against infectious diseases. A higher percentage takes recommendation from doctors rather than the over the counter medication.

And the most used antipyretic medication among this group of subject is paracetamol of 71.4% (Figure 2).

It is observed among the different groups of subject the research was carried on, the health workers had higher understanding of the occurrence of fever, due to their health knowledge and experiences in their work field.

66 students were interviewed, 37 females and 29 male. It was observed that high rate of students interviewed, view fever to be a huge problem to the health, some view it to be a disease. 15.2% strongly agree that fever is the body defense mechanism against infectious diseases. High percent of students did not understand that fever means high body temperature. 56.1% students measure their body temperature by feeling the hotness of their body while 25.8% uses digital thermometer and 7.6% electronic thermometer. It was observed that the 63.6% students interviewed get "over the counter drug" rather than getting recommendation of medication from doctor. And the most used medication is paracetamol (Figure 3).

The highest frequency of 42.4% students interviewed does not know the antipyretic drug they are allergic to.

This research has shown the level of knowledge about fever, the view of what fever is all about and its management among the three groups.

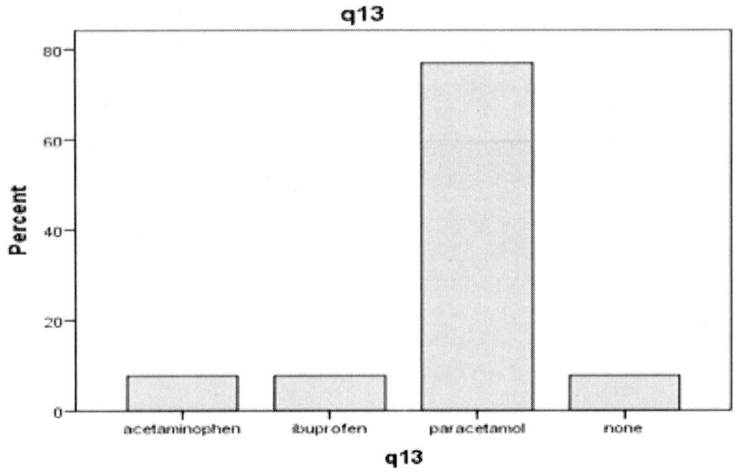

Figure 2: The use of the most antipyretic.

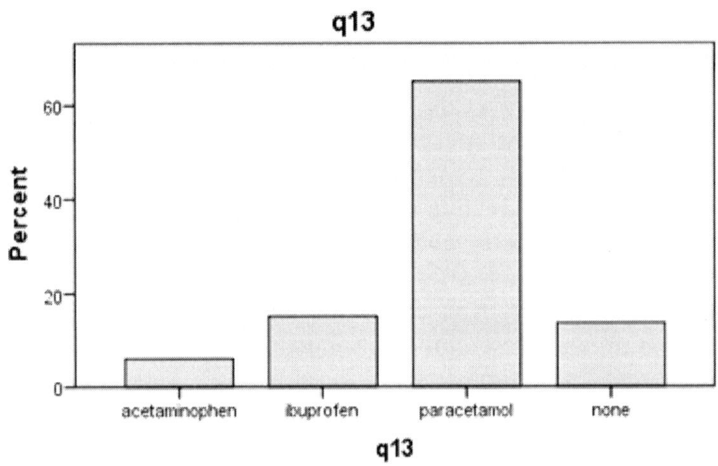

Figure 3: The highest frequency of students. .

CONCLUSION

Fever (high body temperature) is sign/symptoms not actually a disease. Our study has shown that there is high rate of fear among parents when their children experience fever. Fever can be managed at home without the use of medication but it becomes complicated, individual can seek for medical attention.

People should develop an attitude of taking recommendations from a physician for diagnostic test whenever a symptom of high temperature is experienced. It can be as a result of a disease. Fever is a symptom or sign that shows that there is an imbalance in the internal body environment.

REFERENCES

1. http://search.ebscohost.com/login.aspx?direct=true&db=cmedm&AN=26165100&site=eds-live
2. http://search.ebscohost.com/login.aspx?direct=true&db=a9h&AN=108306720&site=eds-live
3. http://search.ebscohost.com/login.aspx?direct=true&db=cmedm&AN=26179160&site=eds-live
4. http://search.ebscohost.com/login.aspx?direct=true&db=cmedm&AN=26569627&site=ehost-live
5. http://search.ebscohost.com/login.aspx?direct=true&db=cmedm&AN=26518691&site=ehost-live
6. http://search.ebscohost.com/login.aspx?direct=true&db=cmedm&AN=14677667&site=ehost-live
7. http://search.ebscohost.com/login.aspx?direct=true&db=a9h&AN=JOE136948359408&site=ehost-live
8. http://search.ebscohost.com/login.aspx?direct=true&db=uvt&AN=182353&site=ehost-live
9. http://www.medicinenet.com/aches_pain_fever/page5.htm#what_is_the_treatment_for_a_fever
10. http://www.medicalnewstoday.com/articles/168266.php

11. http://www.webmd.com/first-aid/fevers-causes-symptoms-treatments#1

9

CHAPTER

Data and Analysis Considerations in Oncology Clinical Trials

Bin Yao[1]*, Yining Ye[2] and Hua Yu[3]

[1]Puma Biotechnology Inc., Los Angeles, CA, USA

[2]Puma Biotechnology Inc., South San Francisco, CA, USA

[3]BioMarin Pharmaceutical Inc., Brisbane, CA, USA

ABSTRACT

Background: Oncology clinical trials are distinct from trials in other disease areas in its unique patient population, treatment and toxicity monitoring, endpoint assessment and follow-up. Promising innovative therapies to treat and prevent cancer have made oncology a fertile ground to conduct clinical research.

Purpose: To raise awareness and discuss relevant data and analysis issues that are critical to the ultimate success of oncology clinical trials.

Methods: We review data collection, cleaning, and analysis considerations in oncology clinical trials in the area of dosing, adverse events, tumor assessments, and survival follow-up. Operational issues relating to statistical analysis milestones and validation are also discussed.
Results: Upfront planning and careful considerations in data collection, monitoring, cleaning, and analyses have major impacts on the quality and conduct of the trial. Clear and appropriate data

presentations not only enhance the interpretability of the results but also boost the confidence in the analyses.

Conclusion: Collaboration and coordination among multiple stakeholders and different functions of the trial sponsor are essential at all stages of a clinical trial. Special emphasis should be given to systematic approaches to collect appropriate data and to monitor data issues as early as possible to ensure quality in execution and clarity in reporting of oncology clinical trials.

Keywords: Oncology; Clinical Trial; Treatment Emergent Adverse Event; Dose Intensity; RECIST criteria; Data cut-off Date; Event-driven Analysis; Analysis Validation

ABBREVIATIONS

AE: Adverse Event; CDISC: Clinical Data Interchange Standards Consortium; AR: Adherence Ratio; CRF: Case Report Forms; DI: Dose Intensity; EDC: Electronic Data Capture; FDA: Food and Drug Administration; ICH: International Conference on Harmonisation; OS: Overall Survival; PD: Progressive Disease; PD-I: Prescribed Dose Intensity; PFS: Progression Free Survival; P-RDI: Prescribed Relative Dose Intensity; PT: Prefer Term; RDI: Relative Dose Intensity; RECIST: Response Evaluation Criteria in Solid Tumors; TEAE: Treatment Emergent Adverse Event

INTRODUCTION

Clinical trials have become a more complex undertaking. Trials that enroll patients globally are commonplace. Biomarker trials involving companion diagnostics become more sophisticated and require coordination and seamless execution from multiple stakeholders. Innovative trial designs involve upfront planning and attention to details in execution. These factors along with regulatory requirements have placed a greater burden on the sponsors to ensure that the data collected from the trials have unimpeachable integrity, quality, and validity to draw conclusions with respect to the objectives of the trials.

Data are arguably the ultimate measure of clinical trial performance. Appropriate trial design, well-thought-out case report forms (CRF) and clear CRF completion instructions are among the first steps to ensure data are consistenly collected in order to achieve the trial objectives. These efforts are augmented by ongoing data cleaning and monitoring to ensure data accuracy. Monitoring visits are one of the most resource-intensive activities to ensure valid data are collected against source documents. The US Food and Drug Administration (FDA) has provided guidance [1] on an integrated approach to monitor clinical trial quality and subject safety through a risk-based centralized monitoring approach. The main idea is to implement a central, systematic, and ongoing review of data which allows the monitoring to be more focused and data-driven. Continued advances in technology, data sharing standards including Clinical Data Interchange Standards Consortium (CDISC) [2], and the increasing sophistication of data visualization tools promise to increase efficiency and reduce clinical trial cost.

In this article, we focus on data collection and analysis issues in oncology clinical trials. In particular, we will take a deeper dive on data related to dosing, adverse events (AEs), tumor assessments, and overall survival. Special emphases are given to considerations in collecting relevant data and in identifying data issues in oncology clinical trials. We strongly believe that the biggest bang for the buck in monitoring trial conduct and ensuring quality comes from early identification of issues and trends so preventative and remedial actions can be put in place to avoid costly damages to the trial. Analysis and reporting considerations are also discussed to highlight the need for effective and clear presentation of data.

METHODS

Treatment exposure

In oncology trials, treatment exposure is not only informative in its own right but also acts as an indirect measure of tolerability and even efficacy.

***Actual versus prescribed dose*:** Dosing information is commonly captured in a log format with key elements such as start date, stop date, actual dose, and dose change reasons. When a dose is withheld due to AE, a record with zero actual dose and dose change reason as "withheld due to AE" is expected. When dosing records do not cover a period of time continuously, it is common to assume that there are no doses given during the gap. However, one cannot be certain if this is due to data entry error (that there is actually no dosing gap). Even though it's cumbersome, dosing records should cover the treatment period continuously with zero dose records always entered and the appropriate dose change reason provided when does are not given (either intentionally withheld due to AE or missed by accident by patients).

Table 1: A sample dosing CRF and dose intensity calculations.

Start Date	Stop Date	Prescribed Daily Dose	Actual Daily Dose (mg)	Reason for Prescribed Dose Change	Reason for Administered Dose Change (if different from prescribed dose)
1/1/2000	1/2/2000	200	200		
1/3/2000	1/4/2000	200	0		01
1/5/2000	1/5/2000	200	200		
1/6/2000	1/10/2000	100	100	01	
Prescribed Dose Change Codes:					
01 Reduced due to adverse events					
02 Withhold due to adverse events					
03 Resumed to previous dose level					
04 Other (specify)					
Administered Dose Change Codes:					
01: adverse event					
02: Other					
In the above example,					
DI = (200mg/day × 2+ 200mg/day ×1 + 100mg/day × 5)/10=110 mg/day					
P-DI = (200mg/day × 5 + 100mg/day ×5)/10 =150mg/day					
RDI = DI/ (200mg/day) = 55%					
P-RDI = P-DI/(200mg/day)=75%					
AR = DI/P-DI = 73.3%					
If the protocol specified treatment duration is 20 days, then the patient stopped after only 10 days of treatment. An alternative (unconditional) dose intensity and relative dose intensity may be derived as the following:					
DI = (200mg/day × 2+ 200mg/day × 1 + 100mg/day × 5)/20=55 mg/day					
RDI = DI/ (200mg/day) = 27.5%					

Some sponsors collect prescribed dose in the dosing log along with the actual dose. We think it provides useful information and suggest that care be given to the CRF design. In a hypothetical example, a patient may be prescribed with a reduced dose due to AE but accidently doesn't take the dose. A CRF with both the prescribed and actual dose along with the respective reasons of dose change can accurately capture the scenario. Table 1 outlines a sample dosing CRF incorporating the actual dose and prescribed dose.

Pill Counts: For orally administered treatment, bottles of pills are dispensed to patients to be taken home. Patients are usually asked to keep dosing records in a diary. Upon return to the clinic, they are to return the unused pills and are dispensed with a new supply. As a part of the protocol procedure, sites are required to review and discuss the dosing diary with patients and to account for the returned pills. In addition, some sponsors design specific CRFs to capture each transaction of dispense and return of the bottles and pills. In theory, one can take the difference between each dispense and return to obtain the exact number of pills consumed and therefore the total amount of dose. In reality, such efforts do not always yield reliable results. Patients may forget to bring back a dispensed bottle at a visit; a bottle may be lost; sites may only guesstimate the number of returned pills as the actual counting is time-consuming for busy clinics. Any one of these issues poses challenges to rely on pill counts to capture actual dose administered. We view data collected from pill counts as a nice-to-have and potentially redundant to the dosing information collected in the log format described above.

Dose intensity and compliance: Dose intensity (DI) is expressed as the amount of dose per unit of time. It is calculated by dividing the actual cumulative dose by treatment duration. It is common in trials where treatment is given until disease progression. Dose intensity calculation is straightforward based on the above definition. However, in settings where treatment is given for a fixed period of time, for example in the adjuvant breast cancer setting where the standard of care is one year of trastuzumab treatment after surgery, for patients with HER2-positive disease, alternative definition of dose intensity may be relevant. If the protocol specified treatment period is for one year and a subject has stopped treatment after 6 months on drug, dose intensity may be calculated for this patient as the cumulative dose over 6 months or over one year. The former definition may be viewed as dose intensity conditional on the patient being treated. The latter definition insists on the protocol specified treatment duration regardless of the actual treatment duration (unconditional). While we are not advocating one definition of dose intensity over the other as the emphasis may be different depending on the situation, we recommend greater clarity and transparency when reporting results. In calculating treatment duration, it is common practice to add the dosing interval after the last dose. If prescribed dose is collected, prescribed dose intensity (P-DI) can also be obtained similarly.

Relative dose intensity (RDI) is calculated as the (actual) dose intensity divided by the protocol specified dose intensity. It compares the actual dose and schedule captured in dose intensity with the protocol specified intensity (protocol specified dose and schedule). With the exception of over-dose (which should be monitored and flagged), a higher RDI represents closer adherence to the protocol specified dose and schedule. Prescribed relative dose intensity (P-RDI) can also be obtained analogously reflecting prescribed rather than the actual dose and schedule relative to the protocol dosing specification. One may also be interested in calculating adherence ratio (AR), defined as the ratio between the (actual) dose intensity divided by the prescribed dose intensity. AR compares the actual dose relative to the prescribed dose with the understanding that prescribed dose has taken into account dose changes, if any, prescribed by the treating physician. It can be shown that AR may also be expressed as RDI/P-RDI.

Table 1 also includes hypothetical data of a patient to illustrate dose intensity and adherence calculations. By providing the details, we wish to highlight the nuances in summarizing dose exposure and intensity.

Dose intensity is a single summary measure incorporating both dose and treatment duration.When a treatment is given in cycles, as is common in oncology, summary measuressuch as dose received per cycle and percent of planned dose received per cycle may be more appealing. However, dose intensity and relative dose intensity may still be relevant as they capture delays of cycle time due to the need to manage treatment toxicities.

Adverse events

The collection of adverse events include description of the event, start date, stop date, seriousness, severity, relationship to study drug, actions taken and outcome. Typically, AEs are collected during the screening phase after informed consent has been signed and continues until the end of the protocol specified safety follow-up time. Ensuring the quality of safety data capture is the foundation of all pharmacovigilence activities. Common checks of the AE data include review of overlapping dates when more than one episodes of the same event of different severity are reported. Actions taken due to an AE should also be cross-checked against dosing data if it leads to a dose reduction or against the end of treatment reason if it leads to the discontinuation of treatment. A more complete suite of cross checks with other data in the database such as labs, concomitant medication, death, or hospitalization should be a part of the standard built-in data cleaning process.

Treatment-emergent adverse events: Because AEs are collected after the date the informed consent is signed which may be prior to the initiation of treatment, treatment emergent adverse events (TEAEs) are often the primary focus of the safety analyses. The idea of TEAE is to include any AE that occurs or worsens after the initiation of treatment and before a pre-defined period of time (e.g. 30 days) after the last dose of treatment. ICH E9 [3] defines TEAE as an event that emerges during treatment but having been absent during pre-treatment, or worsens relative to the pre-treatment state. There are some controversies when implementing this. The following (Figure 1 & Table 2) present four cases that illustrate the key issues. It seems that cases 1 and 3 may not be considered as TEAEs since case 1 may be considered as a continuation of the same event and case 3 may be a continuation of the same event but with a lower grade. However, for cases 2 and 4, the AEs are recorded by investigators as separate episodes starting on Day 5. Because the severity grades are no worse than the pre-existing episode, one may argue the events are pre-existing and should not be counted as TEAEs. Following this logic, what about events of the same severity which start on Day 15 rather than on Day 5? One may be hard pressed to not include separate events long after a subject has received the first dose and has continued to receive doses. We advocate a simple and inclusive approach in that any AEs with a start date on or after the first dose date (and within the pre-defined period after the last dose) should be considered as TEAE regardless of pre-treatment conditions. The TEAE summary should be complemented by a separate summary of any AEs not considered as treatment emergent (AEs occurred pre-treatment or post the pre-defined period after the last dose). When applicable, and depending on the disease area, more in-depth summaries of TEAE taking into account of pre-treatment conditions may be explored. Finally, we want to emphasize the importance of providing clear and specific CRF completion instructions to the sites on adverse events that should be recorded as separate events and events that should be considered as continuing without an end date. In our experiences, this is an area that sponsors should proactively engage the sites during the study setup phase.

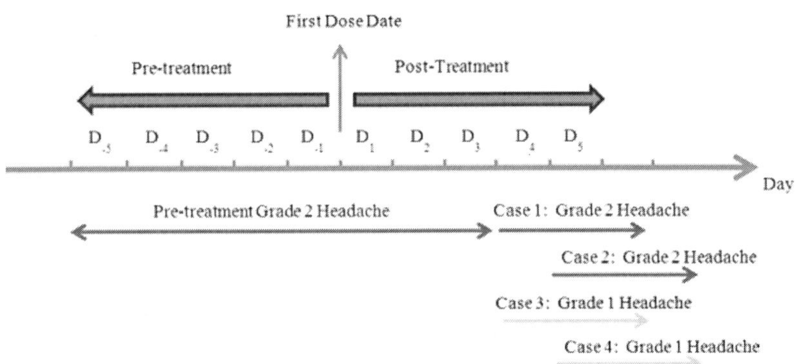

Figure 1: Determining treatment emergent adverse events (TEAEs).

Table 2: Determining treatment emergent adverse events (TEAEs).

Pre-Treatment AE Records	Post treatment AE (recorded as a separate entry from the pre-treatment record)		Comments
Grade 2 headache started 5 days before the first dose, ended on Day 3 (Day 1 is the first dose)	Case 1	Grade 2 headache started on Day 4.	Data query, potentially the same event as the pre-treatment.
	Case 2	Grade 2 headache started on Day 5	A new event of the same grade.
	Case 3	Grade 1 headache started on Day 4.	A continuing event of a lower grade.
	Case 4	Grade 1 headache started on Day 5.	A new event of a lower grade.

Incidence by severity grade: A popular way to present AE incidence table is to layer in the severity grade. For illustration purpose, we provide a simple example to highlight the issues when incorporating worst grade in the AE summary. In this example, ten subjects are given treatment A and have experienced AEs with system organ class of nervous system disorders (with preferred terms of headache and dizziness) and eye disorders (with preferred terms of dry eye and eye pain). Table 3 appears to yield some surprising results where, in the column of worst grade 1, 5 patients have reported grade 1 headache which is larger than the 2 patients reporting any grade 1 AE and the 4 patients reporting grade 1 nervous system disorders as the system organ class. This may be counter intuitive but is not an error. A patient experiencing a grade 1 headache is counted as grade 1 under headache (preferred term), but the same patient also has a grade 3 event (e.g., vision blurred) and is counted in the "Any AE" row under worst grade 3. The same applies when a patient has different severity of two preferred terms associated with the same system organ class . This can be, admittedly, quite confusing. We recommend that AE tables by severity grade using the layout as in Table 3 be shown with preferred terms (PTs) only, skipping the customary first row of "Any AEs" and the system organ class rows. A separate summary table on system organ class may be provided. An alternative layout (Table 4) avoids the issue by displaying the by-grade summary for PT only in rows rather than in columns. This is the recommended layout if one wants to include both the system organ class and preferred terms in the table.

Table 3: AE by worst grade with system organ class and preferred term.

	Arm A (N=10)					
	All Grades	Grade 1	Grade 2	Grade 3	Grade 4	Grade 5
Any AEs	10	2	3	3	1	1
Nervous System Disorder	7	4	2	1	0	0
Headache	6	5	1	0	0	0
Dizziness	6	3	2	1	0	0
Eye Disorder	8	1	3	2	1	1
Vision Blurred	6	1	3	1	1	0
Eye Pain	5	1	2	1	0	1

Tumor assessments

Tumor may be assessed over time by multiple modalities in oncology trials. These assessments contribute to the definition of key endpoints such as response rate and progression free survival (PFS). Response Evaluation Criteria in Solid Tumors (RECIST) version 1.1 [4] is a set of standardized and widely accepted criteria used to assess tumor. Any modifications by the sponsor of the criteria should be documented in the protocol and in a radiology review charter.

Automated response assessment: There are three components in the overall tumor response assessment when RECIST criteria are used: target lesion response, non-target lesion response, and the appearance of a new lesion. Each individual lesion identified at the baseline (target or non-target lesion) are tracked and entered into the CRF. Investigator assessments of response of the target, non-target, and new lesions along with an overall response assessment are provided at each protocol specified tumor assessment time. Typically, investigators are expected to do their own derivations following the RECIST criteria and then provide the response

Table 4: AE by worst grade with system organ class and preferred term.

	Arm A (N=10)
Any AEs	10
Nervous System Disorder	**7**
Headache	6
Grade 1	5
Grade 2	1
Grade 3	0
Grade 4	0
Grade 5	0
Dizziness	**6**
Grade 1	3
Grade 2	2
Grade 3	1
Grade 4	0
Grade 5	0
Eye Disorder	**8**
Vision Blurred	**6**
Grade 1	1
Grade 2	3
Grade 3	1
Grade 4	1
Grade 5	0
Eye Pain	**5**
Grade 1	1
Grade 2	2
Grade 3	1
Grade 4	0
Grade 5	1

assessment. Invariably, some errors occur along the way as some tumor burden calculations are in reference to baseline and some are in reference to the nadir (e.g., progressive disease), Sponsors may pick up these errors during the data cleaning process and issue queries. Since these queries may arrive long after the assessments have been done, investigators may or may not recall all the details why a particular response assessment is given. The time lag can be overcome by implementing a real time automated response derivation within the EDC so the investigators will get immediate feedback on any derivation errors or inconsistencies with the RECIST. Investigators should be allowed to overwrite the automated response assessment and ideally provide reasons for the discrepancy. We believe such an automated response system implemented in real time will help improve the efficiency of data cleaning and more importantly enhance the quality of the data. In addition, the investigators are given the flexibility to differ from the automated derivation to reflect the autonomy of investigator assessments.

Date of response and date of progression: In addition to the overall response assessment at each time point during the study, assessment date is also critical when it comes to defining a time-to-event endpoint such as PFS. Some sponsors require the date associated with the overall response assessment be provided in the CRF. Other sponsors require dates in the individual CRFs of target or non-target lesions but not dates of the overall response assessment. Regardless of the approach, clear instructions will need to be provided to the sites on how to fill in the dates when they are expected to provide an overall responseassessment date based on potentially different dates from each component of the assessment. The same instructions should be provided to data management and statistical programming staff tasked to derive the dates for analysis purposes. As a general principle, consistent with the FDA guidance [5], for progression based on unequivocal progression of non-target lesion or a new lesion, the disease progression (PD) date is the earlier date when PD is detected. If progression is based on target lesions where scans may be obtained at different times, the target lesion PD date is the date of the later scan when complete information is available to establish PD. For the overall response assessment when PD may be due to target lesions, non-target-lesion, or new lesions, the earliest date when PD is identified from any source is the date of PD. However, for time-to-response endpoint (partial response or complete response), the date of response is the last date when complete information is available to establish response.

Central Radiology Review: While RECIST is the standard for solid tumor assessments, its implementation in practice and consistency across global sites in a clinical trial setting can be challenging. As a result, independent radiology review is set up to assess response in a centralized and blinded fashion (although the trial may be open label) [6,7]. For the central review to be successful, a great deal of coordination and collaboration is essential among the study sites, sponsors, vendors, and central review providers. A charter is required to outline all the requisite steps and the handoffs. Data quality checks are important to be imbedded in the central review process.

Recognizing the independent nature of the central review, we recommend minimum sponsor involvement in influencing the data review. However, we encourage a thorough testing of the central review system at the beginning of the trial using a suite of pre-determined test cases to ensure that the data checks in place are compliant with the RECIST so the quality of the data can be relied upon by the sponsor at the time of the analysis.

Overall survival: Overall Survival (OS) is an objective endpoint and it's the gold standard to demonstrate clinical benefit in oncology trials. A key consideration in trial design and analysis when OS endpoint is involved is to minimize loss to follow-up. The trial protocol must draw clear distinctions between withdrawal from treatment and withdrawal from follow-up. Patients may withdraw treatment for any reason; however, every effort should be made to ensure that patients are followed up for OS and long term safety after terminating treatment. It's common to focus on deaths when the number of deaths may be used to trigger the analysis. Equal emphasis should be given to the adequacy of follow-up to patients who are censored. When there are substantial gaps in follow-up, censoring patients using the snapshot date is not advised. In addressing the loss to follow-up, some sponsors undertake public record search to identify death information. Such an approach is not without controversies as it may introduce bias because of different local regulatory and legal requirements. If data from public records are used in the analyses, we recommend the information obtained from this source be clearly flagged in the data to allow for additional sensitivity analyses.

Statistical Analysis

Design and analysis methods: For pivotal oncology trials, group sequential designs [8-10] allow for flexibility of one or more interim analyses and are the most commonly used designs. A complexity is introduced when more than one primary endpoint is involved in a group sequential design. The group sequential Holm procedure [11] has been proposed to handle both multiple primary endpoints (e.g. PFS and OS) and multiple analyses while controlling for the overall type I error rate.

Study adaptation [12-14] has been an area of fertile research although it has not gained wide-spread adoption in practice. Adaptations such as sample size re-estimation, switch of hypotheses (e.g. between non-inferiority and superiority), switch of analysis populations defined by a biomarker, dropping of an arm in a seamless phase 2/3 design are among the most researched. The growing interests in adaptive designs have prompted the U.S. FDA to issue a guidance document [15].

Bayesian designs and analyses have been adopted in phase 1 or phase 2 oncology trials with aims including dose finding or identification of winners among multiple treatments. For example, the I-SPY 2 [16] trial is a phase 2 randomized trial which used an adaptive design based on biomarker subtypes to evaluate novel agents in the neoadjuvant breast cancer setting. It employed response adaptive randomization based on Bayesian modelling of accumulating data. I-SPY 2 has the potential to speed the process of screening drugs with the goal of bringing safe and effective new drugs to market more efficiently.

Event trigger and data cut-off: In oncology trials, analyses are commonly event driven, i.e. the analyses will only occur when a pre-specified number of events (e.g. OS or PFS) are reached. Event goals are specified in the protocol and statistical analysis plan to ensure appropriate study power. In tracking the events, sponsors typically employ a statistical model [17-19] to project the time the event goal may be reached based on accumulating data. When the event goal is nearly reached, sponsors may project a data cut-off date in the future upon which all events up to the date will be included in the analysis whether the final number of events is more or less than the event goal. Alternatively, a sponsor may decide a data cut-off date upon actually observing the event goal. The data cut-off date needs to be communicated to all sites to ensure not only the event goals are reached as close as possible but also a clear understanding from sites that all data on or prior to the cut-off date must be entered and verified in a timely fashion. For interim analysis, if a different number of events from the protocol is obtained, some adjustment is necessary in the analysis, for example, the interim boundaries.

Data snapshot and filtering: For a live clinical database with EDC, data entry across global sites may occur at any moment in time either before or after the data cut-off date. Since the data cleaning and query resolution are unlikely to finish on the same day of data cut-off, a period of several weeks are commonly required to accomplish these activities. By the time a snapshot of the database is taken, a mixture of cleaned data (data prior to the cut-off date) and uncleaned data (data post the cut-off date and up to the snapshot date) is unavoidable.

This begs the question whether all data contained in the snapshot should be the basis for the analysis. Strictly speaking, the intended analysis is to include data up to the data cut-off date both from the perspective of event triggering and data cleaning. The fact that one ends up with additional data post the cut-off date has more to do with practicality than the intent. Sponsors opting to emphasize the original intent will necessarily want to filter out data contained in the snapshot that are beyond the data cut-off date. This is not a simple undertaking and requires careful planning. For example, an adverse event may have a start date before the data cut-off date but with a stop date post the data cut-off date. The stop date should not be used in calculating duration of the AE if one wants to strictly enforce the data cut-off in the analysis. It's also possible that an event (e.g. death) occurred post data cut-off. Assuming it's agreed that the death should not be counted as event in the main analysis, it's not always clear whether knowing the subject's death post data cut-off can be used to infer that the subject is alive on the data cut-off date (therefore the subject is censored on the date). We recommend using only data within the declared data cut-off date for all analysis purposes since there's no assurance that all sites enter data in a timely manner post the data cut-off date.

While "data filtering" described above is tempting with sound rationales, the benefits may not outweigh the time and efforts involved. This is especially true for interim analyses when data cleanliness is not of paramount concern compared to data timeliness. For final analyses, these extra efforts may be worthwhile.

Validation: Statistical analysis of the final or interim data is the climax of a clinical trial. The final analysis represents the fruit of labor from the patients, sites, sponsor and numerous collaborators around the world. The stakes are even higher when a phase 3 trial is reported. Since the results may be considered material for many publically traded pharmaceutical and biotech companies, time is a luxury that the sponsors do not have. To ensure accuracy of the results released to the sponsor management and then to the public, meticulous planning and seamless execution are essential. In our experiences, analysis outputs are typically generated by statistical programmers working in collaboration and under the guidance of statisticians. Programmers are expected to follow sponsor standard procedures in performing validation which forms the first line of defense. However, this alone may not be adequate as programmers tend to focus on data processing from raw data to analysis data (e.g. data conforming to CDISC standards) and from analysis data to analysis displays. We recommend a parallel, independent validation path from raw data directly to analysis results performed by statisticians or programmmers (more than one validators if necessary) for key endpoints so analyses are connected to the raw data. It reduces the risk of relying on the intermediate datasets and boosts the confidence on the final results.

CONCLUSION

Oncology clinical trials are among the most exciting and challenging. Enormous amount of interest, resources, time, and money are invested in oncology drug development. In the end, it all boils down to the data. Data quality and integrity are the cornerstones of all clinical trials. We have highlighted specific issues to consider in collecting, monitoring, and analyzing a wide range of data collected in oncology trials. These are by no means exhaustive nor should they be limiting. We have deliberately emphasized on issues that may be taken for granted in practice. We hope by sharing our experiences and recommendations, more awareness is raised toward designing and executing high quality oncology trials.

CONFLICT OF INTEREST STATEMENT

The Authors declare that there is no conflict of interest. This research received no specific grant from any funding agency in the public, commercial, or not-for-profit sectors.

REFERENCES

1. http://www.fda.gov/RegulatoryInformation/Guidances/ucm127004.htm 2006.
2. http://www.cdisc.org/standards-and-implementations.
3. http://www.ich.org/products/guidelines/efficacy/efficacy-single/article/statistical-principles-for-clinical-trials.html.
4. Eisenhauer EA, Therasse P, Bogaerts J, Schwartz LH, Sargent D, et al. (2009) New response evaluation criteria in solid tumours: Revised RECIST guideline (version 1.1). Eur J Cancer 45(2): 228-247.
5. http://www.fda.gov/downloads/Drugs/Guidances/ucm071590.pdf.
6. http://www.dovepress.com/subjective-endpoints-in-clinical-trials-the-case-for-blinded-independe-peer-reviewed-article-OAJCT#.
7. http://www.fda.gov/downloads/Drugs/GuidanceComplianceRegulatoryInformation/Guidances/UCM268555.pdf.
8. Pococok SJ (1977) Group sequential methods in the design and analysis of clinical trials. Biometrika 64(2): 191-199.

9. O' Brien PC, Fleming TR (1979) A multiple testing procedure for clinical trials. Biometrics 35(3): 549-556.

10. Lan KKG, Demets DL (1983) Discrete sequential boundaries for clinical trials. Biometrika 70(3): 655-660.

11. Ye Y, Li A, Liu L, Yao B (2013) A group sequential Holm procedure with multiple primary endpoints. Stat Medicine 32(7): 1112-1124.

12. Bauer P, Köhne K (1994) Evaluation of experiments with adaptive interim analyses. Biometrics 50(4): 1029-1041.

13. Cui L, Hung HMJ, Wang SJ (1999) Modification of sample size in group sequential clinical trials. Biometrics 55(3): 853-857.

14. Müller HH, Schäfer H (2001) Adaptive group sequential designs for clinical trials: Combining the advantages of adaptive and of classical group sequential approaches. Biometrics 57(3): 886-891.

15. http://www.fda.gov/downloads/Drugs/GuidanceComplianceRegulatoryInformation/Guidances/UCM201790.pdf.

16. Park JW, Liu MC, Yee D, Yau C, van 't Veer LJ, et al. (2016) Adaptive Randomization of Neratinib in Early Breast Cancer. Engl J Med 375(1): 11-22.

17. Ying GS, Heitjan DF (2008) Weibull prediction of event times in clinical trials. Pharm Stat 7(2): 107-120.

18. Ying GS, Heitjan DF, Chen TT (2004) Nonparametric prediction of event times in randomized clinical trials. Clinical Trials 1(4): 352-361.

19. Bagiella E, Heitjan DF (2001) Predicting analysis times in randomized clinical trials. Statistics in Medicine 20(14): 2055-2063.

10

CHAPTER

Analysis of Small-Sample Clinical Genomics Studies Using Multi-Parameter Shrinkage: Application to High-Throughput RNA Interference Screening

Mark A van de Wiel[1], Renée X de Menezes[1], Ellen Siebring-van Olst[2,3], Victor W van Beusechem[2]

[1]Department of Epidemiology and Biostatistics, VU University Medical Center, PO Box 7057, 1007 MB Amsterdam, the Netherlands.

[2]RNA Interference Functional Oncogenomics Laboratory (RIFOL), Department of Medical Oncology, VU University Medical Center, Amsterdam, the Netherlands.

[3]Department of Pulmonary Diseases, VU University Medical Center, Amsterdam, the Netherlands.

ABSTRACT

High-throughput (HT) RNA interference (RNAi) screens are increasingly used for reverse genetics and drug discovery. These experiments are laborious and costly, hence sample sizes are often very small. Powerful statistical techniques to detect siRNAs that potentially enhance treatment are currently lacking, because they do not optimally use the amount of data in the other dimension, the feature dimension.

We introduce ShrinkHT, a Bayesian method for shrinking multiple parameters in a statistical model, where 'shrinkage' refers to borrowing information across features. ShrinkHT is very flexible in fitting the effect size distribution for the main parameter of interest, thereby accommodating skewness that naturally occurs when siRNAs are compared with controls. In addition, it naturally down-weights the impact of nuisance parameters (e.g. assay-specific effects) when these tend to have little effects across siRNAs. We show that these properties lead to better ROC-curves than with the popular limma software. Moreover, in a 3 + 3 treatment vs control experiment with 'assay' as an additional nuisance factor, ShrinkHT is able to detect three (out of 960) significant siRNAs with stronger enhancement effects than the positive control. These were not detected by limma. In the context of gene-targeted (conjugate) treatment, these are interesting candidates for further research.

INTRODUCTION

Many clinical genomics studies suffer from low power and low reproducibility caused by small sample sizes. Small sample sizes may be due to high costs per sample, low availability of genomic material (e.g. for rare diseases) or even juridical restrictions (e.g. when administering an experimental drug to patients). The philosophy behind our method is to increase power and reproducibility by retrieving as much information as possible from the vertical data direction (feature space: genes, tags, small interference RNAs (siRNAs), etc.) for estimating differential treatment effects from the horizontal data direction (sample space).

In statistical terms the latter is referred to as 'shrinkage'. In a classical setting, a shrinkage estimator is a weighted average between the estimator from the concerning feature and a pooled estimator from all features. Shrinkage of dispersion-related parameters, like σ^2 for the Normal distribution, is now commonly applied to genomics data and has been implemented in popular analysis software like limma [1]. We take a step further. We show that shrinking additional parameters, including the main parameter of interest, e.g. the treatment effect, may further enhance power and reproducibility. Our approach is an Empirical Bayes framework around a Full Bayes fitting method called Integrated Nested Laplace Approximation (INLA [2]). Here, INLA provides a fast, flexible, versatile and accurate alternative to MCMC, whereas our framework uses the high-dimensional aspect of the data to estimate priors, which effectuates shrinkage.

For the analysis of RNA-seq count data, we introduced ShrinkSeq [3]. We showed its improved performance in terms of Receiver Operating Characteristic (ROC)-curves with respect to other methods like edgeR, baySeq and DESeq, in particular when the data contain many zeros and sample sizes are small. Here, we provide several extensions and new insights: 1) ability to handle high-dimensional Gaussian data; 2) model selection properties when nuisance parameters are involved; 3) flexible and powerful inference with potentially asymmetric priors.

High-throughput (HT) RNA interference (RNAi) screens [4] are increasingly used for reverse genetics and drug discovery. Statistical methods used for HT screens data analysis are commonly borrowed from small-molecule screens or even other types of high-dimensional data methods. However, HT screens data differs from other high-dimensional data in fundamental ways. Firstly, HT screens data are more susceptible to technical effects, as the cell culture plates are handled several times over a multiple day period, and the various experimental steps are performed by a variety of equipment. Secondly, studies currently involve a very small (1-3) number of replicates per condition. Hence, statistical inference is often absent in HT RNAi studies: only fold changes and standard deviations are mentioned. Thirdly, HT screens data typically involve a large amount of observations for controls, which serve as references for condition effect but are not of primary interest, and a very limited number of observations per siRNA, which are the primary interest. This highly unbalanced design essentially means that classic statistical methods are underpowered to find siRNA-specific effects.

Ideally, HT screens contain two types of controls: a negative one, which in a treatment sensitization setting can be used to estimate the effect of treatment alone, and a positive one, which is a gene known to have an (additional) effect on the response, e.g. cell viability, when silenced. While comparisons to both controls are of interest and our method applies to both, we focus on the one relative to the positive control. Then the lack of power is particularly relevant: an siRNA can only be significant (in comparison with the positive control) when the differential siRNA-specific cell viability between treatment and 'no treatment' conditions exceeds that of the positive control. Most data information then arises from treatment effect for controls, with generally hundreds of measures per replicate, whilst the main goal typically is to draw conclusions about siRNA-specific treatment sensitivity, for which only a single measure is available per replicate. There is thus great need for methods that can borrow information across features (siRNAs), to improve the chance of finding relevant siRNAs.

In this work, we use data from a cisplatin sensitization HT screen. Cisplatin is a DNA damaging agent that has been used for over 30 years to treat cancer and is part of standard therapy for some cancer-types, including non-small cell lung cancer. Unfortunately, results are suboptimal and some patients react better than others. Chemo-resistance is a major problem, for which the molecular cause is largely unknown. Cisplatin sensitization screens aim at identifying genes involved with the sensitivity to cisplatin. This knowledge may render useful biomarkers for treatment response, and elucidate which pathways are involved in resistance to cisplatin. Moreover, the identified genes are potential targets for more effective treatment when cisplatin is combined with an inhibitor of the corresponding gene product.

The data were produced as follows. Cells from the established non-small cell lung cancer (NSCLC) cell line A549 were seeded in 96 well plates. Next day, these cells were transfected with siRNAs targeting a selected set of 960 genes, using a robotic set up. This renders two sets of 24 plates for which each well contains a pool of siRNA targeting one gene. The following day a low dose of cisplatin was added to the wells of one set of plates, while the other set received an equal volume of culture medium without cisplatin. Four days after cisplatin exposure, read out of viability commenced for both sets. This procedure was repeated twice. The positive control,*BIRC7*, is a known inhibitor of apoptosis-related genes and sensitises A549 cells to cisplatin. The negative control consists of a pool of siRNAs that do not target a known human mRNA. The cisplatin concentration used was relatively low: 0.45 μg/ml. At that concentration, the reduction of viability by cisplatin in *BIRC7* silenced cells, compared to cells treated with non-targeting siRNAs, is most profound. Reducing cisplatin in a clinical setting while preserving toxic effect on the tumor is likely to reduce cytotoxic side effects like kidney and auditory nerve damage.

The HT screen data was read into R and normalized by correcting for a plate or assay effect using a linear regression model on the logarithm of the data values, considering all six screens simultaneously. Subsequently, the treatment effect was estimated for positive controls only, also controlling for possible remaining assay-specific effects. The remaining siRNA observations, corrected for control-related treatment effect, were then studied using two alternative empirical-Bayes approaches. The first one involved studying treatment effect in the corrected siRNA data by using limma. This approach shrinks the effect's variance only, which leads to a modified *t*-test. The second one is ShrinkHT, which shrinks multiple parameters: effect variance, effect size and possibly also nuisance effects like the assay-specific ones for data with Gaussian errors.

METHODS

Introduction to (Bayesian) shrinkage

Consider a simple data set, for which features (e.g. siRNAs) X_2, ..., X_p are measured on n = 6 subjects (divided in two groups) only. For illustration purpose assume feature X_1 is measured on the same 6 subjects, but also in 4 other studies (so 5 in total) with the same technology and study design. Feature X_1 will be used to illustrate the potential beneficial effect of shrinkage. A simple Analysis of Variance (ANOVA)-type model for groups j = 1 and j = 2 is:

$$Y_{jk} = \alpha + \beta_j + \varepsilon_{jk}, \tag{1}$$

where Y_{jk} is the data for subject k in group j, α is a common intercept and ε_{jk} follows a central Normal distribution. In addition, β_1 is set to zero, so β_2 can be interpreted as the mean log-fold change between groups. In a Bayesian setting, model (1) is not complete: priors need to be specified for all parameters. Let us focus on the prior for β_2. In a conventional Bayesian analysis, a flat prior would be used, e.g. a Gaussian with very large variance, f.e. $N(0; 100^2)$. This reflects a complete lack of prior believe or evidence on the size and direction of the log-fold change. Refer to model (1) with this prior as model m1. Now our method allows to estimate a prior from $X_2 \ldots, X_p$ (or from $X_1 \ldots, X_p$: because p is large X_1 has a negligible effect on the estimate, so we do not violate the 'do not use the data twice' principle). Suppose the log-fold changes tend to be much more concentrated, reflected by an estimated shrinkage prior $N(0, \tau^2)$, with $\tau = 0.5$. Use of this prior defines model m2. Suppose their is no effect for feature X_1, so $\beta_2 = 0$. Figure 1(a) illustrate estimates of β_2 for X_1 for the five studies under models m1 and m2. We observe two beneficial effects of the shrinkage prior: the means are shrunken towards zero (and hence better reproducible), and the standard deviations are markedly smaller than for the vague prior. For large sample sizes the differences between the shrunken estimates and the ones based on a vague prior diminish (see Figure 1(b)), because the data then dominates the prior.

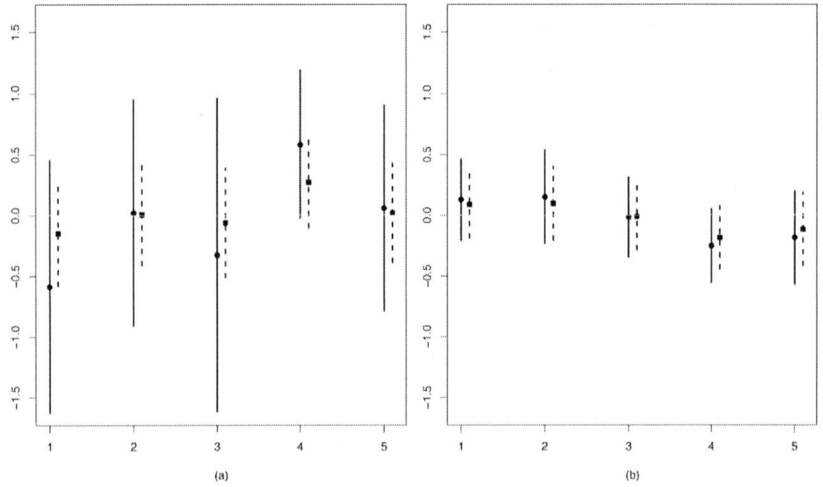

Figure 1. Illustration of shrinkage effect. Estimates of β_2 (mean ± standard deviation) for five studies, using model m1 (vague prior; circle/solid line) and model m2 (shrinkage prior; square/dashed). (a): $n = 6$, (b): $n = 40$. Data are generated from model (1) with $\beta_2 = \beta_1 = 0$ and εjk=dN(0,1).

Use of a shrinkage prior effectuates (Bayesian) shrinkage: (posterior) estimates of the feature-specific log-fold changes are shrunken towards the overall mean log-fold change by using a prior that is concentrated around this mean. Here, the high-dimensional aspect of our data plays an important role: the availability of X_1, ..., X_p, with p large, allows us to *estimate* a common prior, rather than assuming it. In our example, the shrunken prior is correctly positioned for X_1. However, if the true β_2 is not well supported by the prior, shrinkage may do more harm than good, because it may introduce a bias. This is the reason why we allow flexible, non-parametric priors, which can accommodate a wide variety of distributional properties such as skewness or heavy tails. Below we discuss estimation of such priors.

Design of cisplatin sensitization HT screening experiment

The analysis of the HT screening data consists of three parts: 1) Estimation of the hyper-parameters (parameters of priors), which effectuates shrinkage; 2) Estimation of the model parameters; 3) Inference. The design of the experiment is given in Table 1. Next, we describe the model for the HT screening data.

Table 1. Design of the study

		Measurement			
y_{11}	y_{21}	y_{12}	y_{22}	y_{13}	y_{23}
Untreated	Treated	Untreated	Treated	Untreated	Treated
Assay 1	Assay 1	Assay 2	Assay 2	Assay 3	Assay 3

Design of the cisplatin sensitization HT screening experiment

Model

The model is the same for all siRNAs and hence we drop the siRNA index when not referring to a specific siRNA. Then, Y_{jk} is the jth observation for the kth assay for a given siRNA, where $j = 1$ corresponds to 'no treatment' and $j = 2$ to 'treatment'.

$$
\begin{aligned}
Y_{jk} &= \text{offset}_{jk} + \beta_0 + \beta_j^{\text{treat}} + \beta_k^{\text{assay}} + \varepsilon_{jk} \\
\varepsilon_{jk} &=^d N(0, \sigma^2) \\
\beta_k^{\text{assay}} &=^d N(0, \tau^2) for\ k \geq\ 2;\ \beta_1^{\text{assay}} = 0 \\
\beta_2^{\text{treat}} &=^d F_{NP};\ \beta_1^{\text{treat}} = 0 \\
\sigma^{-2} &=^d \Gamma(\alpha_1, \alpha_2)
\end{aligned} \quad (2)
$$

Here, offset$_{jk}$ is trivially computed from the positive control data. It is the estimated effect of the positive controls for treatment level j and assay k using the same model as above, but with vague priors for all parameters. Since the amount of data on the positive controls is large (288 measurements), and the standard deviations of the estimates are small, we do not further propagate the uncertainty of these estimates.

The crux behind our method is that we empirically estimate hyper-parameters τ^2, α_1, α_2 and F_{NP}, which is a non-parametric, log-concave distribution function [5]. The latter provides maximum flexibility for the main parameter of interest, βtreat2. In the Results section we show that this flexibility is essential for detecting significant siRNAs.

Estimation of hyper-parameters

Let us first consider the empirical estimation of the Gaussian variance parameter τ^2. Suppose we initially do not estimate τ^2 and just set it to some large value (eg 10^6) which reflects a vague prior for βassayk. Likewise other hyper-parameters are initialized to induce vague priors, including a vague Gaussian prior to initialize F_{NP}. Then, INLA provides posterior distributions of all parameters. Now write m_{ik} and v_{ik} as the posterior mean and variance of βassayik, where we add index i to indicate siRNA i. In other words, m_{ik} and v_{ik} are means and variances conditional on the data for siRNA i. Using the well-known variance propagation rule, $V(A) = V_B(E(A|B)) + E_B(V(A|B))$, we may now simply re-estimate the unconditional, prior variance by

$$\hat{\tau}^2 = \hat{V}(m_{ik}) + \bar{v}_{ik}, \quad (3)$$

where V^ is the sample variance estimator. Now, the procedure may be repeated until convergence, where new posteriors are computed under the updated prior variance τ^2. Figure2(b) shows an example of central Gaussian priors that result from iterative estimates of τ2. The rationale behind this iterative procedure is as follows. Posteriors are a compromise between the prior and the likelihoods (the data). Hence, as long as the common prior 'conflicts' with the data, pooling the posteriors, which is what (3) does, leads to a prior that, in a global sense, is more in line with the data. Of course, here it is quintessential to have much data in the vertical direction, siRNAs, to ensure that the prior does not tune to one particular siRNA.

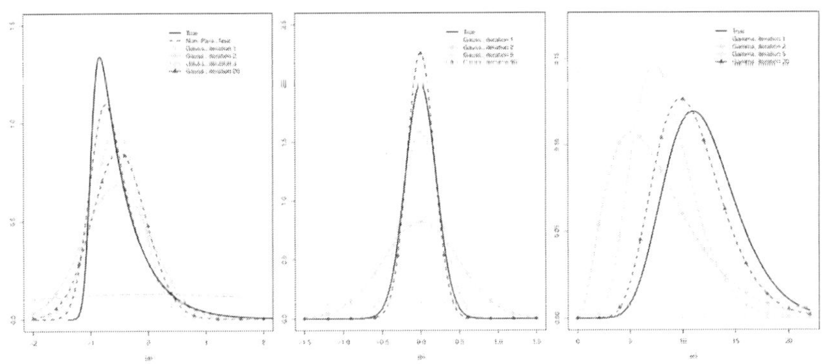

Figure 2. Iterative estimates of priors. (a) Treatment parameter βtreat2; (b) Nuisance parameters βassayk; (c) Precision σ^{-2}.

For non-Gaussian, parametric distributions the above moment-estimator is replaced by a maximum likelihood-based one. Importantly, the procedure above may trivially be extended to estimate multiple priors: at each iteration INLA provides posteriors given *all* priors, hence accounting for potential interdependencies, whereas the re-estimation of the priors depends only on the marginal posteriors of the concerning parameter.

Finally, let us shortly explain how F_{NP} in model (2) is estimated. INLA can currently not deal with non-parametric priors. Hence, in the above joint iterative procedure we have to assume a parametric prior for βtreat2, e.g. Gaussian. Denote this prior with $\pi(\beta)$. Now suppose we want to replace this prior by a non-parametric one $\pi^*(\beta)$, the density corresponding to distribution function F_{NP}. INLA returns posteriors $\pi(\beta/Y)$ under prior $\pi(\beta)$. The following re-weighting allows to compute a posterior $\pi^*(\beta/Y)$ under prior $\pi^*(\beta)$:

$$\pi^*(\beta\backslash Y) = \frac{\pi(\beta\backslash Y)\,\pi^*(\beta)/\pi(\beta)}{\int \pi(\beta\backslash Y)\,\pi^*(\beta)/\pi(\beta)\,d\beta},$$

where the denominator scales the numerator to ensure that $\pi*(\beta|Y)$ is a density integrating to one. The principle for estimating $\pi*(\beta)$ (and hence F_{NP}) is the same as with the above joint iterative procedure: iteratively and alternatingly update $\pi*(\beta)$ and $\pi*(\beta|Y)$. Here, the new update of $\pi*(\beta)$ is just a log-concave fit to a large sample of the empirical mixture of posteriors of βtreati2, where log-concavity helps to stabilize the tails.

Hence, the joint iterative procedure is followed by a marginal iterative procedure (which updates only one prior) and together they provide estimates of τ^2, α_1, α_2, F_{NP} and the posteriors of βtreati2. Several (mathematical) details of the procedure, such as approximate equivalence to maximum marginal likelihood, convergence criteria and various types of parametric priors are further discussed in [3].

INFERENCE

An important feature of HT screening is that, due to the interpretation of the βtreati2 (treatment sensitization effect relative to a positive control), one is mostly interested in βtreati2>0 This implies that inference needs to be one-sided. This is particularly important in an FDR setting: if the inference is performed two-sided, so also aims at detecting βtreati2<0, this may heavily bias the results for βtreati2>0, even when those are a posteriori selected. The reason is that the many 'significant' results for βtreati2<0 (which are to be expected: many siRNAs will have smaller effects than the positive control) push the FDR downwards. This asymmetry for the positive and negative effects is further highlighted in the Results section.

In [3] we argued that in a shrinkage context the posterior probability $p_{0i} = 1 - p_i = 1-P(\beta treati2>0||Yi)$ can be interpreted as a local false discovery rate [6], which for cut-off $t$leads to Bayesian False Discovery Rate (BFDR [7]) when averaged over all $p_{0i} \leq t$. This can be used analogously to ordinary FDR.

RESULTS

Successful estimation of the priors

To assess whether priors can be successfully estimated in this very challenging setting with only 6 measurements per siRNA, two conditions and the presence of a three-level nuisance factor (assay), we set up a simulation that is strongly motivated from the data: the model is the same as (2) except for the offset which is not relevant here. Moreover, the effect size distribution $F_{NP}$is an asymmetric one: $\Gamma(1, 0.5)$ shifted to the left by $\Delta = -1$, where our main interest is in the positive tail. Finally, α_1 and α_2 are set to 12 and 1, respectively, such that the resulting Gamma distribution mimics the observed one for the estimates of σ^{-2} and $\tau = 0.2$ which implies small assay effects, as observed in the data as well. Thousand siRNAs are simulated. The results of the iterative algorithms are displayed in Figure 2.

Given the sample sizes and the number of model parameters per siRNA, the results are very accurate. From (b) and (c) we conclude that the final parametric estimates (Iteration 20) are fairly close to the true ones for the nuisance parameter and the precision. For the first, the final estimate is $\hat{\tau}=0.18$, whereas for the latter it is $(\hat{\alpha}1, \hat{\alpha}2) = (10.90, 1.01)$. From (a) it is clear that the non-parametric estimate can provide a substantial improvement with respect to the Gaussian one for the parameter of interest. Note that the left-tail is somewhat more difficult to estimate due to its steepness, whereas the right-tail (reflecting positive effects, in which we are interested) is very accurately estimated.

COMPARISON

We compare ShrinkHT with limma in a data-based simulation set-up. Here, the functional screening data serves as a template for the sample sizes, number of features and noise levels. More specifically, we simulate two groups of three samples for 960 features from Gaussian distributions with standard deviations equalling those of the corresponding data estimates. For the main parameters of interest, the differences of means, we assume that 80% of these equal exactly 0. The remaining 20% is simulated from four differential effect size distributions: Gamma(0.5, 0.75), halfNormal(0, 0.47), Gamma(0.25, 0.75) and halfNormal(0, 0.25). Here, the half-Normal distributions contain twice the mass of the positive part of the central Normal ones. The first two distribution corresponds to a mean differential effect of $\delta = 0.375$, whereas the latter two correspond to $\delta/2$.

The simulated data were analyzed with ShrinkHT and limma. In this setting, the two approaches differ essentially in only one aspect: in addition to the standard deviations, ShrinkHT shrinks the mean differential effects whereas limma does not. After the analysis, significance results are ranked for both approaches, enabling computation of the False Positive Rate (FPR; 1-specificity) and True Positive Rate (TPR; sensitivity). Figure 3 displays the resulting ROC-curves. For all comparisons we show partial ROC-curves and partial Area-Under-the-Curve (AUC) because in a testing setting only small FPR (we use FPR ≤ 0.2) is relevant [8]. Partial AUC (pAUC) is expressed in terms of relative AUC (rAUC), rAUC = pAUC = $(0.2^2 * 0.5)$, where the denominator is the expected AUC for a non-informative decision procedure.

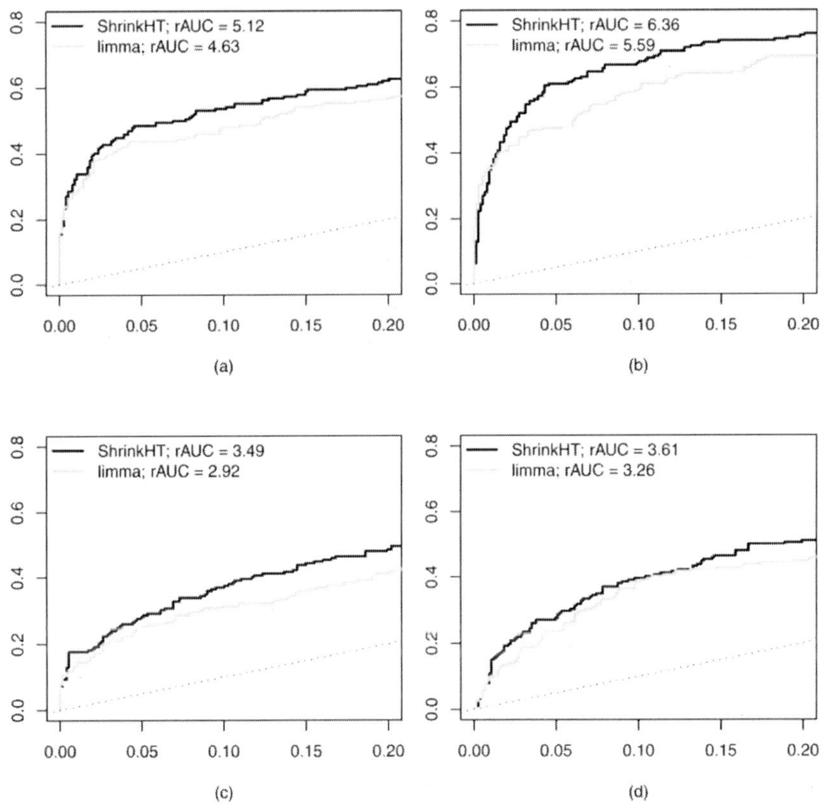

Figure 3. ROC-curves for four effect size distributions. X-axis: False Positive Rate (1-specificity), y-axis: True Positive Rate (sensitivity). (a) Gamma(0.5; 0.75); (b) halfNormal(0, 0.47); (c) Gamma(0.25, 0.75); (d) halfNormal(0, 0.25).

Figure 3 clearly shows the benefit of additional shrinkage in ShrinkHT. For example, for FPR = 0.05, the TPRs of ShrinkHT are 1.11, 1.29, 1.13 and 1.16 times higher than those of limma for cases (a)-(d), respectively.

Analysis of HT screening data

To illustrate the effect of several levels of shrinkage, we compute *eqN*: the 'equivalent number of replicates', which equals $eqN = N/p^*$, with total sample size $N = 6$ and p^* the effective number of parameters in the model [9]. High values of *eqN* lead to more precise, and hence more reproducible, estimates of the parameters. Shrinkage can potentially decrease p^* and hence increase *eqN*. We consider four scenarios: 1) no shrinkage (flat priors); 2) shrinkage of sd σ only; 3) shrinkage of σ and βtreat2; 4) shrinkage of σ, βtreat2 and βassayk.

In scenario 1) *eqN* equals 1.5 for all siRNAs. This is to be expected, because with flat priors and Gaussian models p^* is just the number of free parameters [9], which is 4 in model (2). In scenario 2) *eqN* also equals 1.5 for all siRNAs, because σ is a hyper-parameter in the hierarchical model, which does not contribute to the computation of p^* [9]. Hence shrinkage of this parameter has no effect on *eqN*. For scenario 3) the mean *eqN* equals 1.73 (sd: 0.01), whereas for scenario 4) the mean *eqN* equals 3.21 (sd: 0.08). Hence, in particular shrinkage of the 2 free assay parameters has a very beneficial effect on *eqN*. In fact, under scenarios 1) and 2) sample size N should be more than doubled to obtain approximately the same value of *eqN*: $N' = 13$ would result in $\text{eqN}' = 13 = 4 = 3.25$. The gain in *eqN* for scenario 4 is due to the strong reduction of p^*, which results from the very narrow central Gaussian prior for βassayk: standard deviation $\hat{\tau}$=0.095. Hence, the assay parameters are strongly shrunken towards 0, which illustrates the quasi-parameter-selection property of our method.

An interesting aspect of HT screens data is that when comparing treatment enhancement effect of siRNAs with that of the positive control it is likely that relatively many siRNAs are less effective than the positive control. Here, we show that it is quintessential to account for this potential asymmetry in the statistical analysis. Figure 4 shows the estimated Gaussian (and hence estimated) treatment effect size distribution, and the flexible, non-parametric one, which allows for skewness. Importantly, the two differ strongly on the area of primary interest, the positive area, reflected in the 0.0529/0.0397 = 1.33 times larger mass in this area for the non-parametric one. More importantly, the practical consequence is that at a 0.1 cut-off for the BFDR the non-parametric prior leads to 3 detections of siRNAs that have a stronger effect than the positive control, whereas the Gaussian prior results in only 1 detection (see Table 2). At Benjamini-Hochberg FDR cut-of 0.1, limma returns no detections when one-sided testing is used. However, the comparison with limma should be interpreted tentatively, because the true false positive rate is unknown.

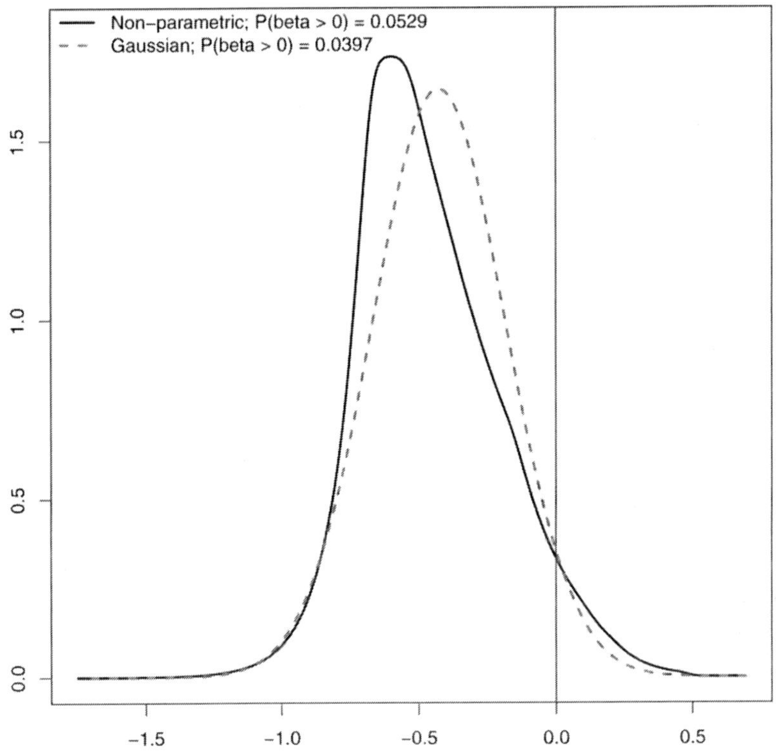

Figure 4. Estimates of Gaussian and non-parametric prior. Gaussian and non-parametric estimates of the treatment sensitization effect size (βtreat2) density and the prior probabilities P(βtreat2>0): the area under the positive part of the curves.

Table 2. Results of the analysis

Id	Untreated			Treated			$\hat{\beta}_{i2}^{treat}$	ShrinkHT NP; BFDR	ShrinkHT G; BFDR	limma FDR
608	-0.63	0.22	-0.14	-1.20	-1.29	-1.37	0.337	0.0136	0.080	0.727
749	0.22	0.28	0.43	-0.51	-0.42	-0.25	0.255	0.0362	0.115	0.413
176	0.38	0.39	0.59	-0.06	-0.31	0.11	0.175	0.0738	0.169	0.727

1st column: siRNA id; 2nd to 7th column: log_2 cell viability data for untreated and treated cell lines, corrected for the differential effect in positive control; 8th column: estimate of treatment sensitization effect ('untreated - treated') in excess of the positive control when ShrinkHT is used with a non-parametric prior; 9th and 10th column: BFDRs when using a non-parametric and Gaussian prior; 11th column: Benjamini-Hochberg corrected FDR for limma results

Table 2 also shows the posterior mean estimates of βtreati2 when using the non-parametric treatment effect size prior. So, for example, the enhancement effect of siRNA 608 on cell viability is estimated to be $2^{0.337} = 1.26$ times larger than that of the positive control. Note that our shrinkage implies that this estimate is intrinsically corrected for selection bias [10].

CONCLUSION

We discussed ShrinkHT, a new method for analyzing HT screening data. Its efficiency and power were demonstrated in both simulation and real data settings. We showed that it is able to detect siRNAs that sensitize cells to cisplatin with a stronger effect than the positive control. It is important to have several candidates that exhibit strong effects, because in the trajectory of further validation many siRNAs are likely to fail. HT screens are expensive and laborious which explains the small sample sizes (often smaller than 3 vs 3) found in literature. Still, even when such small sample size studies are considered as pilots it is important to select the right features for further experiments and to have a good estimate of the false discovery rate to minimize the risk of wasting resources and time.

While we focused on the comparison with the positive control, the comparison with the negative control is at least as important. Here, the gain of ShrinkHT with respect to other methods is relatively less when considering treatment sensitization, because these effects tend to be large when compared to the negative control. On the other hand, the siRNAs that sensitize the treatment *less* than the negative control are also of interest, because these may protect the cells against the treatment. Those protective effects are likely to be smaller and less prevalent than enhancement effects. The adaptivity of the prior towards non-symmetric situations like these renders ShrinkHT very suitable to find such protective effects.

For some HT screens many siRNAs have significantly larger effects than the negative control, whereas none of these has a significantly stronger effect than the positive control (or a good positive control is lacking). For example, silencing of the commonly used positive control gene*PLK1* usually completely kills cells irrespective of the treatment modality. Then, inference with respect to the controls is only partly helpful for selecting siRNAs that sensitize treatment for further validation. In such a case, our method allows a potentially useful alternative: inference with respect to the mean or mode. In an empirical Bayes setting, the prior can be assumed known when estimating marginal posteriors and hence also when drawing inference from these. Hence, we may base the 'null-hypothesis' on e.g. the mean of the prior of the primary parameter of interest, βtreat, and declare an siRNA significant if its effect is significantly larger than this mean. Since the prior mean reflects the average posterior mean over all siRNAs, such significance should be interpreted as a relative statement: the concerning siRNA has a significantly larger effect than the average. In our setting, 181 siRNAs showed such a significant effect at BFDR ≤ 0.1.

In silico validation of our approach is not straightforward. Large sample HT screens are not available, which disallows a sample splitting approach like we performed for RNA-seq data [3]. For those data we demonstrated better reproducibility of the results from our approach with respect to others. On genome-wide screens, pathway (enrichment) analysis could be useful, but our selected set of 960 genes is likely too small for this purpose. Biological validation of significant siRNAs (hits) is planned for the near future. Follow up in RNAi screens with pools of siRNAs targeting the mRNA of one gene, such as in our example data set, starts with the process called deconvolution; each of the single siRNAs from a hit pool is tested to see if it elicits the same effect. Often this is accompanied by quantification of the knock down of the targeted mRNA, in order to detect possible off target effects of the siRNAs. In this particular screen, deconvolution will be combined with a dose response curve to cisplatin to truly assess the sensitizing effect of siRNAs targeting the gene of interest.

ShrinkHT is part of the R-package 'ShrinkBayes', under the function name 'ShrinkGauss'. ShrinkBayes also includes ShrinkSeq for the analysis of RNA-seq data. The package is available from http://www.few.vu.nl/~mavdwiel. We are convinced that ShrinkHT contributes to powerful and reliable detection of siRNAs which, in the context of gene-targeted (conjugate) treatment, are interesting candidates for further validation.

ACKNOWLEDGEMENTS

We thank Ida van der Meulen-Muileman for technical assistance in liquid handling.

Ellen Siebring-van Olst is supported by the Walter Bruckerhoff Stiftung. High-throughput screens were conducted at the RNA Interference Functional Oncogenomics Laboratory (RIFOL) core facility at the VUmc Cancer Center Amsterdam, which was established with support from the Stichting VUmc CCA.

DECLARATIONS

The publication costs for this article were shared by all authors: the Departments of Epidemiology & Bio-statisics, Medical Oncology and Pulmonary Diseases, VU University Medical Center, Amsterdam, provided funding in three equal parts.

This article has been published as part of *BMC Medical Genomics* Volume 6 Supplement 2, 2013: Selected articles from the Second Annual Translational Bioinformatics Conference (TBC 2012). The full contents of the supplement are available athttp://www.biomedcentral.com/bmcmedgenomics/supplements/6/S2.

COMPETING INTERESTS

The authors declare that they have no competing interests.

AUTHORS' CONTRIBUTIONS

MvdW developed the analysis method and software (ShrinkHT). MvdW and RdM performed statistical analyses. ESvO, VvB and RdM designed the RNAi HTS experiment. ESvO performed the experiment.

MvdW drafted the manuscript. All authors read and approved the final manuscript.

REFERENCES

1. Smyth GK: Linear models and empirical Bayes methods for assessing differential expression in microarray experiments. Stat Appl Genet Mol Biol. 2004, 3: Article3

2. Rue H, Martino S, Chopin N: Approximate Bayesian inference for latent Gaussian models by using integrated nested Laplace approximations (with discussion). J R Statist Soc B. 2009, 71: 319-392.

3. Van de Wiel M, Leday G, Pardo L, Rue H, van der Vaart A, van Wieringen W: Bayesian analysis of RNA sequencing data by estimating multiple shrinkage priors. Biostatistics. 2013, 14: 113-128.

4. Mullenders J, Bernards R: Loss-of-function genetic screens as a tool to improve the diagnosis and treatment of cancer. Oncogene. 2009, 28: 4409-4420.

5. Lutz D, Rufibach K: logcondens: Computations related to univariate log-concave density estimation. J Statist Software. 2011, 39: 1-28.

6. Efron B, Tibshirani R, Storey JD, Tusher V: Empirical Bayes analysis of a microarray experiment. J Amer Statist Assoc. 2001, 96: 1151-1160.

7. Ventrucci M, Scott EM, Cocchi D: Multiple testing on standardized mortality ratios: a Bayesian hierarchical model for FDR estimation. Biostatistics. 2011, 12: 51-67.

8. Dodd LE, Pepe MS: Partial AUC estimation and regression. Biometrics. 2003, 59: 614-623. Spiegelhalter DJ, Best NG, Carlin BP, van der Linde A: Bayesian measures of model complexity and fit. J R Statist Soc B. 2002, 64: 583-639.

9. Crager MR: Gene identification using true discovery rate degree of association sets and estimates corrected for regression to the mean. Stat Med. 2010, 29: 33-45.

11
CHAPTER

Modifying the Classical F Test for Microarray Experiments

Bourget G

Department of Mathematics, California State University, Fullerton, CA, USA

ABSTRACT

Microarray data has a high dimensional data structure that makes statistical inference drawn from this type of data challenging. Since current statistical methods are generally for "small p and large n", these methods can be insufficient to draw valid conclusions for microarray data. Nevertheless, some of these methods, such as ANOVA (F test), are still widely used. One of the assumptions of the classical F test is that populations (genes) are assumed to be independent. This assumption is obviously violated in microarray experiments because gene-gene interactions can naturally occur. In this paper, we use an effective "column" size idea to take correlations among genes into account to modify the classical F test. We consider various magnitudes of correlation among genes in Monte Carlo simulation studies. We compare the proposed test (F-MOD) with the classical F test and multivariate Hotelling's T^2 test through validity and power analyses. We also demonstrate the proposed test with real type 2 diabetes mellitus gene expression data, which was obtained from the Gene Expression Omnibus (GEO) database with accession number GSE25724.

Keywords: Effective sample size; High dimensional data; Hotelling's T^2 test; Microarray

INTRODUCTION

Completion of the human genome sequence allows researchers to study expression of 20,000-30,000 genes in a single assay. There are three types of platforms: short oligonucleotide (25-30 base), long oligonucleotide (50-80 base), and cDNA. However, the most two common platform are based on collections of cDNA clones [1] or short (25 base) oligonucleotides synthesized in situ by photolithographic methods [2]. Although microarrays are the most extensively used technology for studying gene expression, it has a high dimensional data structure that makes statistical inference from this type of data challenging [3]. Several methods such as clustering and classification have been used to identify groups of genes that share similar functions [4,5]. However, while clustering and classification are useful techniques to search for similar genes, these techniques do not answer the question of which genes are differentially expressed under different conditions (e.g. cancer cells versus normal cells). The answer to the question requires hypothesis testing with null hypothesis of no difference in the means of gene expressions under different conditions. Various statistical tests have been proposed involving fold change, linear models, as well as Bayesian methods [6-8]; however, progress has been slow in adopting these methods in microarray analysis. Moreover, all of these methods have the common characteristic of being univariate methods.

A common characteristic of high dimensional data is that it has high dimension (p), and relatively small sample size (n). This kind of data structure is called "large p and small n". Besides having high dimensional data, microarray data also have correlation structure [9]. Most of the current methods either ignore high dimensional data structure or fail to efficiently take correlations among genes into account. Multivariate analysis can take correlations among genes into account by analyzing genes jointly. Consequently, multivariate analysis methods have recently being used in microrray data [10,11].

However, these methods are not straightforward, and most importantly ignore the multidimensional structure of the gene expression data.

Hotelling's T^2 test is one of the multivariate analysis methods that takes correlations among genes into account to identify differentially expressed genes. It has been applied in genome association studies [12], microarray process control [13], and data control charts [14]. However, Hotelling's T^2 test does not take high dimensional data structure into account. For example, in a comparison of two groups, this test requires an explicit condition on data dimension and sample size: for fixed p, $p < n_1 + n_2 - 1$, where p is the number of genes, n_1 is the sample size of the group 1, and n_2 is the sample size of the group 2. Lu, *et al.* [15] presented a new T^2 statistic for analyzing microarray data. They used first a multiple forward search algorithm to select a subset of feature vectors in a high-dimensional microarray dataset to reduce the dimension (i.e., p) to satisfy the restriction $p < n_1 + n_2 - 1$, and then they implemented the Hotelling's T^2 test.

Moreover, as an alternative test to Hotelling's T^2, Chen, *et al.* [16] proposed a two-sample test for the means of high-dimensional data.

In this paper, we present a different approach proposed in Lu, *et al.* [15]. Our approach is more general and practical than that of in [15], and moreover does not implement Hotelling's T^2 test but the simple classical F test. The proposed modified$F$ test is denoted by F-MOD. We use an effective sample size idea to take correlation among genes into account [17-19]. The effective sample size formula was originally proposed by Clifford, *et al.* [20], and was improved for small sample sizes by Dutilleul, *et al.* (1993) [21]. Also, the same effective sample size formula was used in modified F tests to assess multiple correlation between one spatial process and several others [22], and to assess correlation between two time series [23]. We implement the same effective sample size formula described in [21] to compute effective column size not effective sample size. Henceforth, we introduce a new nomenclature term "effective column size". To adopt the formula in [21], we consider the same structure of the design matrix (1) in the Methods section.

An another statistical technique for finding significant genes in a set of microarray experiments is Significance Analysis of Microarray (SAM) proposed by Tusher, *et al.* [24]. The SAM uses repeated permutations of the data to determine if the expression of any genes are significantly related to the response. It uses a set of gene-specific *t* tests. Since, the classical *F*, Hotellings T^2, and *F*-MOD tests use global *F* tests and not individual *t* tests as in SAM, we do not consider the SAM as one of the methods to be compared in this paper. Also, the goal of SAM is to handle gene-specific fluctuations by considering a statistic based on the ratio of change in gene expression to standard deviation in the data for that gene. However, in this paper, our goal is to handle gene-gene interactions and not in gene-specific fluctuations, which are two different problems to tackle.

The remainder of the paper is organized as follows. In the Methods section, we describe Hotelling's T^2, classical *F*, and *F*-MOD tests, and in the Results section we outline Monte Carlo simulation studies, present its findings, and analyze gene expression data of type 2 diabetes mellitus. Finally, we draw conclusions in the Discussion section.

METHODS

Comparing Mean Vectors from Two Populations

A s ingle multivariate observation is the collection of measurements on *p* different variables (genes) taken from the same trial (array). If *n* observations have been obtained, the entire data set can be represented in an $n \times p$ matrix

$$\mathbf{X} = \begin{bmatrix} X_{11} & X_{12} & \cdots & X_{1p} \\ X_{21} & X_{22} & \cdots & X_{2p} \\ \vdots & \vdots & \ddots & \vdots \\ X_{n1} & X_{n2} & \cdots & X_{np} \end{bmatrix} = \begin{bmatrix} \mathbf{X}'_1 \\ \mathbf{X}'_2 \\ \vdots \\ \mathbf{X}'_n \end{bmatrix} \quad (1)$$

The row vector $\mathbf{X}'_j$ represents the *jth* multivariate observation. The matrix X represents *p* genes each having *n*observations. Now, consider a microarray experiment of n_1 and n_2 samples from populations 1 and 2, respectively. For example, population 1 can represent the disease group, while population 2 can represent the healthy group. Suppose that the expression levels of p genes are measured and matrix representations of populations 1 and 2 are defined in (1) as X and Y. The observations on p variables can be arranged as follows:

$$\text{Population 1:} \qquad \mathbf{X}'_1, \mathbf{X}'_2, \ldots, \mathbf{X}'_{n_1}$$

$$\text{Population 2:} \qquad \mathbf{Y}'_1, \mathbf{Y}'_2, \ldots, \mathbf{Y}'_{n_2}$$

Our goal in this paper is to only make inferences about the differences of the vector mean of the populations. That is, we want to know if $\mu_1 = \mu_2$, or equivalently if $\mu_1 - \mu_2 = 0$. However, one further can investigate which means are different if the hypothesis of $\mu_1 - \mu_2 = 0$ is concluded. We need to make some assumptions to provide answers to these questions. The assumptions are:

1. The sample $\mathbf{X}'_1, \mathbf{X}'_2, \ldots, \mathbf{X}'_{n_1}$ is a random sample of n_1 from a p-variate population with mean vector μ_1 and covariance matrix Σ_1.
2. The sample $\mathbf{Y}'_1, \mathbf{Y}'_2, \ldots, \mathbf{Y}'_{n_2}$ is a random sample of n_2 from a p-variate population with mean vector μ_2 and covariance matrix Σ_2.
3. The samples $\mathbf{X}'_1, \mathbf{X}'_2, \ldots, \mathbf{X}'_{n_1}$ are independent of the samples $\mathbf{Y}'_1, \mathbf{Y}'_2, \ldots, \mathbf{Y}'_{n_2}$.

For large samples, these assumptions are enough to make an inference about $\mu_1 - \mu_2$. However, when the sample sizes $n_1$and n_1 are small we need to have the following assumptions as well.

1. Both populations are multivariate normal, and
2. $\Sigma_1 = \Sigma_2$.

The null (H_0) and alternative (H_a) hypotheses we are interested are:

$$H_0: \mu_1 - \mu_2 = 0 \qquad \text{versus} \qquad H_a: \mu_1 - \mu_2 \neq 0 \tag{2}$$

where $\mu_1 = (\mu_{11}, \mu_{12}, \ldots, \mu_{1p})'$ is the vector mean expression level of population 1, and $\mu_2 = (\mu_{21}, \mu_{22}, \ldots, \mu_{2p})'$ is the vector mean expression level of population 2. The null and alternative hypotheses can also be rewritten as

$$H_0 : (\mu_{11} - \mu_{21}, \mu_{12} - \mu_{22}, \ldots, \mu_{1p} - \mu_{2p})' = (0, 0, \ldots, 0)'$$
$$H_a : (\mu_{11} - \mu_{21}, \mu_{12} - \mu_{22}, \ldots, \mu_{1p} - \mu_{2p})' \neq (0, 0, \ldots, 0)' \quad (3)$$

or equivalently

$$H_0 : \mu_{11} = \mu_{21}, \mu_{12} = \mu_{22}, \ldots, \mu_{1p} = \mu_{2p}$$
$$H_a : \text{at least one } \mu_{1i} = \mu_{2i}, (i = 1, 2, \ldots, p) \quad (4)$$

Note that, we test the mean expression of p genes all together not the individual mean expressions in (2) - (4). That is, we consider a global test not an individual test.

Hotelling's T^2 Test

We consider a microarray experiment composing of n_1 samples from population 1 and n_2 samples from population 2. Let X_{ij} be the expression level for gene j of sample i from population 1, and Y_{kj} be the expression level for gene j of sample $k$from population 2. The expression level vectors for sample i from population 1 can be expressed as $X_i = (X_{i1}, \ldots, X_{ip})'$. The mean expression level of gene j in population 1 is defined as

$$\overline{X}_j = \frac{1}{n_1} \sum_{i=1}^{n_1} X_{ij} \quad (5)$$

Then, the mean expression level vector for p genes for population 1 is given by $\bar{\mathbf{X}} = (\bar{X}_1, \bar{X}_2, \ldots, \bar{X}_p)'$ We can similarly define these expressions for population 2. The pooled variance-covariance matrix of p genes for populations 1 and 2 can be written as

$$\begin{aligned} \mathbf{S} &= \frac{(n_1-1)\mathbf{S}_X+(n_2-1)\mathbf{S}_Y}{n_1+n_2-2} \\ &= \frac{1}{n_1+n_2-2}[\sum_{i=1}^{n_1}(\mathbf{X}_i-\overline{\mathbf{X}})(\mathbf{X}_i-\overline{\mathbf{X}})' \\ &\quad +\sum_{j=1}^{n_2}(\mathbf{Y}_i-\overline{\mathbf{Y}})(\mathbf{Y}_i-\overline{\mathbf{Y}})'] \end{aligned} \quad (6)$$

where S_X and S_Y are the sample variance covariance matrices of populations 1 and 2. Note that correlation among genesare taken into account through sample variance covariance matrices.

The Hotelling's T^2 test [25] is defined as

$$T^2 = \frac{n_1 n_2}{n_1+n_2}(\overline{\mathbf{X}}-\overline{\mathbf{Y}})'\mathbf{S}^{-1}(\overline{\mathbf{X}}-\overline{\mathbf{Y}}) \quad (7)$$

By Central Limit Theorem,

$$\frac{n_1+n_2-p-1}{p(n_1+n_2-2)}T^2 \quad (8)$$

has classical *F* distribution with *p* degrees of freedom for the numerator and $n_1 + n_2 - p - 1$ degrees of freedom for the denominator. This test requires that the degrees of freedoms are positive, that is, it forces the condition $p < n_1 + n_2 - 1$. However, this restriction makes it almost impossible to implement Hotelling's T^2 test in microarray experiments.

Classical *F* Test

The classical *F* test compares the means of the columns of X, and assumes that these columns are independent (univariate case). In microarray experiment, we want to compare the differences of the *p* means of X and Y. Since we want to compare multivariate (Hotelling's T^2) and univariate (classical *F*) methods, we adopt the data structure from the multivariate to univariate case by considering the observations as the *differences* of the data matrices X and Y. That is, we compute $X_{ij} - Y_{ij}$, and apply the univariate F test on these observations. The F test is defined as

$$F_{\text{obs}} = \frac{\text{MST}}{\text{MSE}} \tag{9}$$

where MST is the mean square for treatments (genes), and MSE is the mean square for errors. The F_{obs} in (9) follows an Fdistribution with $p - 1$ degrees of freedom for the numerator and $p(n - 1)$ degrees of freedom for the denominator, where $n_1 = n_2 = n$.

F –MOD Test

When the assumptions are not satisfied by sample data, there are two general remedies: (1) to transform the data so that the assumptions are satisfied, or (2) to develop a modified inferential method in which the assumptions are relaxed at the estimation stage, or deviations from the assumptions are taken into account at the testing stage.

In linear models, the autocorrelation of errors has an impact on the inefficiency of slope estimators and the invalidity of significance levels. When regressors have fixed structure, the only source of autocorrelation comes from errors. However, when regressors also have random structures, their autocorrelations along with correlations of errors have an impact on estimation and testing [17-19,26,27]. Since the autocovariances of stochastic processes bias the variance of sample correlation coefficients [28], the incorporation of effective sample size into modified t-tests were proposed [20,21]. The effective sample size $\hat{n}$ in [20] was defined as

$$\hat{n} = \hat{\sigma}^{\vdash 2} + 1 \quad \text{with} \quad \hat{\sigma}^2 = \text{tr}(\hat{\Sigma}_{\mathbf{X}}\hat{\Sigma}_{\mathbf{Y}})/[\text{tr}(\hat{\Sigma}_{\mathbf{X}})\text{tr}(\hat{\Sigma}_{\mathbf{Y}})] \tag{10}$$

where $\hat{\Sigma}_X$ and $\hat{\Sigma}_Y$ were the estimated covariance matrices of X and Y, respectively. Dutilleul (1993) proposed an improved effective sample size for small sample sizes [21]. However, the effective sample sizes prosed in [20] and [21] behave similarly for large sample sizes. The effective sample size in [21] was defined as

$$\hat{n} = \hat{\sigma}^{-2} + 1 \quad \text{with} \quad \hat{\sigma}^2 = \mathrm{tr}(\mathrm{B}\hat{\Sigma}_{\mathrm{X}}\mathrm{B}\hat{\Sigma}_{\mathrm{Y}})/[\mathrm{tr}(\mathrm{B}\hat{\Sigma}_{\mathrm{X}})\mathrm{tr}(\mathrm{B}\hat{\Sigma}_{\mathrm{Y}})] \tag{11}$$

where B $= n^{-1}(\mathrm{I} - n^{-1}\mathrm{J})$, J is the $n \times n$ matrix of ones, and I is the identity matrix.

In this paper, we use equation (11) defined in [21] to compute effective column size to identify differentially expressed genes in microarray data. We considered the following steps for F-MOD test in the simulation runs: first, we computed the effective column size, $\hat{P}$, as in equation (11).

The estimated covariance matrices $\hat{\Sigma}_X$ and $\hat{\Sigma}_Y$ were computed using the raw data of X and Y, respectively. Second, we replaced p by $\hat{P}$ in the degrees of freedoms of the classical F test defined in (9). Finally, we computed the p-value of the global F test in (9) with $\hat{P} - 1$ and $\hat{P}(n-1)$ degrees of freedoms for the numerator and denominator degrees of freedoms, respectively. Note that, the sample size is $n_1 = n_2 = n$.

RESULTS AND DISCUSSION

Simulation

We generated two multivariate normal distributions: MVN(μ_1, Σ_1) and MVN(μ_2, Σ_2), each with dimension p (genes). The variance covariance matrices are defined as

$$\Sigma_1 = \Sigma_2 = \begin{pmatrix} \Sigma_\rho & 0 & 0 & \cdots & \cdots & \cdots \\ 0 & \Sigma_{(-\rho)} & 0 & 0 & \cdots & \vdots \\ 0 & 0 & \Sigma_\rho & 0 & \cdots & \vdots \\ \vdots & 0 & 0 & \Sigma_{(-\rho)} & 0 & \vdots \\ \vdots & \vdots & \vdots & 0 & \ddots & \vdots \\ \cdots & \cdots & \cdots & \cdots & \cdots & \ddots \end{pmatrix}_{p \times p}$$

where

$$\Sigma_\rho = l \begin{pmatrix} 1 & \rho & \dots & \rho^{g-2} & \rho^{g-1} \\ \rho & 1 & \dots & \dots & \rho^{g-2} \\ \vdots & \ddots & \ddots & \ddots & \vdots \\ \rho^{g-2} & \dots & \vdots & \vdots & \rho \\ \rho^{g-1} & \rho^{g-2} & \dots & \rho & 1 \end{pmatrix}_{g \times g} \qquad (12)$$

where $l = \sigma^2/\sqrt{1-\rho^2}$. We can similarly define $\Sigma_{(-\rho)}$ by replacing ρ by $(-\rho)$ in (12).

The matrices $\Sigma_{(\rho)}$ and $\Sigma_{(-\rho)}$ have dimensions $g \times g$, and the matrices $\Sigma_1 = \Sigma_2$ have dimensions $p \times p$. The constant term l is cancelled out in the computation of the effective column size in (11), hence, it has no effect on the effective column size. However, this term is considered to generate the data matrices X and Y with covariance matrices defined in (12).

Actually, the simulation setup has sound basis in methodologies used in analyzing real microarray data. It is common knowledge that genes are networked together in pathways. Although, it is true that weak connections between groups may exist, independence between groups is a reasonable assumption. Also, within each group, genes are either positively or negatively correlated, and due to their relative distance in the regulatory pathway, the further apart two genes, the less correlation between them. These are exactly the reasons why we considered the structures of Σ_1 and Σ_2 defined in (12) for microarray data.

We assumed that both populations have equal sample sizes (i.e., $n_1 = n_2$), and there are 10 matrices on the diagonals of $\Sigma_1$and Σ_2. For example, if $p = 100$ then there are 10 matrices on the diagonal of Σ_1 and Σ_2 with 10 genes in each matrix (i.e., $g= 10$). To assess the effects of correlation among genes, we took $\rho = 0, 0.1, 0.2, \dots, 0.9$ as various magnitudes of correlations. We also set the variances of each gene at 0.01 (i.e., $\sigma^2 = 0.01$). Even though the value of σ^2 is needed to generate X and Y, it has no effect on the computation of the effective column size. Two different significance levels, $\alpha = 0.01$ and 0.05, were used in validity and power analyses.

The null hypothesis in validity analysis was set to $\mu_1 = \mu_2$ |= $(0,0,0,.....,0)'(p \times p)$ whereas in power analysis $\mu_1 \neq \mu_2$ with

$\mu_1 = (0,0,0,.....,0)'(p \times 1)$ and $\mu_2 = (\underbrace{0.5,\ldots,0.5}_{0.02*p},\underbrace{0,0,\ldots,0}_{0.98*p})'_{(p\times 1)}$.

More precisely, the first 2% of the means of the genes were set to 0.5, and the rest were set to 0 in μ_2. If $0.02 * p$ was not an integer value, then we used ceiling function in R that takes a single numeric argument a and returns a numeric value containing the smallest integers not less than the corresponding elements of a.

The simulation program was written and run in R, which is a free software environment for statistical computing and graphics. We ran 10,000 data sets to test the null hypothesis. We computed empirical significance levels (p-values) and powers of the tests to draw conclusions about the testing procedures.

Lu, *et al.* [15], Chen, et al. [16], and SAM [24] methods were not compared in the simulation. The SAM handles gene-specific fluctuations by considering a statistic based on the ratio of change in gene expression to standard deviation in the data for that gene. However, in this paper, our goal is to handle gene-gene interactions and not gene-specific fluctuations. Also, Lu, *et al.* [15] modified the degrees of freedom in Hotellings T^2 test but F-MOD modified the degrees of freedom of the classical F test. Moreover, the method of Chen, *et al.* [16] was not compared because they proposed a two-sample test, and we used a test that modified the global F-test.

VALIDITY AND POWER ANALYSIS

The *strict* definition of a testing procedure to be valid at a significance level α is that if the actual p-value, which is the probability of rejecting the null hypothesis when in fact the null hypothesis is true, is less than or equal to α. To take variability among generated data into account in simulation runs, one may consider the upper limit of the approximate 95% confidence interval for the actual p-value. Under binomial distribution model, for α and m simulation runs, the approximate 95% confidence interval is $\alpha \pm 2\sqrt{\alpha(1-\alpha)/m}$. In simulation runs, we took $\alpha = 0.01$ and 0.05, and $m = 10,000$. The upper limits are

$$\alpha = 0.01 \Longleftrightarrow 0.01 + 2\sqrt{(0.01 \cdot 0.99)/10,000} = 0.012$$

$$\alpha = 0.05 \Longleftrightarrow 0.05 + 2\sqrt{(0.05 \cdot 0.95)/10,000} = 0.054$$

Therefore, we assessed the validity of the testing procedures based on the strict definition of the validity and the variability associated with the data generation. That is, the validity conditions are p-value ≤ 0.012 when $\alpha = 0.01$, and p-value ≤ 0.054 when $\alpha = 0.05$ in Table 1 and 2.

In Table 1, we investigated the validit y of the tests at $\alpha = 0.01$ and 0.05 when $p < n_1 + n_2 - 1$. We need this restriction to perform the Hotelling's T^2 test, but not the other two tests. Table 1 showed that the classical F test suffered lack of validity when correlations among genes were between mild and strong. The Hotelling's T^2 test is known to be not well-defined when p is much greater than n because the variance-covariance matrices Σ_1 and Σ_2 become singular. As a result, Hotelling's T^2 test becomes unstable. This phenomena was ascertained in Table 1 when $p > 60$. Therefore, we suggest not to use Hotelling's T^2 test when $p > 60$. In contrast, the proposed F-MOD test always provided valid tests for any ρ, except only in two cases ($p = 50$ when $\alpha = 0.05$ and $\alpha = 0.01$), which might be solely due to variation among data.

We studied the validity of F and F-MOD tests without the restriction $p < n_1 + n_2 - 1$ in Table 2. Since F MOD performed very well up to $p = 80$, we ran simulations for $p = 100$ and 200 to better understand the performance of the test for larger number of genes. Both tests performed similarly as in Table 1. That is, F test was only valid when correlation among genes did not exist or the magnitudes of the correlations were very weak. The F-MOD test always provided valid testings, except in one case.

Table 1: Validity analysis with restriction $p < n1 + n2 - 1$, where p is the number of columns (e.g., the number of genes) and n is the number of sample size (e.g., the number of individuals.)

$p = 50, n_1 = n_2 = 26$											
		ρ									
α	Test	0	0.1	0.2	0.3	0.4	0.5	0.6	0.7	0.8	0.9
0.05	F	0.049	0.056	0.054	0.060	0.076	0.084	0.094	0.108	0.130	0.144
	F-MOD	0.049	0.055	0.049	0.049	0.054	0.052	0.048	0.048	0.052	0.044
	Hotelling's	0.049	0.051	0.051	0.048	0.054	0.049	0.049	0.048	0.048	0.052
0.01	F	0.011	0.011	0.012	0.013	0.019	0.029	0.038	0.048	0.063	0.087
	F-MOD	0.012	0.011	0.011	0.009	0.011	0.011	0.013	0.011	0.011	0.009
	Hotelling's	0.011	0.011	0.011	0.012	0.009	0.012	0.011	0.009	0.009	0.009
$p = 60, n_1 = n_2 = 31$											
0.05	F	0.046	0.049	0.053	0.061	0.068	0.081	0.095	0.123	0.136	0.167
	F-MOD	0.046	0.049	0.048	0.049	0.049	0.046	0.047	0.052	0.046	0.045
	Hotelling's	0.050	0.052	0.049	0.046	0.051	0.052	0.048	0.048	0.050	0.051
0.01	F	0.009	0.013	0.013	0.016	0.019	0.032	0.034	0.051	0.069	0.092
	F-MOD	0.009	0.013	0.010	0.011	0.009	0.012	0.010	0.009	0.011	0.010
	Hotelling's	0.009	0.009	0.009	0.009	0.009	0.009	0.010	0.011	0.010	0.011
$p = 80, n_1 = n_2 = 41$											
0.05	F	0.051	0.052	0.053	0.058	0.072	0.086	0.101	0.12	0.146	0.176
	F-MOD	0.051	0.050	0.047	0.046	0.049	0.049	0.049	0.048	0.047	0.045
	Hotelling's	0.000	0.000	0.000	0.000	0.000	0.000	0.000	0.000	0.000	0.000
0.01	F	0.011	0.009	0.011	0.015	0.019	0.028	0.039	0.058	0.078	0.113
	F-MOD	0.011	0.008	0.009	0.009	0.011	0.011	0.011	0.011	0.011	0.008
	Hotelling's	0.000	0.000	0.000	0.000	0.000	0.000	0.000	0.000	0.000	0.000

Table 2: Validity analysis without restriction $p < n1 + n2 - 1$, where p is the number of columns (e.g., the number of genes) and n is the number of sample size (e.g., the number of individuals.)

$p = 100, n_1 = n_2 = 20$											
		ρ									
α	Test	0	0.1	0.2	0.3	0.4	0.5	0.6	0.7	0.8	0.9
0.05	F	0.051	0.056	0.055	0.066	0.075	0.088	0.104	0.127	0.152	0.188
	F-Mod	0.052	0.055	0.049	0.052	0.053	0.049	0.048	0.048	0.047	0.047
0.01	F	0.011	0.011	0.013	0.013	0.020	0.029	0.044	0.063	0.088	0.121
	F-Mod	0.011	0.010	0.010	0.010	0.012	0.011	0.012	0.012	0.009	0.011
$p = 200, n_1 = n_2 = 20$											
0.05	F	0.047	0.053	0.055	0.064	0.072	0.099	0.114	0.135	0.175	0.213
	F-Mod	0.048	0.052	0.049	0.050	0.048	0.050	0.048	0.049	0.048	0.045
0.01	F	0.010	0.010	0.013	0.015	0.022	0.033	0.050	0.067	0.098	0.147
	F-Mod	0.010	0.009	0.010	0.010	0.010	0.012	0.011	0.011	0.010	0.010

Table 3 provided power analysis at $\alpha = 0.01$ and 0.05 when $p < n_1 + n_2 - 1$. Since F test suffered lack of validity when $\rho > 0.2$, we did not analyze the power values in the table; these values were provided only for completeness of the Table. Hence, the power of F test should be ignored when $\rho > 0.2$. While Hotelling's T^2 test provided better power when correlations among genes were not too strong, the power decreased as correlations among genes got stronger. The Hotelling's T^2 test actually became powerless as p increased. This is not an unusual observation because it is known that even when $p \leq n$, the Hotelling's T^2 test perform poorly if p is nearly as large as n. The performance of the Hotelling's T^2test under $p, n \to \infty$ with $p/n \to 1 - \epsilon$ was studied in [29], which they showed that the asymptotic power of the test suffered for small values of $\epsilon > 0$. A number of improvements to give better power on the Hotelling's T^2 test in high-dimensional data have been proposed in [16, 29-31]. It was interesting to observe that Hotelling's T^2 test was more powerful when $\alpha = 0.05$ than when $\alpha = 0.01$. Its powers were more than 88.5% when $\alpha = 0.05$, but not more than 35.4% when $\alpha = 0.01$. In contrast, the F-MOD always provided powers at 100%.

We did not provide a table for power analysis when the restriction $p < n_1 + n_2 - 1$ was because held because it provided similar results to those in Table 3.

Effective Column Size

Table 4 shows average effective column sizes computed from (11) when 10,000 simulation runs were performed. The effective column sizes decreased as correlations among genes got stronger. As expected, when genes are independent (i.e., $\rho = 0$) the effective column size was the same as the original number of genes (p).

Table 3: Power analysis with restriction $p < n1 + n2 - 1$, where p is the number of columns (e.g., the number of genes) and n is the number of sample size (e.g., the number of individuals.)

$p = 50, n_1 = n_2 = 26$											
		ρ									
α	Test	0	0.1	0.2	0.3	0.4	0.5	0.6	0.7	0.8	0.9
0.05	F	1.000	1.000	1.000	1.000	1.000	1.000	1.000	1.000	1.000	1.000
	F-MOD	1.000	1.000	1.000	1.000	1.000	1.000	1.000	1.000	1.000	1.000
	Hotelling's	0.893	0.894	0.891	0.893	0.894	0.895	0.888	0.885	0.890	0.888
0.01	F	1.000	1.000	1.000	1.000	1.000	1.000	1.000	1.000	1.000	1.000
	F-MOD	1.000	1.000	1.000	1.000	1.000	1.000	1.000	1.000	1.000	1.000
	Hotelling's	0.257	0.252	0.249	0.255	0.256	0.259	0.256	0.249	0.252	0.252
$p = 60, n_1 = n_2 = 31$											
0.05	F	1.000	1.000	1.000	1.000	1.000	1.000	1.000	1.000	1.000	1.000
	F-MOD	1.000	1.000	1.000	1.000	1.000	1.000	1.000	1.000	1.000	1.000
	Hotelling's	0.976	0.967	0.961	0.949	0.938	0.928	0.915	0.906	0.899	0.887
0.01	F	1.000	1.000	1.000	1.000	1.000	1.000	1.000	1.000	1.000	1.000
	F-MOD	1.000	1.000	1.000	1.000	1.000	1.000	1.000	1.000	1.000	1.000
	Hotelling's	0.354	0.330	0.317	0.305	0.294	0.281	0.267	0.258	0.255	0.248
$p = 80, n_1 = n_2 = 41$											
0.05	F	1.000	1.000	1.000	1.000	1.000	1.000	1.000	1.000	1.000	1.000
	F-MOD	1.000	1.000	1.000	1.000	1.000	1.000	1.000	1.000	1.000	1.000
	Hotelling's	0.000	0.000	0.000	0.000	0.000	0.000	0.000	0.000	0.000	0.000
0.01	F	1.000	1.000	1.000	1.000	1.000	1.000	1.000	1.000	1.000	1.000
	F-MOD	1.000	1.000	1.000	1.000	1.000	1.000	1.000	1.000	1.000	1.000
	Hotelling's	0.000	0.000	0.000	0.000	0.000	0.000	0.000	0.000	0.000	0.000

Table 4: Effective column size p for p when $n1 = n2 = n$

		ρ									
p	n	0	0.1	0.2	0.3	0.4	0.5	0.6	0.7	0.8	0.9
50	26	17.4	17.3	17	16.6	15.9	15.1	14.1	12.8	11.3	9.6
60	31	60.1	59.2	56.5	52.3	46.8	40.6	33.9	27.2	20.9	15.4
80	41	80.1	78.8	74.9	68.9	61.3	52.5	43.2	33.9	25.0	17.1
100	20	100.6	98.9	93.9	86.1	76.2	64.9	52.9	41.0	29.4	19.1
200	20	200.8	197.6	186.7	169.9	149.1	125.4	100.3	75.4	51.3	28.9

Real Data: Type 2 Diabetes Mellitus

We used the gene expressions of type 2 diabetes from the data base Gene Expression Omnibus (GEO) with accession number GSE25724 [32] (data was not collected by us). The normalized gene expression data of p = 22, 283 genes was obtained from six type 2 diabetic human islets (population 1, n_1 = 6) and seven non-diabetic human islet (population 2, $n_2 = 7$). In over all design, human islets were isolated from the pancreas of organ donors by collagenase digestion followed by density gradient purification, then hand-picked and cultured two days in M199 culture medium. The platform GPL96 [HG-U133A]) by Affymetrix was used.

The programming codes to analyze gene expression data were written in R software. The dimensions of the matrices X and Y were 6 × 22, 283, and 7 × 22, 283, respectively. Since F-MOD test required the differences of the observations from two populations, six non-diabetic patients were chosen to have equal sample sizes for both populations ($n_1 = n_2 = 6$). That is, the dimension of the difference matrix was 6 × 22, 283. The data structure was high dimensional ($p =$ 22, 283 genes, and $n = 6$ observations), which caused memory exhaustion in R. However, we used built-in functions such as "as.big.matrix" to do matrix operations and "bigcor" to compute correlation and covariance matrices of size 22, 283 × 22, 283. The effective column size in (11) was easily computed using the as.big.matrix function to multiply two or four matrices of sizes 22, 283 × 22, 283.

Before analyzing the data, we verified that the assumptions of the fixed one-way ANOVA were satisfied: (1) our data did not violate the assumption of normal distribution, because fixed one-way ANOVA is considered a robust test against the normality assumption. (2) the equality of variances were not violated because it is well known that when the error variances are unequal, the F test for equality of means with the fixed one-way ANOVA model is only slightly affected if all factor level sample sizes are equal or do not differ greatly. In real data, the sample size was six in each gene, hence this assumption was not violated. However, 3) the independence of the populations were violated. To show dependency, we computed the correlation matrices for both populations. The correlation matrix has entries of correlations for pairwise genes. The number of pairwise genes for 22,283 genes is $\binom{22,283}{2} = 2.48254903 \times 10^8$. We counted the pairwise correlations that are more than 0.5, 0.7, and 0.9 in absolute values. The result is shown in Table 5. We concluded that genes were correlated in both populations, and hence the classical F test was not performed. The Hotelling's T^2 was also not performed because 22, 283 $\nless 6 + 6 - 1$. Therefore, we only considered F-MOD test to analyze the data.

Table 5: The number of pairwise correlations from the correlation matrices for non-diabetic and diabetic groups

Correlations greater than in absolute value	Non-diabetic	Diabetic
0.5	117,610,455	107,977,419
0.7	62,064,682	52,999,817
0.9	11,663,163	8,784,875

Table 6: The significant genes of Type 2 Diabetes Mellitus at α = 0.01/22283 = 4.49 × 10-7 when genes are matched with GeneCards data base

No.	Gene Symbol	ID	PVAL	Gene Title
1	ACP1	201630 _s_at	4.06e-12	acid phosphatase 1, soluble
2	ALDOB	217238_s_at	3.5e-07	aldolase B, fructose-bisphosphate
3	ARG2	203946_s_at	1.34e-11	arginase, type II
4	CAT	201432_at	1.07e-08	catalase
5	CPE	201117_s_at	3.35e-08	carboxypeptidase E
6	CPE	201116_s_at	8.65e-14	carboxypeptidase E
7	CXCL10	204533_at	1.17e-11	chemokine (C-X-C motif) ligand 10
8	CYB5R4	219079_at	2.3e-07	cytochrome b5 reductase 4
9	FTL	213187_x_at	3.83e-07	ferritin, light polypeptide
10	FUCA1	202838_at	4.38e-07	fucosidase, alpha-L- 1, tissue
11	GAD2	206780_at	2.96e-07	glutamate decarboxylase 2 (pancreatic islets and brain, 65kDa)
12	GAPDH	*	1.92e-07	glyceraldehyde-3-phosphate dehydrogenase
13	GAPDH	**	3.45e-11	glyceraldehyde-3-phosphate dehydrogenase
14	GC	204965_at	7.04e-09	group-specific component (vitamin D binding protein)
15	GCG	206422_at	5.33e-10	glucagon
16	GNAI1	209576_at	9.24e-09	guanine nucleotide binding protein (G protein), alpha inhibiting activity polypeptide 1
17	GNAS	200981_x_at	1.79e-08	GNAS complex locus
18	GNAS	214548_x_at	6.95e-08	GNAS complex locus
19	GNAS	200780_x_at	1.17e-07	GNAS complex locus

20	GNAS	212273_x_at	1.21e-08	GNAS complex locus
21	GNAS	214157_at	7.59e-13	GNAS complex locus
22	GPX3	214091_s_at	2.08e-08	glutathione peroxidase 3 (plasma)
23	GREM1	218468_s_at	7.55e-13	gremlin 1
24	GREM1	218469_at	7.54e-11	gremlin 1
25	GYG1	201554_x_at	1.72e-08	glycogenin 1
26	HMGCR	202539_s_at	6.44e-12	3-hydroxy-3-methylglutaryl-CoA reductase
27	HPRT1	202854_at	1.95e-08	hypoxanthine phosphoribosyltransferase 1
28	HSPA8	210338_s_at	1.08e-12	heat shock 70kDa protein 8
29	IAPP	207062_at	1.95e-18	islet amyloid polypeptide
30	IARS2	217900_at	2.22e-08	isoleucyl-tRNA synthetase 2, mitochondrial
31	LEPROT	202377_at	1.57e-07	leptin receptor overlapping transcript
32	LIPA	201847_at	1.28e-08	lipase A, lysosomal acid, cholesterol esterase
33	NAMPT	217738_at	1.13e-09	nicotinamide phosphoribosyltransferase
34	NEUROD1	206282_at	2.51e-07	neurogenic differentiation 1
35	PCSK1	205825_at	8.42e-18	proprotein convertase subtilisin/kexin type 1

Table 7: Table 6 continues

No.	Gene Symbol	ID	PVAL	Gene Title
36	PEX2	210296_s_at	3.26e-12	peroxisomal biogenesis factor 2
37	PFKM	210976_s_at	8.3e-08	phosphofructokinase, muscle
38	PLAGL1	209318_x_at	3.36e-09	pleiomorphic adenoma gene-like 1
39	PSMC6	201699_at	3.54e-08	proteasome (prosome, macropain) 26S subunit, AT-Pase, 6
40	PTGS2	204748_at	4.32e-07	prostaglandin-endoperoxide synthase 2 (prostaglandin G/H synthase and cyclooxygenase)
41	PTPRN2	203029_s_at	1.82e-07	protein tyrosine phosphatase, receptor type, N polypeptide 2
42	PTS	209694_at	3.06e-07	6-pyruvoyltetrahydropterin synthase
43	RBP4	219140_s_at	5.06e-14	retinol binding protein 4, plasma
44	SCD	200832_s_at	4.2e-08	stearoyl-CoA desaturase (delta-9-desaturase)
45	SDHB	202675_at	2.37e-09	succinate dehydrogenase complex, subunit B, iron sulfur (Ip)
46	SEL1L	202061_s_at	8.62e-10	sel-1 suppressor of lin-12-like (C. elegans)
47	SSBP1	202591_s_at	1.64e-10	single-stranded DNA binding protein 1
48	TFPI	210665_at	1.64e-09	tissue factor pathway inhibitor (lipoprotein-associ-ated coagulation inhibitor)
49	TFRC	207332_s_at	1.28e-10	transferrin receptor (p90, CD71)
50	TTR	209660_at	5.23e-08	transthyretin
51	USO1	201832_s_at	2.12e-08	USO1 vesicle docking protein homolog (yeast)
52	VDAC1	212038_s_at	3.59e-09	voltage-dependent anion channel 1

Table 8: The significant genes of Type 2 Diabetes Mellitus at $\alpha = 0.05/22283 = 2.24 \times 10{-}6$ when genes are matched with GeneCards data base

No.	Gene Symbol	ID	PVAL	Gene Title
1	ACP1	201630_s_at	4.06e-12	acid phosphatase 1, soluble
2	ALDOB	217238_s_at	3.5e-07	aldolase B, fructose-bisphosphate
3	APC	203525_s_at	4.7e-07	adenomatous polyposis coli
4	ARG2	203946_s_at	1.34e-11	arginase, type II
5	ATP5B	201322_at	1.28e-06	ATP synthase, H+ transporting, mitochondrial F1 complex, beta polypeptide
6	CAT	201432_at	1.07e-08	catalase
7	CFTR	215702_s_at	1.06e-06	cystic fibrosis transmembrane conductance regulator (ATP-binding cassette sub-family C, member 7)
8	CPE	201116_s_at	8.65e-14	carboxypeptidase E
9	CPE	201117_s_at	3.35e-08	carboxypeptidase E
10	CTGF	209101_at	8.4e-07	connective tissue growth factor
11	CX3CL1	823_at	9.49e-07	chemokine (C-X3-C motif) ligand 1
12	CXCL10	204533_at	1.17e-11	chemokine (C-X-C motif) ligand 10
13	CYB5R4	219079_at	2.3e-07	cytochrome b5 reductase 4
14	CYCS	208905_at	1.85e-06	cytochrome c, somatic
15	FABP5	202345_s_at	2.08e-06	fatty acid binding protein 5 (psoriasis-associated)
16	FTL	213187_x_at	3.83e-07	ferritin, light polypeptide
17	FUCA1	202838_at	4.38e-07	fucosidase, alpha-L- 1, tissue
18	GAD2	206780_at	2.96e-07	glutamate decarboxylase 2 (pancreatic islets and brain, 65kDa)
19	GAPDH	*	1.92e-07	glyceraldehyde-3-phosphate dehydrogenase
20	GAPDH	**	3.45e-11	glyceraldehyde-3-phosphate dehydrogenase
21	GC	204965_at	7.04e-09	group-specific component (vitamin D binding protein)
22	GCG	206422_at	5.33e-10	glucagon
23	GFPT1	202722_s_at	5.72e-07	glutamine–fructose-6-phosphate transaminase 1
24	GLO1	200681_at	7.17e-07	glyoxalase I
25	GNAI1	209576_at	9.24e-09	guanine nucleotide binding protein (G protein), alpha inhibiting activity polypeptide 1
26	GNAS	200981_x_at	1.79e-08	GNAS complex locus
27	GNAS	212273_x_at	1.21e-08	GNAS complex locus
28	GNAS	200780_x_at	1.17e-07	GNAS complex locus
29	GNAS	214157_at	7.59e-13	GNAS complex locus
30	GNAS	214548_x_at	6.95e-08	GNAS complex locus
31	GPX3	214091_s_at	2.08e-08	glutathione peroxidase 3 (plasma)
32	GREM1	218469_at	7.54e-11	gremlin 1
33	GREM1	218468_s_at	7.55e-13	gremlin 1
34	GYG1	201554_x_at	1.72e-08	glycogenin 1
35	HMGCR	202539_s_at	6.44e-12	3-hydroxy-3-methylglutaryl-CoA reductase

Table 9: Table 8 continues

No.	Gene Symbol	ID	PVAL	Gene Title
36	HPRT1	202854_at	1.95e-08	hypoxanthine phosphoribosyltransferase 1
37	HSPA8	210338_s_at	1.08e-12	heat shock 70kDa protein 8
38	HSPA8	208687_x_at	1.58e-06	heat shock 70kDa protein 8
39	HSPD1	200806_s_at	1.24e-06	heat shock 60kDa protein 1 (chaperonin)
40	IAPP	207062_at	1.95e-18	islet amyloid polypeptide
41	IARS2	217900_at	2.22e-08	isoleucyl-tRNA synthetase 2, mitochondrial
42	INS	206598_at	5.49e-07	insulin
43	ISL1	206104_at	1.75e-06	ISL LIM homeobox 1
44	LEPROT	202377_at	1.57e-07	leptin receptor overlapping transcript
45	LIPA	201847_at	1.28e-08	lipase A, lysosomal acid, cholesterol esterase
46	NAMPT	217738_at	1.13e-09	nicotinamide phosphoribosyltransferase
47	NEUROD1	206282_at	2.51e-07	neurogenic differentiation 1
48	NUCB2	203675_at	1.8e-06	nucleobindin 2
49	OGT	209240_at	1.32e-06	O-linked N-acetylglucosamine (GlcNAc) trans ferase(UDP-N-acetylglucosamine:polypeptide-N-acetylglucosaminyl transferase)
50	PCSK1	205825_at	8.42e-18	proprotein convertase subtilisin/kexin type 1
51	PDHX	203067_at	1.11e-06	pyruvate dehydrogenase complex, component X
52	PEX2	210296_s_at	3.26e-12	peroxisomal biogenesis factor 2
53	PFKM	210976_s_at	8.3e-08	phosphofructokinase, muscle
54	PLAGL1	209318_x_at	3.36e-09	pleiomorphic adenoma gene-like 1
55	PON2	210830_s_at	6.93e-07	paraoxonase 2
56	PROS1	207808_s_at	1.88e-06	protein S (alpha)
57	PSMC6	201699_at	3.54e-08	proteasome (prosome, macropain) 26S subunit, AT-Pase, 6
58	PTGS2	204748_at	4.32e-07	prostaglandin-endoperoxide synthase 2 (prostaglandin G/H synthase and cyclooxygenase)
59	PTPN12	202006_at	5.75e-07	protein tyrosine phosphatase, non-receptor type 12
60	PTPRN2	203029_s_at	1.82e-07	protein tyrosine phosphatase, receptor type, N polypeptide 2
61	PTS	209694_at	3.06e-07	6-pyruvoyltetrahydropterin synthase
62	RBP4	219140_s_at	5.06e-14	retinol binding protein 4, plasma
63	SCD	200832_s_at	4.2e-08	stearoyl-CoA desaturase (delta-9-desaturase)
64	SDHB	202675_at	2.37e-09	succinate dehydrogenase complex, subunit B, iron sulfur (Ip)
65	SEL1L	202061_s_at	8.62e-10	sel-1 suppressor of lin-12-like (C. elegans)
66	SSBP1	202591_s_at	1.64e-10	single-stranded DNA binding protein 1
67	SST	213921_at	8.11e-07	somatostatin
68	TFPI	210665_at	1.64e-09	tissue factor pathway inhibitor (lipoprotein-associated coagulation inhibitor)
69	TFPI	210664_s_at	6.24e-07	tissue factor pathway inhibitor (lipoprotein-associated coagulation inhibitor)
70	TFRC	207332_s_at	1.28e-10	transferrin receptor (p90, CD71)
71	TTR	209660_at	5.23e-08	transthyretin
72	USO1	201832_s_at	2.12e-08	USO1 vesicle docking protein homolog (yeast)
73	VDAC1	212038_s_at	3.59e-09	voltage-dependent anion channel 1

The second column shows the name of the genes from UniGene bank. The third column shows the Entrez Gene Database UID number. The fourth column shows the p-values adjusted by Bonferroni correction. The last column shows the title of the gene represented by the probe set. In column three, * and ** symbols are replaced for AFFX-HUMGAPDH/M33197_M_at and AFFX-HUMGAPDH/M33197_5_at, respectively.ene represented by the probe set. In column three, ? symbol is replaced for AFFX-HUMGAPDH/M33197_5_at respectivel

In column three, * and ** symbols are replaced for AFFX-HUMGAPDH/M33197_M_at and AFFX-HUMGAPDH/M33197_5_at, respectively

In the simulation study, we were only interested in the hypotheses defined in (2) or (3). That is, if there was a difference in the vector means of the populations. In the data analysis we proceeded one step further to identify differentially expressed genes if the null hypothesis in (2) or (3) was rejected. The statistic in (9) was F_{obs} = 5.609043, and the effective column size in (11) was computed as $\hat{P}$ = 9.424243. Since p-value= 4.13 × 10^{-5} was smaller than the significance levels α = 0.01 or α = 0.05, we rejected the null hypothesis, and concluded that 22,283 genes were differentially expressed together. We then run t tests for each genes with the adjusted degree of freedoms $\hat{P}(n_1 - 1)$ with and without Bonferroni corrections at α = 0.01 and α = 0.05 significance levels. Below, we only presented the number of significant genes without the Bonferroni corrections but provided the list of significant genes with the Bonferroni corrections in Tables 6-9. With or without Bonferroni corrections, we then compared these significant genes with significant genes listed at the GeneCards database. GeneCards is a searchable, integrated database of human genes that provides comprehensive, updated, and user-friendly information on all known and predicted human genes (http://www.genecards.org). The search is automatically extracted from more than 100 carefully selected web sources, and uses standard nomenclature and approved gene symbols. Moreover, it presents a rich subset of data for each gene by providing links to the original sources for further examination. Its use is free for academic non-profit institutions. We identified 1083 significant genes related to type 2 diabetes by searching the keywords "type 2 diabetes mellitus".

There were 4215 significant genes at $\alpha = 0.01$ significance level (without Bonferroni correction) in which 297 of them were matched with GeneCards database (results were not shown).

After Bonferroni correction, there were 674 significant genes at $\alpha = 0.01/22283 = 4.49 \times 10^{-7}$ significance level in which 52 were matched with GeneCards database (Table 6 and 7). Without Bonferroni correction at $\alpha = 0.05$ significance level, there were 7116 significant genes in which 554 of them were matched with the GeneCards (results were not shown). With Bonferroni correction at $\alpha = 0.05/22, 283 = 2.24 \times 10^{-6}$, there were 901 significant genes in which 73 of them were matched with the GeneCards data (Table 8 and 9).

We used PANTHER classification system, which is a comprehensive, curated database of protein families, trees, subfamilies and functions [33,34], for the significant genes identified in Tables 6-9. The tool is available at http://pantherdb.org. The results are presented in Tables 10-12. The main goals of PANTHER are to make accurate inference of genes and protein functions over large sequence databases. PANTHER extrapolates phylogenetic trees to represent gene family evolution. It also identifies subfamilies and protein class. In Tables 10-12, we presented families/subfamilies and protein class for each gene. The significant genes were grouped in the following protein classes: peptide hormones and protein hormones (have an effect on the endocrine system of animals and humans); DNA-binding proteins (can incorporate domains as the zinc finger, the helix-turn-helix, and the leucine zipper that facilitate binding to nucleic acid); acetyltransferase or transacetylase (is a type of transferase enzyme that transfers an acetyl group); carbohydrate kinase domain also known as CARKD; chemokines (are a family of small cytokines, or signaling proteins secreted by cells); hydrolase (is an enzyme that catalyzes the hydrolysis of a chemical bond); dehydrogenase also called DHO (is an enzyme belonging to the group of oxidoreductases that oxidizes a substrate by a reduction reaction that transfers one or more hydrides (H-) to an electron acceptor); peroxidases (are a large family of enzymes); and reductase (is an enzyme that catalyzes a reduction reaction).

Table 10: Functional classification of the genes in Tables 6-9 by PANTHER

No.	Gene Symbol	Panther family/subfamily	PANTHER Protein Class
1	APC	Adenomatous polyposis coli protein (pthr12607:sf11)	
2	FTL	Ferritin light chain (pthr11431:sf47)	storage protein
3	HMGCR	3-hydroxy-3-methylglutaryl-Coenzyme a reductase (pthr10572:sf2)	
4	PEX2	Peroxisome biogenesis factor2 PEX2 ortholog	
5	PLAGL1	Zinc finger protein plagl1 (pthr10032:sf227)	KRAB box transcription factor
6	PTGS2	Prostaglandin g/h synthase 2 (pthr11903:sf8)	oxygenase
7	ATP5B	Atp synthase subunit beta, mito-channel; Chondrial (pthr15184:sf44)	ATP ligand-gated ion channel; DNA binding protein; hydrolase
8	GC	Vitamin d-binding protein (pthr11385:sf11)	
9	GNAI1	Guanine nucleotide-binding Protein g(i) subunit alpha-1 (pthr10218:sf227)	heterotrimeric G-protein
10	GYG1	Glycogenin-1 (pthr11183:sf18)	glycosyltransferase
11	INS	Insulin-related (pthr11454:sf9)	growth factor; peptide hormone
12	PON2	Serum paraoxonase/arylesterase 2 (pthr11799:sf17)	
13	FABP5	Fatty acid-binding protein, Epidermal-related (pthr11955:sf58)	
14	GREM1	Gremlin-1 (pthr15283:sf3)	
15	HPRT1	Hypoxanthine-guanine phosphoribo-syltransferase (pthr22573:sf38)	glycosyltransferase; mutase
16	IAPP	Islet amyloid polypeptide (pthr10505:sf4)	peptide hormone
17	IARS2	Isoleucine–trna ligase, mitochon-Drial (pthr11946:sf82)	aminoacyl-tRNA synthetase
18	PCSK1	Prosaas (pthr15531:sf0)	
19	PTS	6-pyruvoyl tetrahydrobiopterin syn- 1hase (pthr12589:sf1)	
20	ARG2	Arginase-2, mitochondrial (pthr11358:sf18)	hydrolase
21	CTGF	Connective tissue growth factor (pthr11348:sf7)	growth factor
22	FUCA1	Tissue alpha-l-fucosidase (pthr10030:sf2)	

Table 11: Table 10 continues

No.	Gene Symbol	Panther family/subfamily	PANTHER Protein Class
23	GAPDH	Glyceraldehyde-3-phosphate dehy- Droge-nase (pthr10836:sf51)	Dehydrogenase
24	GLO1	Lactoylglutathione lyase (pthr10374:sf8)	
25	ISL1	Insulin gene enhancer protein isl-1 (pthr24204:sf3)	Homeobox transcription factor; zinc finger transcription factor; nucleic acid binding
26	OGT	Udp-n-acetylglucosamine–peptide N-acetylglucosaminyltransferase 110 Kda subunit (pthr23083:sf364)	Glycosyltransferase
27	PCSK1	Neuroendocrine convertas 1 (pthr10795:sf407)	Serine protease
28	PSMC6	26s protease regulatory subunit 10b (pthr23073:sf31)	Hydrolase
29	PTPN12	Tyrosine-protein phosphatase non-receptor type 12 (pthr19134:sf283)	Protein phosphatase
30	SSBP1	Single-stranded dna-binding pro- Tein, mitochondrial (pthr10302:sf0)	DNA binding protein
31	TFRC	Transferrin receptor protein 1 (pthr10404:sf26)	Receptor
32	CFTR	Cystic fibrosis transmembrane conductance regulator (pthr24223:sf19)	Anion channel
33	CXCL10	C-x-c motif chemokine 10 (pthr10179:sf47)	Chemokine
34	NEUROD1	Neurogenic differentiation factor 1 (pthr19290:sf88)	Basic helix-loop-helix transcription factor; nuclease
35	NUCB2	Nucleobindin-2 (pthr19237:sf22)	Nucleic acid binding; annexin; calmo-dulin
36	PDHX	Pyruvate dehydrogenase pro-Tein x component, mitochondrial (pthr23151:sf57)	Acetyltransferase
37	PFKM	6-phosphofructokinase, muscle type (pthr13697:sf13)	Carbohydrate kinase
38	RBP4	Retinol-binding protein 4 (pthr11873:sf2)	transfer/carrie protein
39	SCD	Acyl-coa desaturase (pthr11351:sf31)	
40	SEL1L	Protein sel-1 homolog 1 (pthr11102:sf70)	Enzyme modulator
41	SST	Somatostatin (pthr10558:sf2)	Peptid hormone
42	USO1	General vesicular transport factor P115 (pthr10013:sf0)	Membrane traffic protein
43	CYCS	Cytochrome c pthr11961:sf15)	

Table 12: Table 10 continues

No.	Gene Symbol	Panther family/subfamily	PANTHER Protein Class
44	GNAS	Guanine nucleotide-binding protein G(s) subunit alpha isoforms xlas (pthr10218:sf36)	
45	LEPROT	Leptin receptor gene-related protein (pthr12050:sf3)	Cytokine receptor
46	TTR	Transthyretin (pthr10395:sf12)	Transporter; transfer/carrier
47	ALDOB	Fructose-bisphosphate aldolaseb (pthr11627:sf2)	
48	CAT	Catalase (pthr11465:sf9)	Peroxidase
49	CPE	Carboxypeptidase e (pthr11532:sf59)	Metalloprotease
50	CYB5R4	Cytochrome b5 reductase 4 (pthr19370:sf122)	Reductase
51	GCG	Glucagon (pthr11418:sf0)	Peptide hormone
52	GFPT1	Glutamine-fructose-6-phosphate Aminotransferase [isomerizing] 1 (pthr10937:sf2)	Transaminase
53	LIPA	Lysosomal acid lipase/cholesteryl es- Ter hydrolase (pthr11005:sf26)	Lipase
54	NAMPT	Nicotinamide phosphoribosyltrans-Ferase (pthr11098:sf15)	Cytokine
55	PROS1	Vitamin k-dependent proteins (pthr24040:sf0)	
56	VDAC1	Voltage-dependent anion-selective channel protein 1 (pthr11743:sf13)	Anion channel; voltage-gated ion channel
57	ACP1	Low molecular weight phosphortyrosine protein phosphatase (pthr11717:sf7)	Protein phosphatase; reductase
58	CX3CL1	Fractalkine (pthr12015:sf92)	Chemokine
59	GAD2	Glutamate decarboxylase 2 (pthr11999:sf77)	Decarboxylase
60	GPX3	Glutathione peroxidase 3 (pthr11592:sf32)	Peroxidase
61	HSPA8	Heat shock cognate 71 kda protein (pthr19375:sf239)	Hsp70 family chaperone
62	PTPRN2	Receptor-type tyrosine-protein phos-Phatase n2 (pthr19134:sf266)	Receptor; protein phosphatase
63	SDHB	Succinate dehydrogenase [ubiquinone] iron-sulfur subunit, Mitochondrial (pthr11921:sf29)	Dehydrogenase
64	TFPI	Tissue factor pathway inhibitor (pthr10083:sf238)	Serine protease inhibitor

CONCLUSION

Microarray data has a high dimensional data structure that makes statistical inference from this type of data challenging. The most widely used statistical methods for finding differentially expressed genes from microarray data are univariate. While univariate methods do not take correlations among genes into account, gene-

gene interactions shouldn't be ignored in testing procedures. Multivariate statistical methods can overcome this deficiency of univariate methods by taking gene-gene interactions into account through variance-covariance matrices. However, these methods are sometimes not straightforward, and moreover ignore the multidimensional structure of the gene expression data.

The Hotelling's T^2 test is one of the multivariate analysis methods that takes correlations among genes into account but requires the restriction $p < n_1 + n_2 - 1$, when two populations are considered with sample sizes of n_1 and n_2. In microarray experiments, it is almost impossible to satisfy this condition because p is always larger than n_1 and n_2. That means Hotelling's T^2 suffers to handle curse of dimensionality. One solution is to apply Principal Component Analysis (PCA), or some other methods to satisfy the restriction before implementing the Hotelling's T^2 test. However, even this condition is satisfied, this test still suffers lack of powers when $p, n \to \infty$ with $p/n \to 1 - \epsilon$ for small values of $\epsilon > 0$.

In the Real Data section, we analyzed gene expressions of type 2 diabetes [32]. There were 117,610,455 pairwise genes that had correlations in absolute value more than 0.5 in the non-diabetic group, and 107,977,419 pairwise genes that had correlations in absolute value more than0.5 in the diabetic group. We concluded that the assumptions of independence were violated in both groups, and hence the classical F test was not performed. We also did not implement Hotelling's T^2test because the restriction $22,283 < 6 + 6 - 1$ did not hold. Since F-MOD takes correlations among genes into account, we analyzed the data only using F-MOD test with and without Bonferroni corrections. For example, we identified 901 significant genes in which 73 of them were matched with the GeneCards data at $\alpha = 0.05/22,283 = 2.24 \times 10^{-6}$.

In this paper, we consider F-MOD test that used the novel idea of effective column size concept in microarray data. The test provides valid testings and 100% powers for any ρ. More- over, the computation of F-MOD can easily be performed in R using built-in functions such as "as.big.matrix" and "bigcor" without exhausting the memory in R. To adopt the data structure from the multivariate case to the univariate case, the differences of the data matrices X and Y were considered as observations. If the null hypothesis in (2) is rejected, then we suggest testing to identify differentially expressed genes

$$H_0: \mu_{1i} = \mu_{2i} \qquad \text{versus} \qquad Ha: \mu_{1i} \neq \mu_{2i} \qquad (i = 1, 2, \ldots, p)$$

using the classical t-test with $\hat{p}(n_1 - 1)$ degree of freedoms with Bonferroni correction. Here, μ_1i is the mean expression of gene i from population 1, and μ_{2i} is the mean expression of gene i from population 2.

We suggest for researchers to consider the F-MOD test with a multiple test adjustment correction, such as Boferroni correction, instead of the classical F test if the assumption of independence is in question. Hotelling's T^2 is the second competitive test to F-MOD. However, the restriction $p < n_1 + n_2 - 1$ does not hold in microarray data, and renders this test inapplicable. We believe that the use of effective column size in microarray experiment will be a novel approach that will help practitioners to choose an easy, effective, and powerful testing procedure instead of a complicated or a procedure with restrictions, such as Hotelling's T^2 test.

In future work, it is interesting to investigate the performance of a test that modifies Hotelling's T^2 test by taking into account the effective column size concept in the degrees of freedoms.

ACKNOWLEDGEMENTS

We would like to thank the referees for their valuable comments that helped improve the quality of the article.

REFERENCES

1. Schena M, Shalon D, Davis RW, Brown PO (1995) Quantitative monitoring of gene ex- pression patterns with a complementary DNA microarray. Science 270: 368-71.

2. Lockhart DJ, Dong H, Byrne MC, Follettie MT, Gallo MV, et al. (1996) Expression monitoring by hybridization to high-density oligonucleotide arrays. Nature Biotechnol 14: 1675-80.

3. Mehta T, Tanik M, Allison DB (2004) Towards sound epistemological foundations of statistical methods for high-dimensional biology. Nature Genetics 36: 943-7.

4. Alon U, Barkai N, Notterman DA, Gish K, Ybarra S, et al. (1999) Broad patterns of gene expression revealed by clustering analysis of tumor and normal colon tissues probed by oligonucleotide arrays. Proc Natl Acad Sci U S A 96: 6745-50.

5. Brazma A, Vilo J (2000) Gene expression data analysis. FEBS Letters 480: 17-24.

6. Baldi P, Long AD (2001) A bayesian framework for the analysis of microarray expression data: regularized t -test and statistical inferences of gene changes. Bioinformatics 17: 509-19.

7. Wang S, Ethier S (2004) A generalized likelihood ratio test to identify differentially ex- pressed genes from microarray data. Bioinformatics 20: 100-4.

8. Wettenhall JM, Smyth GK (2004) limmagui: a graphical user interface for linear modeling of microarray data. Bioinformatics 20: 3705-6.

9. Leung YF, Cavalieri D (2003) Fundamentals of cdna microarray data analysis. Trends Genet 19: 649-59.

10. Chilingaryan A, Gevorgyan N, Vardanyan A, Jones D, Szabo A (2002) Multivariate ap- proach for selecting sets of differentially expressed genes. Math Biosci 176: 59-69.

11. Szabo A, Boucher K, Carroll WL, Klebanov LB, Tsodikov AD, et al. (2002) Variable selection and pattern recognition with gene expression data generated by the microarray technology. Math Biosci 176: 71-98.

12. Xiong M, Zhao J, Boerwinkle E (2002) Generalized t2 test for genome association studies. Am J Hum Genet 70: 1257-68.

13. Model F, K¨onig T, Piepenbrock C, Adorj´an P (2002) Statistical process control for large scale microarray experiments. Bioinformatics 18: S155-63.

14. Mason RL, Tracy ND, Young JC (1995) Decomposition of t2 for multivariate control chart interpretation. J Quality Technol 27: 109-19.

15. Lu Y, Liu PY, Xiao P, Deng HW (2005) Hotelling's t2 multivariate profiling for detecting differential expression in microarrays. Bioinformatics 21: 3105-13.

16. Chen SX, Qin YL (2010) A two-sample test for high-dimensional data with applications to gene-set testing. Annals Statist 38:2: 808-35.

17. Alpargu G, Dutilleul P (2003a) Efficiency and validity analyses of two-stage estimation procedures and derived testing procedures in quantitative linear models with ar(1) errors. Comm Statist Simulation Comput 32: 799-833.

18. Alpargu G, Dutilleul P (2003) To be or not to be valid in testing the significance of the slope in simple quantitative linear models with autocorrelated errors. J Statist Comput Simulation 73: 165-80.

19. Alpargu G, Dutilleul P (2006) Stepwise regression in mixed quantitative linear models with autocorrelated errors. Comm Statist Simulation Comput 35: 79-104.

20. Clifford P, Richardson S, H´emon D (1989) Assessing the significance of the correlation between two spatial processes. Biometrics 45: 123-34.

21. Dutilleul P, Clifford P, Richardson S, Hemon D (1993) Modifying the t test for assessing the correlation between two spatial processes. Biometrics 49: 305-14.

22. Dutilleul P, Pelletier B, Alpargu G (2008) Modified f tests for assessing the multiple correlation between one spatial process and several others. J Statist Planning Inference 138: 1402-15.

23. Alpargu G, Buonaccorsi JP (2009) A model free test for assessing dependence between times series. J Agri Biol Envi Statis 14: 115-32.

24. Tusher VG, Tibshirani R, Chu G (2001) Significance analysis of microarrays applied to the ionizing radiation response. Proc Natl Acad Sci U S A 98: 5116-21.

25. Anderson TW (2003) Introduction to multivariate statistical analysis. New York, NY: John Wiley.

26. Alpargu G (2001) Estimation and testing in quantitative linear models with autocorrelated errors. PhD Thesis, Department of Mathematics and Statistics, McGill University.

27. Alpargu G, Dutilleul P (2001) Efficiency analysis of ten estimation procedures for quanti- tative linear models with autocorrelated errors. J Statist Comput Simulation 69: 257-75.

28. Jenkins GM, Watts DG (1968) Spectral Analysis and its Applications. San Francisco, CA: Holden-Day.

29. Bai Z, Saranadasa H (1996) Effect of high dimension: by an example of a two sample problem. Statistica Sinica 6: 311-29.

30. Srivastava MS, Du M (2008) A test for the mean vector with fewer observations than the dimension. J Multivariate Analy 99: 386-402.

31. Srivastava MS (2009) A test for the mean with fewer observations than the dimension under non-normality. Journal of Multivariate Analysis 100: 518-32.

32. Dominguez V, Raimondi C, Somanath S, Bugliani M, Loder MK, et al. (2011) Class ii phosphoinositide 3-kinase regulates exocytosis of insulin granules in pancreatic beta cells. J Biol Chem 286: 4216-25.

33. Mi H, Muruganujan A, Thomas PD (2013) Panther in 2013: modeling the evolution of gene function, and other gene attributes, in the context of phylogenetic trees. Nucl Acids Res 41.

34. Mi H, Muruganujan A, Casagrande JT, Thomas PD (2013) Large-scale gene function analysis with the panther classification system. Nature Protocols 8: 1551 - 66.

12
CHAPTER

A Deterministic Model Predicts the Properties of Stochastic Calcium Oscillations in Airway Smooth Muscle Cells

Pengxing Cao[1], Xiahui Tan[2], Graham Donovan[1], Michael J. Sanderson[2], James Sneyd[1]

[1] Department of Mathematics, University of Auckland, Auckland, New Zealand,
[2]Department of Microbiology and Physiological Systems, University of Massachusetts Medical School, Worcester, Massachusetts, United States of America

ABSTRACT

The inositol trisphosphate receptor (IP_3R) is one of the most important cellular components responsible for oscillations in the cytoplasmic calcium concentration. Over the past decade, two major questions about the IP_3R have arisen. Firstly, how best should the IP_3R be modeled? In other words, what fundamental properties of the IP_3R allow it to perform its function, and what are their quantitative properties? Secondly, although calcium oscillations are caused by the stochastic opening and closing of small numbers of IP_3R, is it possible for a deterministic model to be a reliable predictor of calcium behavior? Here, we answer these two questions, using airway smooth muscle cells (ASMC) as a specific example. Firstly, we show that periodic calcium waves in ASMC, as well as the statistics of calcium puffs in other cell types, can be quantitatively reproduced by a two-state model of the IP_3R, and thus the behavior of the IP_3R is essentially determined by its modal structure. The structure within each mode is irrelevant for function. Secondly, we show that, although calcium waves in ASMC are generated by a stochastic mechanism, IP_3R stochasticity is not essential for a qualitative prediction of how oscillation frequency depends on model parameters, and thus deterministic IP_3R models demonstrate the same level of predictive capability as do stochastic models. We conclude that, firstly, calcium dynamics can be accurately modeled using simplified IP_3R models, and, secondly, to obtain qualitative predictions of how oscillation frequency depends on parameters it is sufficient to use a deterministic model.

INTRODUCTION

Oscillations in cytoplasmic calcium concentration ($[Ca^{2+}]_i$), mediated by inositol trisphosphate receptors (IP_3R; a calcium channel that releases calcium ions (Ca^{2+}) from the endoplasmic or sarcoplasmic reticulum (ER or SR) in the presence of inositol trisphosphate (IP_3)) play an important role in cellular function in many cell types. Hence, a thorough knowledge of the behavior of the IP_3R is a necessary prerequisite for an understanding of intracellular Ca^{2+} oscillations and waves. Mathematical and computational models of the IP_3R play a vital role in studies of Ca^{2+} dynamics. However, over the past decade, two major questions about IP_3R models have arisen.

Firstly, how best should the IP_3R be modeled? Models of the IP_3R have a long history, beginning with the heuristic models of [1]–[3]. With the recent appearance of single-channel data from IP_3R *in vivo* [4], [5], a new generation of Markov IP_3R models has recently appeared [6], [7]. These models show that IP_3R exist in different modes with different open probabilities. Within each mode there are multiple states, some open, some closed. Importantly, it was found [8] that time-dependent transitions between different modes are crucial for reproducing Ca^{2+} puff data from [9]. However, it is not yet clear whether transitions between states within each mode are important, or whether all the important behaviors are captured simply by inter-mode transitions.

Secondly, why do deterministic models of the IP_3R perform so well as predictive models? Deterministic models of the IP_3R have proven to be useful predictive models in a range of cell types. For example, IP_3R-based models have been developed to study Ca^{2+} oscillations in airway smooth muscle cells (ASMC) [10]–[13], and these models have made predictions which have been confirmed experimentally. This shows the usefulness of such models in advancing our understanding of how intracellular Ca^{2+} oscillations and waves are initiated and controlled in ASMC. However, these models are deterministic models which assume infinitely many IP_3R per unit cell volume, an assumption that contradicts experimental findings in many cell types showing that Ca^{2+} puffs and spikes occur stochastically, and that intracellular Ca^{2+} waves and oscillations arise as an emergent property of fundamental stochastic events [9], [14], [15].

Here, we answer these two fundamental modeling questions using data and models from ASMC. Firstly, we show that a simple model of the IP_3R, involving only two states with time-dependent transitions, suffices to generate correct dynamics of Ca^{2+} puffs and oscillations. Secondly, we show that, although Ca^{2+} oscillations in ASMC are generated by a stochastic mechanism, a deterministic model can make the same qualitative predictions as the analogous stochastic model, indicating that deterministic models, that require much less computational time and complexity, can be used to make reliable predictions. Although we work in the specific context of ASMC, our results are applicable to other cell types that exhibit similar Ca^{2+} oscillations and waves.

RESULTS

A two-state model of the IP_3R is sufficient to reproduce function

We have previously shown [8] that the statistics of Ca^{2+} puffs in SH-SY5Y cells can be reproduced by a Markov model of the IP_3R based on the steady-state data of [5] and the time-dependent data of [4]. In this model the IP_3R can exist in 6 different states, grouped into two modes, which we call *Drive* and *Park* (see Fig. 1). The Drive mode (which contains 4 states; 1 open and 3 closed) has an average open probability of around 0.7, while the Park mode (which contains the remaining two states; 1 open and 1 closed) has an open probability close to zero. Transitions between states within each mode are independent of Ca^{2+} and IP_3; only the transitions between modes are ligand-dependent.

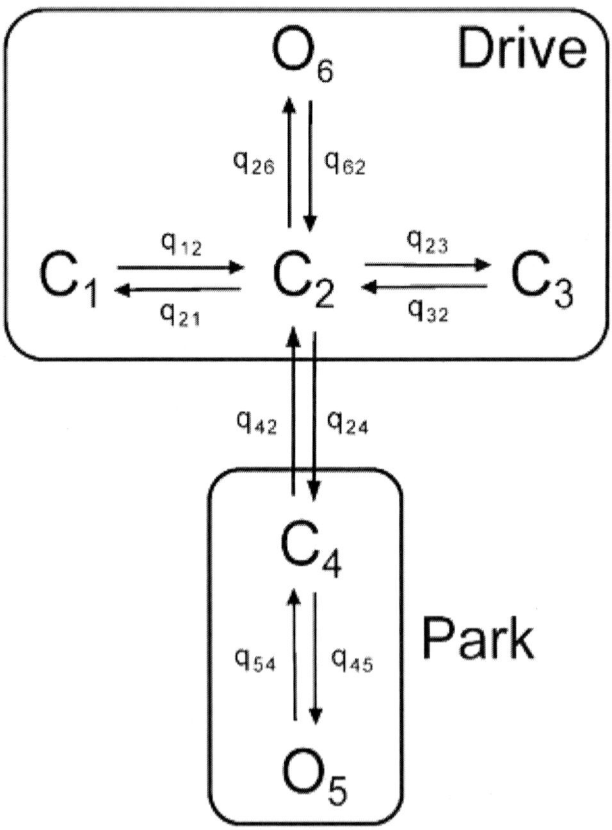

Figure 1. The structure of the Siekmann IP_3R model. The IP_3R model is comprised of two modes. One is the drive mode containing three closed states C_1, C_2, C_3 and one open state O_6. The other is the park mode which includes one closed state C_4 and one open state O_5. qs are rates of state-transitions between two adjacent states and q_{42} and q_{24} are transitions between the two modes[7].

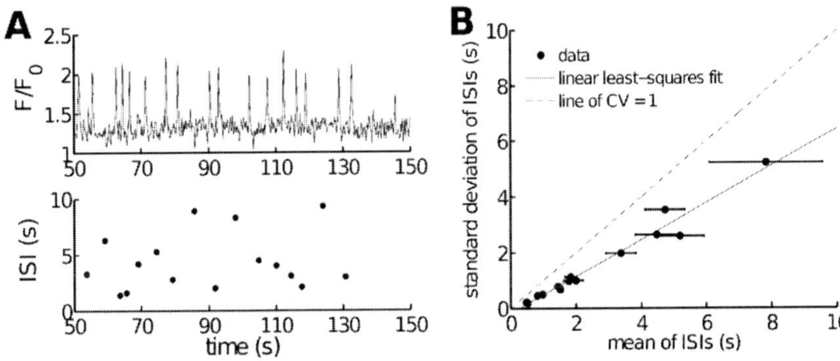

Figure 2. Ca^{2+} oscillations in ASMC in lung slices are generated by a stochastic mechanism. A: experimental Ca^{2+} spiking in ASMC in lung slices, stimulated with 50 nM MCh. In the upper panel we filter out baseline noise by using a low threshold of 1.42 (relative fluorescence intensity) and then choose samples with amplitude larger than 1.75. The ISI calculated from the upper panel is shown in the lower panel. **B**: relationship between the standard deviation and the mean of experimental ISIs. Data obtained from 14 ASMC in 5 mouse lung slices. The relationship is approximately linear with a slope of 0.66, which implies that an inhomogeneous Poisson process governs the generation of oscillations. The dashed line indicates where the coefficient of variation (CV) is 1 (as it is for a pure Poisson process). Variation in ISI is mainly caused by both use of different doses of MCh and different sensitivities of different cells to MCh. Error bars indicate the standard errors of the means (SEM).

In our previous study on calcium puffs [8], we showed that, to reproduce the experimentally observed non-exponential interspike interval (ISI) distribution and coefficient of variation (CV) of ISI smaller than 1, the time-dependent intermodal transitions are crucial. Lack of time dependencies in the Siekmann model leads to exponential ISI distributions and CV=1, which is not the case for calcium spikes in ASMC. Fig. 2A shows an example of Ca^{2+} oscillations generated by 50 nM methacholine (MCh, an agonist that can induce the production of IP_3 by binding to a G protein-coupled receptor in the cell membrane) in ASMC. By gathering data from 14 cells in 5 mouse lung slices, we found that the standard deviation of the interspike interval (ISI) is approximately a linear function of the

ISI mean, with a slope clearly between 0 and 1 (i.e. $CV < 1$), indicating that the spikes are generated by an inhomogeneous Poisson process (a slope of 1 would denote a pure Poisson process) (see Fig. 2B). This shows the necessity of inclusion of time-dependent transitions for mode-switching.

Using a quasi-steady-state approximation, and ignoring states with very low dwell times, it is possible to construct a simplified two-state version of the full six-state model (see *Materials and Methods*). In the simplified model the intramodal structure is ignored, and only the intermodal transitions have an effect on IP_3R behavior. In Fig. 3 we compared the simplified IP_3R model to the full six-state model. Both models have the same distribution of interspike interval, spike amplitude and spike duration. Moreover, by looking at a more detailed comparison between the two model results (Figs. 4A, C and E) and experimental data (Figs. 4B, D and F), we found the 2-state model not only can reproduce the behaviour of the 6-state model, but can also qualitatively reproduce experimental data. The average experimental ISI shows a clear decreasing trend as MCh concentration increases (although a saturation occurs in the data for high MCh), a trend that is mirrored by the model results as the IP_3 concentration increases. Unfortunately, since the exact relationship between MCh concentration and IP_3 concentration is uncertain, a quantitative comparison is not possible. In both model and experimental results, the average peak and duration of the oscillations are nearly independent of agonist concentration. The quantitative difference in spike duration between the model results and the data in Figs. 4E and F are most likely due to choice of calcium buffering parameters. For example, adding 3 or $5\ \mu M$ fast Ca^{2+} buffer (see*Materials and Methods*) increases the average spike duration to 0.54 s or 0.7 s respectively, which are close to the levels shown in the data.

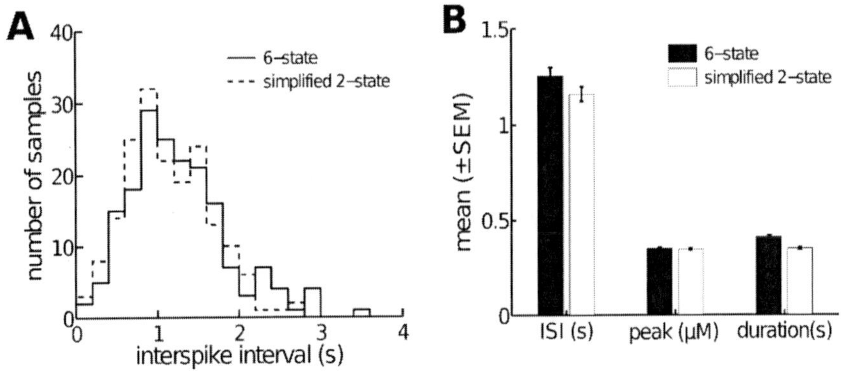

Figure 3. A 2-state open/closed model quantitatively reproduces the 6-state IP_3R model. A: histograms of interspike interval (ISI) distribution for both the 6-state and the simplified models. The ISI is defined to be the waiting time between successive spikes. Each histogram contain an equal number of samples (180). **B**: comparison of average ISI, average peak value of $[Ca^{2+}]_i$ (c in the model) and average spike duration. All distributions were computed at a constant $[IP_3] = 0.15\ \mu M$.

Thus, the intramodal structure of the six-state model is essentially unimportant, as the model behavior (in terms of the statistics of puffs and oscillations) is governed almost entirely by the time dependence of the intermode transitions, particularly the time dependence of the rapid inhibition of the IP_3R by high $[Ca^{2+}]_i$, and the slow recovery from inhibition by Ca^{2+}. The multiple states within each mode are necessary to obtain an acceptable quantitative fit to single-channel data, but are nevertheless of limited importance for function. Hence, even when simulating microscopic events such as Ca^{2+} puffs it is sufficient to use a simpler, faster, two-state model, rather than a more complex six-state model. In the following, we will use the 2-state IP_3R model to generate all the simulation results.

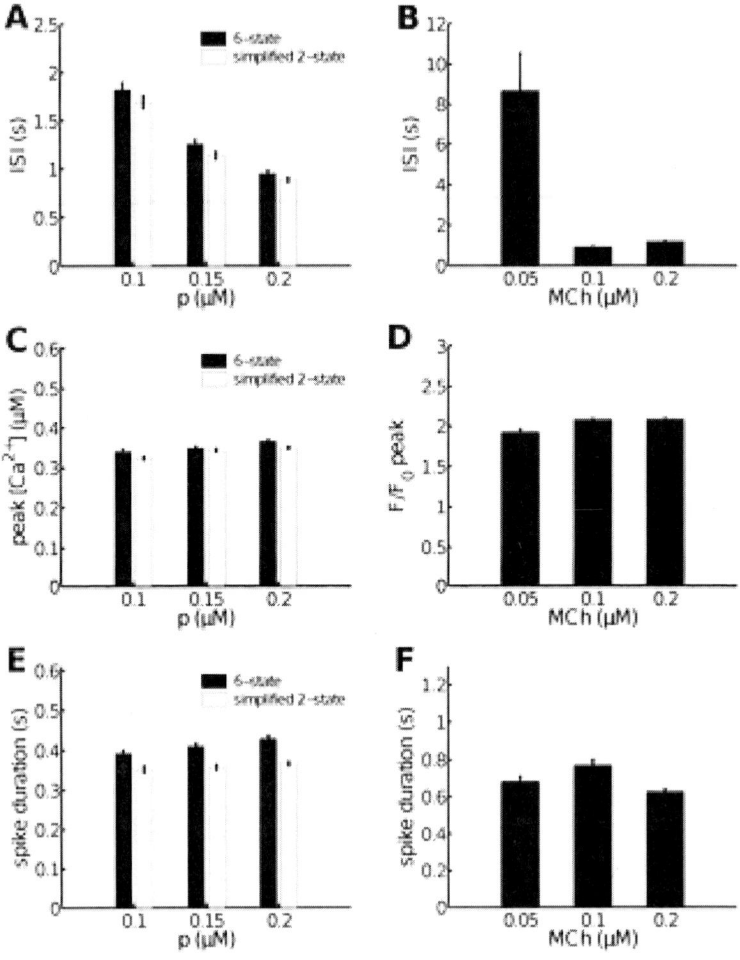

Figure 4. More detailed comparisons between the 2-state and the 6-state IP_3R models, and a comparison to experimental data. As a function of IP_3 concentration (P), the two models give the same ISI (**A**), peak $[Ca^{2+}]_i$ (**C**) and spike duration (**E**). These results agree qualitatively with experimental data, as shown in panels **B**, **D** and **F** respectively. Quantitative comparisons are generally not possible as the relationship between IP_3 concentration and agonist concentration is not known. Error bars represent $\text{mean} \pm \text{SEM}$. Data for each MCh concentration are obtained from at least three different cells from at least two different lung slices.

Prediction of stochastic Ca^{2+} behavior by a deterministic model

Although the data (Fig. 2) show that Ca^{2+} oscillations in ASMC are generated by a stochastic process, not a deterministic one, we wish to know to what extent a deterministic model can be used to make qualitative (and experimentally testable) predictions. Our simplified 2-state Markov model of the IP_3R can be converted to a deterministic model (see *Materials and Methods*). The result is a system of ordinary differential equations (ODEs) with four variables, which takes into account the increased $[Ca^{2+}]_i$ at an open IP_3R pore, as well as the increased $[Ca^{2+}]_i$ within a cluster of IP_3R; the four variables are the $[Ca^{2+}]_i$ outside the IP_3R cluster (c), the $[Ca^{2+}]_i$ within the IP_3R cluster (c_b), the total intracellular Ca^{2+} concentration (c_t) and an IP_3R gating variable (h_{42}). We refer to the reduced 4D model as the deterministic model for all the results and analyses.

Note that there is no physical or geometric constraint enforcing a high local $[Ca^{2+}]_i$; in this case the spatial heterogeneity arises solely from the low diffusion coefficient of Ca^{2+}. Our use of c_b is merely a highly simplified way of introducing spatial heterogeneity of the Ca^{2+}concentration. Since the IP_3R can only "see" c_b (as well as the Ca^{2+} concentration right at the mouth of an open channel, which we denote by c_p), but cannot be influenced directly by c(the experimentally observed Ca^{2+} signal), our approach allows for the functional differentiation of the rapid local oscillatory Ca^{2+} in the cluster, from the slower Ca^{2+} signal in the cytoplasm, without the need for computationally intensive simulations of a partial differential equation model. Quantitative accuracy is thus sacrificed for computational convenience.

Calcium oscillations in the stochastic and deterministic models are shown in Fig. 5A. According to our previous results [8], the average value of h_{42} over the cluster of IP_3Rprimarily regulates the termination and regeneration of individual spikes. This can be seen in the stochastic model by projecting the solution on the c_b, h_{42} phase plane (Fig. 5B). Upon an initial Ca^{2+} release from one or

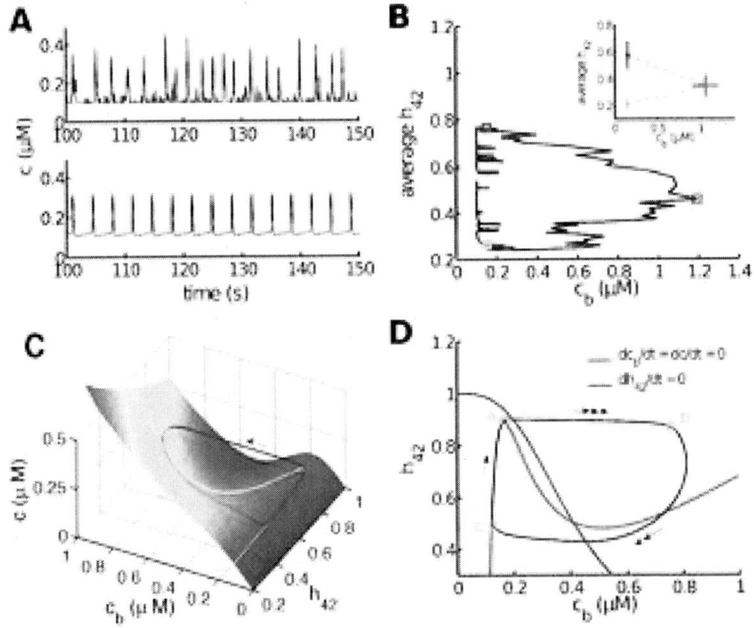

Figure 5. Stochastic and deterministic simulations exhibit similar dynamic properties. A: simulated stochastic (upper panel) or deterministic (lower panel) Ca^{2+} oscillations at $0.1\ \mu M\ IP_3$. **B**: a typical stochastic solution projected on the $c_b - h_{42}$ plane. The average h_{42} represents the average value of h_{42} over the 20 IP_3R. Statistics ($\text{mean} \pm \text{SD}$) of the initiation point (blue square), the peak (red square) and termination point (green square) are shown in the inset. 116 samples are obtained by applying a low threshold of $0.15\ \mu M$ and a high threshold of $0.8\ \mu M$ to c_b. **C**: a typical periodic solution of the deterministic model (black curve), plotted in the c, c_b, h_{42} phase space. The arrow indicates the direction of movement. c_t is the slowest variable so that its variation during an oscillation is very small. This allows to treat c_t as a constant ($c_t = 53.12\ \mu M$ in this case) and study the dynamics of the model in the c, c_b, h_{42} phase space. The color surface is the surface where $dc_b/dt = 0$ (called the critical manifold). The white N-shaped curve is the intersection of the critical manifold and the surface $dc/dt = 0$. **D**: projection of the periodic solution to the c_b, h_{42} plane. The red N-shaped curve is the projection to the c_b, h_{42} plane of the white curve shown in **C**. The evolution of the deterministic solution exhibits three different time scales separated by green circles (labelled by a, b and c) and indicated by arrows (triple arrow: fastest; double arrow: intermediate; single arrow: slowest).

more IP_3R, a large spike is generated by Ca^{2+}-induced Ca^{2+} release (via the IP_3R) during which time a decreasing h_{42} gradually decreases the average open probability of the clustered IP_3R. The spike is terminated when h_{42} is too small to allow further Ca^{2+} release. This phenomenon is qualitatively reproduced by the deterministic model (Fig. 5D). In both the stochastic and deterministic models the decrease in average IP_3R open probability of a cluster of IP_3R caused by Ca^{2+} inhibition is the main reason for the termination of each spike.

According to Figs. 5B and D, regeneration of each spike requires a return of h_{42} back to a relatively high value (i.e., recovery of the IP_3R from inhibition by Ca^{2+}). The deterministic model sets a clear threshold for the regeneration, as can be seen in Fig. 5C, where an upstroke in c_b occurs when the trajectory creeps beyond the sharp "knee" of the white curve. When the trajectory reaches the knees of the white curve it is forced to jump across to the other stable branch of the critical manifold, resulting in a fast increase in c_b followed by a relatively fast increase in c (seen by combining Figs. 5C and D).

In contrast, the stochastic model enlarges the contributions of individual IP_3R so that the generation of each spike is also effectively driven by random Ca^{2+} release through the IP_3R, which can be seen in the inset of Fig. 5B where the site of spike initiation (blue bar) exhibits significantly greater variation than that of spike termination (green bar). In spite of this, the essential similarities in phase plane behavior result in both deterministic and stochastic models making the same qualitative predictions in response to perturbations, such as changes in IP_3 concentration ($[IP_3]$), Ca^{2+} influx or efflux. In the following, we illustrate this by investigating a number of experimentally testable predictions. Due to the extensive importance of frequency encoding in many Ca^{2+}-dependent processes, we focus particularly on the change of oscillation frequency in response to parameter perturbations. As a side issue we also investigate how the oscillation baseline depends on physiologically important parameters.

Dependence of oscillation frequency on IP_3 concentration

In many cell types a moderate increase in $[IP_3]$ increases the Ca^{2+} oscillation frequency (seeFig. 2A in [11], Fig. 4E in [16] and Fig. 6B in [17]), a result that is reproduced by both model types (Fig. 6A). As $[IP_3]$ increases, the stochastic model increases the probability of the initial Ca^{2+} release through the first open IP_3R and of the following Ca^{2+} release, thus shortening the average ISI. Although the oscillatory region of the deterministic model is strictly confined by bifurcations which do not apply to the stochastic model, the deterministic model can successfully replicate an increasing frequency by lowering the "knee" of the red curve in Fig. 5D and shortening the time spent from the termination point c to the initiation point a (thus shortening the ISI). Hence, although the deterministic model cannot be used to predict the exact values of $[IP_3]$ at which the oscillations begin and end, as stochastic effects predominate in these regions, it can be used to predict the correct qualitative trend in oscillation frequency.

Dependence of oscillation frequency on Ca^{2+} influx and efflux

In many cell types, including ASMC, transmembrane fluxes modulate the total intracellular Ca^{2+} load (c_t) on a slow time scale [16], [18], and thereby modulate the oscillation frequency[19]. Experimental data can be seen in Fig. 8 in [16] and Fig. 2 in [18]. Figs. 6B and C show that both stochastic and deterministic models predict the same qualitative changes in oscillation frequency in response to changes in membrane fluxes (through membrane ATPase pumps and/or Ca^{2+} influx channels such as receptor-operated channels or store-operated channels).

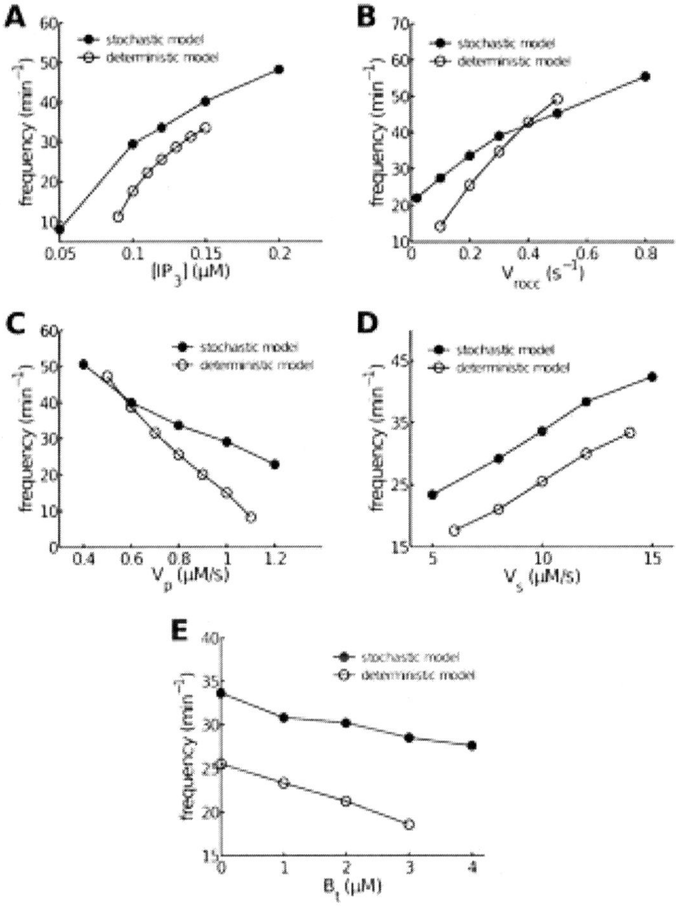

Figure 6. Comparison of parameter-dependent frequency changes in the stochastic and deterministic models. All curves are computed at $0.12\ \mu\mathrm{M}\ \mathrm{IP}_3$ except in panel A, which uses a variety of $[\mathrm{IP}_3]$. Other parameters are set at their default values given in Table 1. **A**: as $[\mathrm{IP}_3]$ increases, Ca^{2+} oscillations in both models increase in frequency. **B**: as Ca^{2+} influx increases (modeled by an increase in receptor-operated calcium channel flux coefficient V_{rocc}), so does the oscillation frequency in both models. **C**: as Ca^{2+} efflux increases (modeled by an increase in plasma pump expression V_p), oscillation frequency decreases. **D**: as SERCA pump expression, V_s, increases, so does oscillation frequency. **E**: as total buffer concentration, B_t, increases, oscillation frequency decreases.

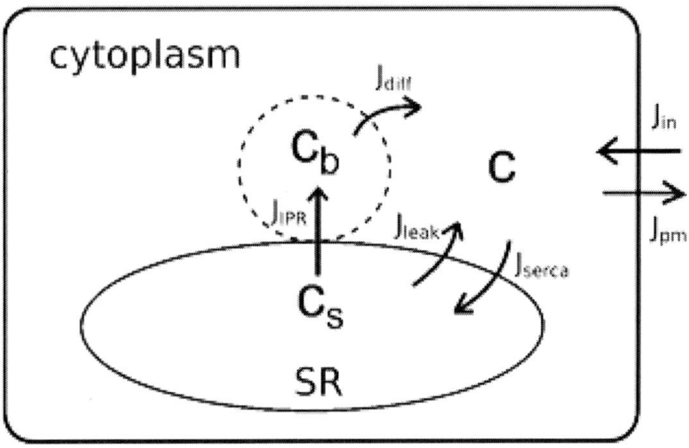

Figure 8. Schematic diagram of the Ca^{2+} model. c represents cytoplasmic Ca^{2+} concentration, excluding a small local Ca^{2+} (whose concentration is denoted by c_b) close to the Ca^{2+} release site (i.e., an IP_3R cluster). Upon coordinated openings of the IP_3R, SR Ca^{2+} (c_s) is first released into the local domain (J_{IPR}) to cause a rapid increase in c_b. High local Ca^{2+} then diffuses to the rest of the cytoplasm (J_{diff}), and is eventually pumped back to the SR (J_{serca}).

Dependence of oscillation frequency on SERCA expression

The level of sarco/endoplasmic reticulum calcium ATPase (SERCA) expression (or capacity) is important for airway remodeling in asthma [20] and ASMC Ca^{2+} oscillations [21]. We thus investigated the predictions of the two models in response to changes in SERCA expression (V_s). As V_s decreases, the deterministic model exhibits a decreasing frequency, in agreement with experimental data (see Figs. 3 and 4 in [21]). The same trend is seen in the stochastic model with only 20 IP_3R (see Fig. 6D).

Dependence of oscillation frequency on Ca^{2+} buffer concentration

Calcium buffers have been shown to be able to change the ISI and spike duration, which in turn change the oscillation frequency [15], [22]. We compared the effects on the two models of varying total buffer concentration (B_t) by adding one buffer with relatively fast kinetics to the models (see *Materials and Methods* for details). In both models the frequency decreases as B_t increases (see Fig. 6E), which is consistent with experimental data (Fig. 2B in [18]). This is not surprising, because increasing B_t can decrease the effective rates of SR Ca^{2+} release and reuptake.

Dependence of oscillation baseline on Ca^{2+} influx and SERCA expression

Sustained elevations of baseline during agonist-induced Ca^{2+} oscillations or transients have been observed experimentally, and are believed to be a result of an increase in Ca^{2+} influx caused by opening of membrane Ca^{2+} channels [13], [16]. Furthermore, there is evidence showing that decreased SERCA expression could also increase the baseline (Fig. 4 in [21]). Those phenomena are successfully reproduced by both models (see Fig. 7).

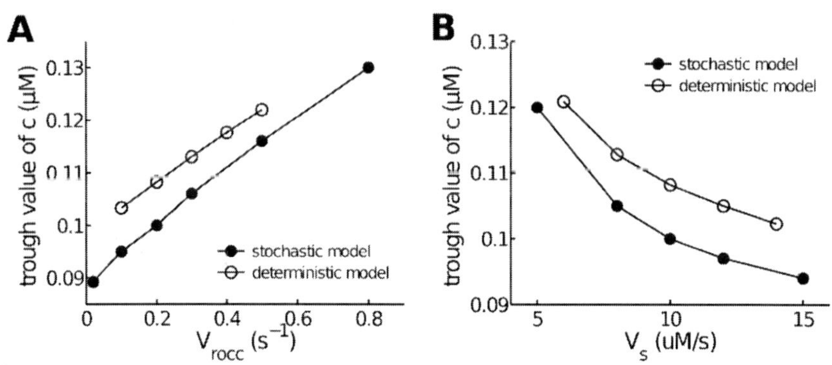

Figure 7. Dependence of calcium oscillation baseline on calcium influx and SERCA expression. **A**: increasing influx (described by V_{rocc}) increases the average trough of Ca^{2+} oscillations. **B**: decreasing SERCA expression (described by V_s) increases the average trough of Ca^{2+} oscillations. All curves are computed at $0.12\ \mu M\ IP_3$.

DISCUSSION

In this paper we address two current major questions in the field of Ca^{2+} modeling. Firstly, we show that Ca^{2+} puffs and stochastic oscillations can be reproduced quantitatively by an extremely simple model, consisting only of two states (one open, one closed), with time-dependent transitions between them. This model is obtained by removing the intramodal structure of a more complex model that was determined by fitting a Markov model to single-channel data [7]. We thus show that the internal structure of each mode is irrelevant for function and mode switching is the key mechanism for the control of calcium release. The necessity for time-dependent mode switching is shown not only by the dynamic single-channel data of [4]), but also by the puff data of [9] and our ASMC data.

Secondly, we investigate the role of stochasticity of IP_3R in modeling Ca^{2+} oscillations in ASMC by comparing a stochastic IP_3R-based Ca^{2+} model and its associated deterministic version, for parameters such that both of the models exhibit Ca^{2+} spikes but the stochastic model cannot necessarily be replaced by a mean-field model. We find that a four-variable deterministic model has the same predictive power as the stochastic model, in that it correctly reproduces the process of spike termination and predicts the same qualitative changes in oscillation frequency and baseline in response to a variety of perturbations that are commonly used experimentally. The mechanism for termination of individual spikes is fundamentally a deterministic process controlled by a rapid inhibition induced by the high local $[Ca^{2+}]_i$ in the IP_3R cluster, whereas spike initiation is significantly affected by stochastic opening of IP_3R. Hence, repetitive Ca^{2+} cycling is primarily induced by the time-dependent gating variables governing transitions of the IP_3R from one mode to another.

Our simplified two-state model of the IP_3R is identical in structure (although not in parameter values) to the well-known model of [23]. It is somewhat ironic that after 20 years of detailed studies of the IP_3R and the construction of a plethora of models of varying complexity, the single-channel data have led us around full circle, back to these original formulations. Excitability is arising via a fast activation followed by a slower inactivation, a combination often seen in physiological processes [24]. Encoding of this fundamental combination results directly from the two-mode structure of the IP_3R. Although similar single-channel data have been used to construct three-mode models [6], [25], neither of these models has yet been used in detailed studies of Ca^{2+} puffs and waves, and it remains unclear whether or not they have a similar underlying structure.

In contrast to previous deterministic ODE models, our four-variable Ca^{2+} model includes a more accurate IP_3R model, as well as local control of clustered IP_3R by two distinct Ca^{2+} microdomains; one at the mouth of an open IP_3R, the other inside a cluster of IP_3R. Neglect of either of these microdomains leads to models that either exhibit unphysiological cytoplasmic Ca^{2+} concentrations or fail to reproduce reasonable oscillations. This underlines the importance of taking Ca^{2+} microdomains into consideration when constructing any model. Our microdomain model is highly simplified, with the microdomain being treated simply as a well-mixed compartment. More detailed modeling of spatially-dependent microdomains is possible, and not difficult in principle, but requires far greater computational resources. It is undeniable that a more detailed model, incorporating the full spatial complexity – and possibly stochastic aspects as well – would make, overall, a better predictive tool. However, our goal is to find the simplest models that can be used as predictive tools.

An important similar study is that of Shuai and Jung [26]. They compared the use of Markov and Langevin approaches to the computation of puff amplitude distributions, compared their results with the deterministic limit, and showed that IP_3R stochasticity does not qualitatively change the type of puff amplitude distribution except for when there are fewer than 10 IP_3R. Here, we significantly extend the scope of their study by exploring the effects of IP_3R stochasticity on the dynamics of Ca^{2+} spikes, and we do this in the context of an IP_3R model that has been fitted to single-channel data. Although this is true in a general sense for the Li-Rinzel model, which is based on the DeYoung-Keizer model, which did take into account the opening time distributions of IP_3R in lipid bilayers, neither model can reproduce the more recent data obtained from on-nuclei patch clamping. When these recent data are taken into account one obtains a model with the same structure, but quite different parameters and behavior.

We find that, in spite of a relatively large variation in spike amplitude which is partially caused by a large variation in ISI (Fig. 5B), the mechanism governing individual spike terminations is the same for both a few or infinitely many IP_3R, which explains why the one-peak type of amplitude distribution is independent of the choice of IP_3R number (see Fig. 6A in [26]).

Another important relevant study was done by Dupont et al. [27], who compared the regularity of stochastic oscillations in hepatocytes for different numbers of IP_3R clusters. They found that the impact of IP_3R stochasticity on global Ca^{2+} oscillations (in terms of CV) increases as the total cluster number decreases. Our study here extends these results, and demonstrates how well stochastic oscillations can be qualitatively described by a deterministic system, even when there is only a small number of IP_3R (which appears to be the case for ASMC, in which the wave initiation site is only $2 \sim 4\ \mu m$ in diameter). Indeed, as we have shown, for the purposes of predictive modeling a simple deterministic model does as well as more complex stochastic simulations.

Ryanodine receptors (RyR) are another important component modulating ASMC Ca^{2+} oscillations [16], [28], [29] but are not included in our model. This is because the role of RyR is not fully understood and may be species-dependent; for example, in mouse or human ASMC, RyR play very little role in IP_3-induced continuing Ca^{2+} oscillations [17], [30], but this appears not to be true for pigs [28]. Our study focuses on the calcium oscillations in mouse and human (as we did in our experiments) where inclusion of a deterministic model of RyR should have little effect. An understanding of the role of RyR stochasticity and how the IP_3R and the RyR interact needs a reliable RyR Markov model, exclusive to ASMC, which is not currently available. Multiple Markov models of the RyR have been developed for use in cardiac cells [31], but these are based on single-channel data from lipid bilayers, and are adapted for the specific context of cardiac cells. Their applicability to ASMC remains unclear.

Although we have not shown that the deterministic model for ASMC has the same predictive power as the stochastic model in all possible cases (which would hardly be possible in the absence of an analytical proof) the underlying similarity in phase plane structure indicates that such similarity is plausible at least. Certainly, we have not found any counterexample to this claim. However, whether or not this claim is true for all cell types is unclear. Some cell types exhibit both local Ca^{2+} puffs and global Ca^{2+} spikes (usually propagating throughout the cells in the form of traveling waves), showing that initiation of such Ca^{2+} spikes requires a synchronization of Ca^{2+} release from more than one cluster of IP_3R [14]. This type of spiking relies on the hierarchical organization of Ca^{2+} signal pathways, in particular the stochastic recruitment of both individual IP_3R and puffs at different levels [32], and therefore cannot be simply reproduced by deterministic models containing only a few ODEs. However, Ca^{2+} oscillations in ASMC, as observed in lung slices, may not be of this type, as IP_3R-dependent puffs have not been seen in these ASMC. It thus appears that, in ASMC in lung slices, every Ca^{2+} "puff" initiates a wave, resulting in periodic waves with ISI that are governed by the dynamics of individual puffs.

MATERIALS AND METHODS

Ethics Statement

Animal experimentations carried out were approved by the Animal Care and Use Committee of the University of Massachusetts Medical School under approval number A-836-12.

Lung slice preparation

BALB/c mice (7–10 weeks old, Charles River Breeding Labs, Needham, MA) were euthanized via intraperitoneal injection of 0.3 ml sodium pentabarbitone (Oak Pharmaceuticals, Lake Forest, IL). After removal of the chest wall, lungs were inflated with ~ 1.1 ml of 1.8% warm agarose in sHBSS via an intratracheal catheter. Subsequently, air (~ 0.3 ml) was injected to push the agarose within the airways into the alveoli. The agarose was polymerized by cooling to $4^\circ C$. A vibratome (VF-300, Precisionary Instruments, San Jose, CA) was used to make $180\ \mu m$ thick slices which were maintained in Dulbecco's Modified Eagle's Media (DMEM, Invitrogen, Carlsbad, CA) at $37^\circ C$ in $10\%\ CO_2$/air. All experiments were conducted at $37^\circ C$ in a custom-made temperature-controlled Plexiglas chamber as described in [17].

Measurement of Ca^{2+} oscillations

Lung slices were incubated in sHBSS containing $20\ \mu M$ Oregon Green 488 BAPTA-1-AM (Invitrogen), a Ca^{2+}-indicator dye, 0.1% Pluronic F-127 (Invitrogen) and $200\ \mu M$ sulfobromophthalein (Sigma Aldrich, St Louis, MO) in the dark at $30^\circ C$ for 1 hour. Subsequently, the slices were incubated in $200\ \mu M$ sulfobromophthalein for 30 minutes. Slices were mounted on a cover-glass and held down with $200\ \mu m$ mesh. A smaller cover-glass was placed on top of the mesh and sealed at the sides with silicone grease to facilitate solution exchange. Slices were examined with a custom-built 2-photon scanning laser microscope with a $\times\ 40$ oil immersion objective lens and images recorded at 30 images per second using Videosavant 4.0 software (IO Industries, Montreal, Canada). Changes in fluorescence intensity (which represent changes in $[Ca^{2+}]_i$) were analyzed in an ASMC of interest by averaging the grey value of a $10\ \times\ 10$ pixel region using custom written software. Relative fluorescence intensity (F/F_0) was expressed as a ratio of the fluorescence intensity at a particular time (F) normalized to the initial fluorescence intensity (F_0).

The calcium model

Inhomogeneity of cytoplasmic Ca^{2+} concentration not only exists around individual channel pores of the IP_3R, where a nearly instantaneous high Ca^{2+} concentration at the pore (denoted by c_p) leads to a very sharp concentration profile, but is also seen inside

an IP_3R cluster where the average cluster concentration (c_b) is apparently higher than that of the surrounding cytoplasm (c) [33]. This indicates that during Ca^{2+} oscillations each IP_3R is controlled by either the pore Ca^{2+} concentration (when it is open) or the cluster Ca^{2+}concentration (when it is closed). Neither of these local concentrations influence cell membrane fluxes or the majority of SERCAs, which we assume to be distributed outside the cluster.

The scale separation between the pore Ca^{2+} concentration and the cluster Ca^{2+}concentration allows to treat c_p as a parameter, providing a simpler way of modeling local Ca^{2+} events (like Ca^{2+} puffs) that has been used in several previous studies [8], [34], [35]. However, evolution of the cluster concentration and wide-field cytoplasm Ca^{2+} concentration are not always separable, so an additional differential equation for the cluster Ca^{2+} is necessary.

A schematic diagram of the model is shown in Fig. 8. The corresponding ODEs are

$$\frac{dc}{dt} = J_{\text{diff}} + J_{\text{leak}} - J_{\text{serca}} + J_{\text{in}} - J_{\text{pm}}, \quad (1)$$

$$\frac{dc_b}{dt} = \gamma_1 (J_{\text{IPR}} - J_{\text{diff}}), \quad (2)$$

$$\frac{dc_t}{dt} = J_{\text{in}} - J_{\text{pm}}, \quad (3)$$

where $c_t = c + c_b/\gamma_1 + c_s/\gamma_2$ representing total intracellular Ca^{2+} concentration, and thus SR Ca^{2+} concentration, c_s is given by $c_s = \gamma_2(c_t - c - c_b/\gamma_1)$. γ_1 and γ_2 are the volume ratios given in Table 1. J_{IPR} is the flux through the IP_3R, J_{leak} is a background Ca^{2+} leak out of the SR, and J_{serca} is the uptake of Ca^{2+} into the SR by SERCA pumps. J_{pm} is the flux through plasma pump, and J_{in} represents a sum of main Ca^{2+} influxes including J_{rocc} (receptor-operated Ca^{2+} channel), J_{socc} (store-operated Ca^{2+} channel) and J_{leakin} (Ca^{2+}leak into the cell). J_{diff} coarsely models the diffusion flux from cluster microdomain to the cytoplasm. Details of the fluxes are

Table 1. Parameter values of the stochastic calcium model.

Parameter	Description	Value/Units
k_{IPR}	IP_3R flux coefficient	$0.05\ s^{-1}$
k_{diff}	Ca^{2+} diffusional flux coefficient	$10\ s^{-1}$
k_{leak}	SR leak flux coefficient	$0.0032\ s^{-1}$
V_s	maximum capacity of SERCA	$10\ \mu M{\cdot}s^{-1}$
K_s	SERCA half-maximal activating $[Ca^{2+}]_i$	$0.26\ \mu M$
n_s	Hill coefficient for SERCA	1.75
J_{leakin}	plasma membrane leak influx	$0.03115\ \mu M{\cdot}s^{-1}$
V_{rocc}	ROCC flux coefficient	$0.2\ s^{-1}$
V_{socc}	maximum capacity of SOCC	$1.6\ \mu M{\cdot}s^{-1}$
K_{socc}	SOCC dissociation constant	$100\ \mu M$
V_p	maximum capacity of plasma pump	$0.8\ \mu M{\cdot}s^{-1}$
K_p	half-maximal activating $[Ca^{2+}]_i$ of plasma pump	$0.5\ \mu M$
n_p	Hill coefficient for plasma pump	2
γ_1	the cytoplasmic-to-microdomain volume ratio	100
γ_2	the cytoplasmic-to-SR volume ratio	10
c_{p0}	an instantaneous high $[Ca^{2+}]_i$ at open channel pore when $c_s = 100\ \mu M$	$120\ \mu M$
N_t	total number of IP_3R channels	20

- Different formulations of J_{IPR} give different types of models:

  a) For the stochastic model, $J_{IPR} = (k_{IPR}/N_t)N_o(c_s - c)$ where k_{IPR} is the maximum conductance of a cluster of N_t IP_3R (here $N_t = 20$). N_o is the number of open IP_3R determined by the states of IP_3R.

  b) For the deterministic model we set $J_{IPR} = k_{IPR} P_o(c_s - c)$ where P_o is the IP_3R open probability, a continuous analogue of N_o/N_t.

To calculate N_o and P_o, we use the IP_3R model of [7], [8], with minor modifications described later.

- $J_{diff} = k_{diff}(c_b - c)$.
- $J_{serca} = V_s c^{n_s}/(K_s^{n_s} + c^{n_s})$ where K_s and n_s are obtained from [36].
- $J_{leak} = k_{leak}(c_s - c)$.

- J_{in} includes a basal leak (J_{leakin}), receptor-operated calcium channel (ROCC, J_{rocc}), store-operated calcium channel (SOCC, J_{socc}). By using the IP_3 concentration (P) as a surrogate indicator of MCh concentration, we assume that $J_{rocc} = V_{rocc}p$. SOCC is modeled by $J_{socc} = V_{socc}K_{socc}^4/(K_{socc}^4 + c_s^4)$ [13].
- $J_{pm} = V_p c^{n_p}/(K_p^{n_p} + c^{n_p})$.

Calcium concentration at open channel pore (c_p) does not explicitly appear in the equations but is used in the IP_3R model introduced later. c_p is assumed to be proportional to SR Ca^{2+}concentration (c_s) and is therefore simply modeled by $c_p = c_{p0}(c_s/100)$ where c_{p0} is the value corresponding to $c_s = 100\ \mu M$. Alternatively, c_p can also be assumed to be a large constant (say greater than $100\ \mu M$) without fundamentally altering the model dynamics. The choice of c_{p0} is not critical as long as it is sufficiently large to play a role in inactivating the open channels. All the parameter values are given in Table 1.

The data-driven IP_3R model

The IP_3R model used in our ASMC calcium model is an improved version of the Siekmann IP_3R model which is a 6-state Markov model derived by fitting to the stationary single channel data using Markov chain Monte Carlo (MCMC) [5], [7], [8]. Fig. 1 has shown the structure of the IP_3R model which is comprised of two modes; the drive mode, containing three closed states C_1, C_2, C_3 and one open state O_6, and the park mode, containing one closed state C_4 and one open state O_5. The transition rates in each mode are constants (shown in Table 2), but q_{42} and q_{24} which connect the two modes are Ca^{2+}-/IP_3-dependent and are formulated as

$$q_{24} = a_{24} + V_{24}(1 - m_{24}h_{24}), \quad (4)$$

$$q_{42} = a_{42} + V_{42}m_{42}h_{42}, \quad (5)$$

where m_{24}, h_{24}, m_{42} and h_{42} are Ca^{2+}-/IP_3-modulated gating variables. a_{24}, a_{42}, V_{24} and V_{42} are either functions of P or constants and are given later. We assume the gating variables obey the following differential equation,

$$\frac{dG}{dt} = \lambda_G(G_\infty - G), \quad (G = m_{24}, h_{24}, m_{42}, h_{42}), \tag{6}$$

where G_∞ is the equilibrium and λ_G is the rate at which the equilibrium is approached. Those equilibria are functions of Ca^{2+} concentration at the cytoplasmic side of the IP_3R, denoted by $\hat{c}$ in the equations, equal to either c_p or c_b depending on the state of the channel). They are assumed to be

$$m_{24\infty} = \frac{\hat{c}^3}{\hat{c}^3 + k_{24}^3}, \tag{7}$$

$$h_{24\infty} = \frac{k_{-24}^2}{\hat{c}^2 + k_{-24}^2}, \tag{8}$$

$$m_{42\infty} = \frac{\hat{c}^3}{\hat{c}^3 + k_{42}^3}, \tag{9}$$

$$h_{42\infty} = \frac{k_{-42}^3}{\hat{c}^3 + k_{-42}^3}. \tag{10}$$

Table 2. Parameter values of the IP_3R model.

Parameter	Value/Units	Parameter	Value/Units
q_{12}	$1240\ s^{-1}$	q_{21}	$88\ s^{-1}$
q_{23}	$3\ s^{-1}$	q_{32}	$69\ s^{-1}$
q_{26}	$10500\ s^{-1}$	q_{62}	$4010\ s^{-1}$
q_{45}	$11\ s^{-1}$	q_{54}	$3330\ s^{-1}$
H	$20\ s^{-1}$	L	$0.5\ s^{-1}$
λ_{m24}	$100\ s^{-1}$	λ_{m42}	$100\ s^{-1}$
λ_{h24}	$40\ s^{-1}$		

Hence, we have stationary expressions of q_{42} and

$$q_{24}, q_{24\infty} = a_{24} + V_{24}(1 - m_{24\infty} h_{24\infty}), \tag{11}$$

$$q_{42\infty} = a_{42} + V_{42} m_{42\infty} h_{42\infty}. \tag{12}$$

The expressions of as, Vs, ns and ks are chosen as follows so that Eq. 11 and Eq. 12 capture the correct trends of experimental values of q_{24} and q_{42} (see Fig. 9) and generate relatively smooth open probability curves (see Fig. 10),

$$V_{24} = 62 + 880/(p^2 + 4) \quad a_{24} = 1 + 5/(p^2 + 0.25)$$
$$V_{42} = 110p^2/(p^2 + 0.01) \quad a_{42} = 1.8p^2/(p^2 + 0.34)$$
$$k_{24} = 0.35 \quad k_{42} = 0.49 + 0.543p^3/(p^3 + 64)$$
$$k_{-24} = 80 \quad k_{-42} = 0.41 + 25p^3/(p^3 + 274.6)$$

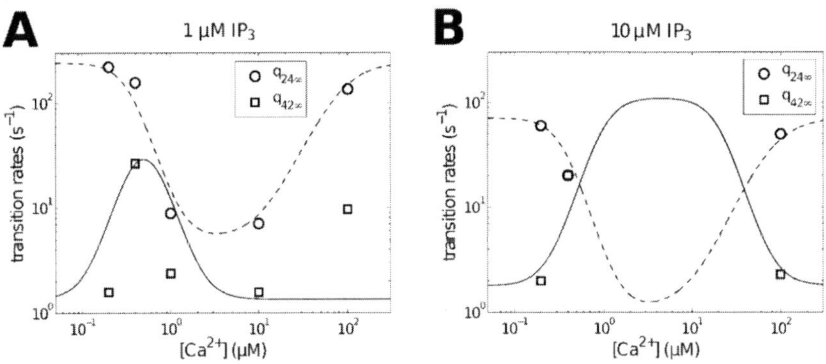

Figure 9. Stationary data and fits of q_{24} and q_{42}. Stationary transition rates of q_{24} and q_{42}, $q_{24\infty}$ and $q_{42\infty}$, as functions of Ca^{2+} concentration were estimated and fitted for two $[IP_3]$, $1\ \mu M$ **(A)** and $10\ \mu M$ **(B)**. Circles and squares represent the means of q_{24} and q_{42} distributions computed by MCMC simulation [7]. Note that MCMC failed to determine the values of q_{24} and q_{42} at $c = 1,\ 10\ \mu M$ for $10\ \mu M\ IP_3$, as the IP_3R was almost in the drive mode for these cases. The corresponding fitting curves (solid for q_{42}; dashed for q_{24}) are produced using Eqs. 7–12.

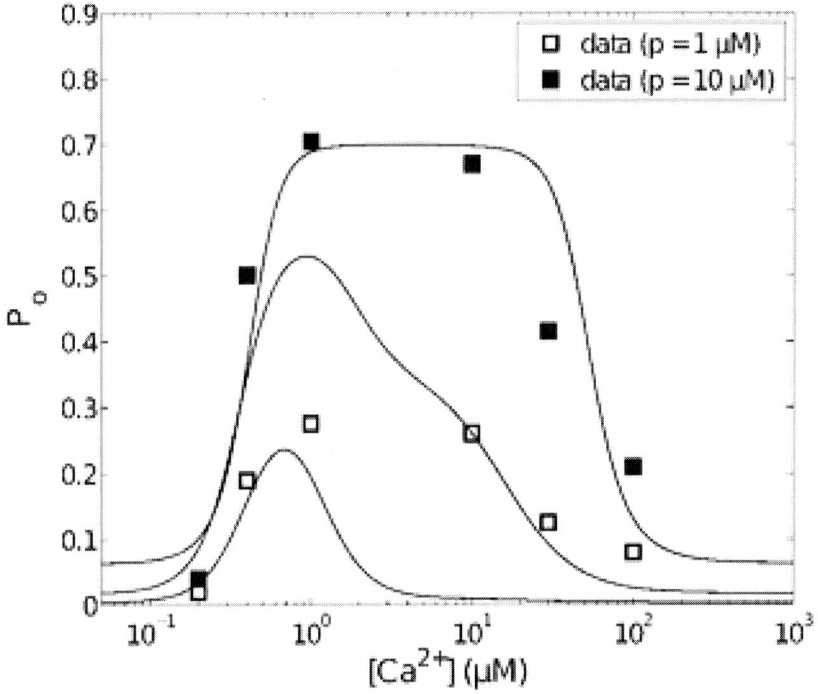

Figure 10. Open probability curves for various $[\mathrm{IP_3}]$. P_o is equal to the sum of probabilities of the $\mathrm{IP_3R}$ in O_5 and O_6. Three representative curves correspond to $0.1\ \mu\mathrm{M}$, $1\ \mu\mathrm{M}$ and $10\ \mu\mathrm{M}\,[\mathrm{IP_3}]$ (from bottom to top) respectively. Data (average open probability) are from [5].

Note that the above formulas are different from the relatively complicated formulas used in [8]. The rates, λ_{m24}, λ_{h24} and λ_{m42}, are constants estimated by using dynamic single channel data[4] and given in Table 2, whereas λ_{h42} is not clearly revealed by experimental data. However we have shown that it should be relatively large for high $\hat{c}$ but relatively small for low $\hat{c}$ for reproducing experimental puff data [8]. By introducing two $\mathrm{Ca^{2+}}$ concentrations, c_b and c_p, λ_{h42} and the state of the $\mathrm{IP_3R}$ channel become highly correlated, so that we can assume λ_{h42} is a relatively large value H if the channel is open and is a relatively small value L if the channel is closed. Hence, λ_{h42} is modeled by the logic function

$$\lambda_{h42} = \begin{cases} H, & \text{if the channel is open;} \\ L, & \text{if the channel is closed.} \end{cases}$$

Values of L and H are chosen so that simulated Ca^{2+} oscillations in ASMC are comparable to experimental observations.

The IP_3R model reduction

Here we reduce the 6-state model to a 2-state open/closed model. The reduction takes the following steps:

- The sum of the probabilities of C_1, C_3 and O_5 is less than 0.03 for any $\hat{c}$, so they are either rarely visited by the IP_3R or have a very short dwell time. This implies they have very little contribution to the Ca^{2+} dynamics. Therefore, we completely remove the three states from the full model.

- Transition rates of q_{26} and q_{62} are about 2 orders larger than that of q_{24} and q_{42}, which allows us to omit the fast transitions by taking a quasi-steady state approximation. This change will affect two aspects. First, we have $O_6 = C_2 q_{26}/q_{62}$ which allows us to combine C_2 and O_6 to be a new state D, which satisfies $D = O_6(q_{62} + q_{26})/q_{26}$. Although this means D is a partially open state with an open probability of $q_{26}/(q_{62} + q_{26})$, it can be used as an fully open state in the stochastic simulations by multiplying the maximum IP_3R flux conductance k_{IPR} by a factor of $q_{26}/(q_{62} + q_{26})$. Secondly, q_{24} needs to be rescaled by $q_{62}/(q_{62} + q_{26})$, i.e., the effective closing rate is $q_{24}q_{62}/(q_{62} + q_{26})$.

- Due to the combination of C_2 and O_6, λ_h is accordingly modified to

$$\lambda_{h42} = \begin{cases} H, & \text{if the channel is in } C_4 \\ L, & \text{if the channel is in } D \text{ (the drive mode)} \end{cases}$$

Hence, the reduced two-state model contains one "open" state D and one closed state C_4 with the opening transition rate of q_{42} and the closing transition rate of $q_{24}q_{62}/(q_{62} + q_{26})$.

Deterministic formulation of the stochastic model

Based on the stochastic calcium model and the reduced 2-state IP_3R model, we construct a deterministic model. We need to modify three things that are used in the stochastic model but inapplicable to fast simulations of the deterministic model. The first is the discrete number of open channels; the second is state-dependent use of c_b and c_p in calculating q_{42} and q_{24}; the last is the logic expression of $\lambda_{h_{42}}$. Details of the modifications are as follows,

- The fraction of open channels (N_o/N_t) is replaced by open probability P_o which is 70% of the probability of state D.
- In the stochastic simulations, q_{24} which only controls the IP_3R closing is primarily governed by c_p, whereas q_{42} which controls IP_3R opening is mainly governed by c_b. Therefore, in the deterministic model, we separate the functions of c_p and c_b

  by assuming and $h_{24\infty}$ are functions of c_p only whereas $m_{42\infty}$ and $h_{42\infty}$ are functions of c_b only. That is, $m_{24\infty}=m_{24\infty}(c_p)$, $h_{24\infty}=h_{24\infty}(c_p)$, $m_{42\infty}=m_{42\infty}(c_b)$ and $h_{42\infty}=h_{42\infty}(c_b)$. Here $c_p=c_{p0}(c_s/100)$ as defined before.
- To describe an average rate that infinitely many receptors are rapidly inhibited by high Ca^{2+} concentration but slowly restored from Ca^{2+}-inhibition. $\lambda_{h_{42}}$ is proposed to be $\lambda_{h_{42}}=(1-D)L+DH$.

Based on the above changes, the full deterministic model containing 8 ODEs is presented as follows,

$$\frac{dc}{dt}=J_{\text{diff}}+J_{\text{leak}}-J_{\text{serca}}+J_{\text{in}}-J_{\text{pm}}, \tag{13}$$

$$\frac{dc_b}{dt}=\gamma_1(J_{\text{IPR}}-J_{\text{diff}}), \tag{14}$$

$$\frac{dc_t}{dt}=J_{\text{in}}-J_{\text{pm}}, \tag{15}$$

$$\frac{dD}{dt} = q_{42}(1 - D) - (\frac{q_{24}q_{62}}{q_{62} + q_{26}})D, \quad (16)$$

$$\frac{dm_{24}}{dt} = \lambda_{m_{24}}(\frac{c_p^3}{c_p^3 + k_{24}^3} - m_{24}), \quad (17)$$

$$\frac{dh_{24}}{dt} = \lambda_{h_{24}}(\frac{k_{-24}^2}{c_p^2 + k_{-24}^2} - m_{24}), \quad (18)$$

$$\frac{dm_{42}}{dt} = \lambda_{m_{42}}(\frac{c_b^3}{c_b^3 + k_{42}^3} - m_{42}), \quad (19)$$

$$\frac{dh_{42}}{dt} = \lambda_{h_{42}}(\frac{k_{-42}^3}{c_b^3 + k_{-42}^3} - h_{42}), \quad (20)$$

where q_{24} and q_{42} are functions of the gating variables given by Eqs. 4 and 5. All the fluxes are the same as those of the stochastic model except $J_{\text{IPR}} = k_{\text{IPR}}(Dq_{26}/(q_{62} + q_{26}))(c_s - c_b)$. All the parameter values of the deterministic model are the same as those of the stochastic model and are therefore given in Tables 1 and2.

Reduction of the full deterministic model

The full deterministic model contains 8 variables which make the model difficult to implement and analyze. Thus, we reduce the full model to a minimal model that still captures the crucial features of the full model. First of all, $\lambda_{m_{42}}$, $\lambda_{m_{24}}$ and $\lambda_{h_{24}}$ are sufficiently large so that we can assume they instantaneously follow their equilibrium functions. Therefore, by taking quasi-steady state approximation to m_{24}, h_{24} and m_{42}, we remove the three time-dependent variables from the full model.

By now, the full model has been reduced to a 5D model,

$$\frac{dc}{dt} = J_{\text{diff}} + J_{\text{leak}} - J_{\text{serca}} + J_{\text{in}} - J_{\text{pm}}, \quad (21)$$

$$\frac{dc_b}{dt} = \gamma_1 (J_{\mathrm{IPR}} - J_{\mathrm{diff}}), \tag{22}$$

$$\frac{dc_t}{dt} = J_{\mathrm{in}} - J_{\mathrm{pm}}, \tag{23}$$

$$\frac{dD}{dt} = q_{42}(1-D) - (\frac{q_{24}q_{62}}{q_{62}+q_{26}})D, \tag{24}$$

$$\frac{dh_{42}}{dt} = \lambda_{h_{42}}(\frac{k_{-42}^3}{c_b^3 + k_{-42}^3} - h_{42}). \tag{25}$$

Second, the rate of change of D approaching its equilibrium, $\lambda_D = (q_{42}q_{62} + q_{42}q_{26} + q_{24}q_{62})/(q_{62}+q_{26})$ (calculated from Eq. 24), is at least one order larger than those of c, c_t and h_{42}, indicating that taking the quasi-steady state approximation to Eq. 24 could not significantly affect the evolutions of c, c_t and h_{42}. That is,

$$D = \frac{q_{42}(q_{62}+q_{26})}{q_{42}q_{62} + q_{42}q_{26} + q_{24}q_{62}}. \tag{26}$$

We emphasize here that the theory of the quasi-steady state approximation has not yet been well established, particularly about the rigorous conditions under which such a reduction is valid. Thus, our criterion of judging the validity of the reduction is checking whether the solutions of the reduced model are capable of qualitatively reproducing that of its original model. For this model, we find the reduction works. Hence, the full model is eventually reduced to a 4D model summarized as follows,

$$\frac{dc}{dt} = J_{\mathrm{diff}} + J_{\mathrm{leak}} - J_{\mathrm{serca}} + J_{\mathrm{in}} - J_{\mathrm{pm}}, \tag{27}$$

$$\frac{dc_b}{dt} = \gamma_1 (J_{\mathrm{IPR}} - J_{\mathrm{diff}}), \tag{28}$$

$$\frac{dc_t}{dt} = J_{\mathrm{in}} - J_{\mathrm{pm}}, \tag{29}$$

$$\frac{dh_{42}}{dt} = \lambda_{h_{42}}\left(\frac{k_{-42}^3}{c_b^3 + k_{-42}^3} - h_{42}\right), \quad (30)$$

where D is given by Eq. 26.

Inclusion of calcium buffers

To check the effect of calcium buffers on oscillation frequency, we introduce a stationary buffer (no buffer diffusion), as mobile buffers are too complicated to be included in the current deterministic model. Since we have two different cytoplasmic Ca^{2+} concentrations, c and c_b, two pools of buffer with the same kinetics should be considered. Hence, the inclusion of a stationary calcium buffer is modeled by the following system,

$$\frac{dc}{dt} = J_{\text{diff}} + J_{\text{leak}} - J_{\text{serca}} + J_{\text{in}} - J_{\text{pm}} - k_+(B_t - b_1)c + k_- b_1, \quad (31)$$

$$\frac{dc_b}{dt} = \gamma_1(J_{\text{IPR}} - J_{\text{diff}}) - k_+(B_t - b_2)c_b + k_- b_2, \quad (32)$$

$$\frac{dc_t}{dt} = J_{\text{in}} - J_{\text{pm}}, \quad (33)$$

$$\frac{db_1}{dt} = k_+(B_t - b_1)c - k_- b_1, \quad (34)$$

$$\frac{db_2}{dt} = k_+(B_t - b_2)c_b - k_- b_2, \quad (35)$$

where b (b_1 and b_2) and B_t represent the concentrations of Ca^{2+}-bound buffer and total buffer respectively. k_+ and k_- are the rates of Ca^{2+}-binding and Ca^{2+}-dissociation, indicating how fast the time scale of the buffer dynamics is. Fast buffer refers to the buffer with relatively large k_+. In the simulations, we use a fast buffer with $k_+ = 100\ \mu M^{-1} \cdot s^{-1}$ and $k_- = 100\ s^{-1}$ and vary B_t to test if the stochastic model and the deterministic model have a qualitatively similar B_t-dependency. Results are given in Fig. 6E.

Numerical methods and tools for deterministic and stochastic simulations

For the stochastic model, Eqs. 1–3 and ODEs of the four gating variables in the IP_3R model are solved by the fourth-order Runge-Kutta method (RK4) and the stochastic states of IP_3R determined by the IP_3R model are solved by using a hybrid Gillespie method with adaptive timing [37]. The maximum time step size is set to be either 10^{-4} s (for the 6-state IP_3R model) or 10^{-3} s (for the reduced 2-state IP_3R model). All the computations are done with MATLAB (The MathWorks, Natick, MA) and the codes are provided in Supporting information (Text S1–S2). For the deterministic model, we use ode15s, an ODE solver in MATLAB. Accuracy is controlled by setting an absolute tolerance of 10^{-8} applied to all the variables.

Statistical analysis

Data analysis is performed on the Ca^{2+} traces with relatively stable baselines and less noise. A moving average of every 3 data points is used to improve the data by smoothing out short-term fluctuations (Fig. 2A is an improved result). Due to large variations in baseline, amplitude, and level of noise in data, we used two thresholds to get samples: a low threshold, 20% of the amplitude of the largest spike above the baseline, to initially filter baseline noise out; and a relatively high threshold, 50% of the amplitude of the largest spike above the baseline, to further remove small spikes that cannot initiate waves. For simulated stochastic traces of variable c, we first convert it to fluorescence ratio (F/F_0) by using $F/F_0 = c(c_0 + K_d)/(c_0 c + c_0 K_d)$ where the dissociation constant of Oregon Green $K_d = 0.17\ \mu M$ and resting $[Ca^{2+}]_i$ $c_0 = 0.1\ \mu M$. We then used the same sampling procedure mentioned above to obtain samples. After samples are chosen, ISIs and spike durations are calculated based on the low threshold. Simulated traces used to calculate average frequency are about 200–400 seconds long. All the samplings and linear least-squares fittings are implemented using MATLAB (see Text S3–S4 for Matlab codes).

ACKNOWLEDGMENTS

We acknowledge many useful conversations with Martin Falcke.

AUTHOR CONTRIBUTIONS

Conceived and designed the experiments: JS GD MJS. Performed the experiments: XT. Analyzed the data: PC. Contributed to the writing of the manuscript: PC JS. Conceived and designed the model: PC JS GD. Performed the simulations: PC.

REFERENCES

1. De Young GW, Keizer J (1992) A single-pool inositol 1, 4, 5-trisphosphate-receptor-based model for agonist-stimulated oscillations in Ca2+ concentration. Proc Natl Acad Sci USA 89: 9895–9899.

2. Dupont G, Goldbeter A (1993) One-pool model for Ca2+ oscillations involving Ca2+ and inositol 1,4,5-trisphosphate as co-agonists for Ca2+ release. Cell Calcium 14: 311–322.

3. Atri A, Amundson J, Clapham D, Sneyd J (1993) A single-pool model for intracellular calcium oscillations and waves in the Xenopus laevis oocyte. Biophys J 65: 1727–1739.

4. Mak DOD, Pearson JE, Loong KPC, Datta S, Fernández-Mongil M, et al. (2007) Rapid ligand-regulated gating kinetics of single IP3R Ca2+ release channels. EMBO Rep 8: 1044–1051.

5. Wagner LE, Yule DI (2012) Differential regulation of the InsP3 receptor type-1 and -2 single channel properties by InsP3, Ca2+ and atp. J Physiol 590: 3245–3259.

6. Ullah G, Mak DOD, Pearson JE (2012) A data-driven model of a modal gated ion channel: the inositol 1,4,5-trisphosphate receptor in insect sf9 cells. J Gen Physiol 140: 159–173

7. Siekmann I, Wagner LE, Yule DI, Crampin EJ, Sneyd J (2012) A kinetic model for IP3R type i and type ii accounting for mode changes. Biophys J 103: 658–668.

8. Cao P, Donovan G, Falcke M, Sneyd J (2013) A stochastic model of calcium puffs based on single-channel data. Biophys J 105: 1133–1142.

9. Smith IF, Parker I (2009) Imaging the quantal substructure of single IP3R channel activity during Ca2+ puffs in intact mammalian cells. Proc Natl Acad Sci USA 106: 6404–6409.

10. Brumen M, Fajmut A, Dobovišek A, Roux E (2005) Mathematical modelling of Ca2+oscillations in airway smooth muscle cells. J Biol Phys 31: 515–524.

11. Sneyd J, Tsaneva-Atanasova K, Reznikov V, Bai Y, Sanderson MJ, et al. (2006) A method for determining the dependence of calcium oscillations on inositol trisphosphate oscillations. Proc Natl Acad Sci USA 103: 1675–1680.

12. Wang IY, Bai Y, Sanderson MJ, Sneyd J (2010) A mathematical analysis of agonist- and kcl-induced Ca2+ oscillations in mouse airway smooth muscle cells. Biophys J 98: 1170–1181.

13. Croisier H, Tan X, Perez-Zoghbi JF, Sandrson MJ, Sneyd J, et al. (2013) Activation of store-operated calcium entry in airway smooth muscle cells: insight from a mathematical model. PLoS ONE 8(7): e69598

14. Marchant JS, Parker I (2001) Role of elementary Ca2+ puffs in generating repetitive Ca2+ oscillations. EMBO J 20: 65–76.

15. Skupin A, Kettenmann H, Winkler U, Wartenberg M, Sauer H, et al. (2008) How does intracellular Ca2+ oscillate: by chance or by the clock? Biophys J 94: 2404–2411.

16. Perez JF, Sanderson MJ (2005) The frequency of calcium oscillations induced by 5-ht, ach, and kcl determine the contraction of smooth muscle cells of intrapulmonary bronchioles. J Gen Physiol 125: 535–553.

17. Bai Y, Edelmann M, Sanderson MJ (2009) The contribution of inositol 1,4,5-trisphosphate and ryanodine receptors to agonist-induced Ca2+ signaling of airway smooth muscle cells. Am J Physiol Lung Cell Mol Physiol 297: L347–L361.

18. .Bird GSJ, Putney JW (2005) Capacitative calcium entry supports calcium oscillations in human embryonic kidney cells. J Physiol 562(3): 697–706.

19. Sneyd J, Tsaneva-Atanasova K, Yule DI, Thompson JL, Shuttleworth TJ (2004) Control of calcium oscillations by membrane fluxes. Proc Natl Acad Sci USA 101: 1392–1396.

20. Mahn K, Hirst SJ, Ying S, Holt MR, Lavender P, et al. (2009) Diminished sarco/endoplasmic reticulum Ca2+ atpase (serca) expression contributes to airway remodelling in bronchial asthma. Proc Natl Acad Sci USA 106: 10775–10780.

21. 21.Sathish V, Leblebici F, Kip SN, Thompson MA, Pabelick CM, et al. (2008) Regulation of sarcoplasmic reticulum Ca2+ reuptake in porcine airway smooth muscle. Am J Physiol Lung Cell Mol Physiol 294: L787–L796.

22. Zeller S, Rüdiger S, Engel H, Sneyd J, Warnecke G, et al. (2009) Modeling of the modulation by buffers of Ca2+ release through clusters of IP3 receptors. Biophys J 97: 992–1002.

23. .Li Y, Rinzel J (1994) Equations for InsP3 receptor-mediated [Ca2+]i oscillations derived from a detailed kinetic model: a hodgkin-huxley like formalism. J Theor Biol 166: 461–473.

24. Keener J, Sneyd J (2009) Mathematical Physiology, Second Edition. Springer, New York.

25. Ionescu L, White C, Cheung KH, Shuai J, Parker I, et al. (2007) Mode switching is the major mechanism of ligand regulation of InsP3 receptor calcium release channels. J Gen Physiol 130: 631–645.

26. Shuai JW, Jung P (2002) Stochastic properties of Ca2+ release of inositol 1,4,5-trisphosphate receptor clusters. Biophys J 83: 87–97.

27. Dupont G, Abou-Lovergne A, Combettes L (2008) Stochastic aspects of oscillatory Ca2+ dynamics in hepatocytes. Biophys J 95: 2193–2202.

28. .Kannan MS, Prakash YS, Brenner T, Mickelson JR, Sieck GC (1997) Role of ryanodine receptor channels in Ca2+ oscillations of porcine tracheal smooth muscle. Am J Physiol 272: L659–L664.

29. Tazzeo T, Zhang Y, Keshavjee S, Janssen LJ (2008) Ryanodine receptors decant internal Ca2+ store in human and bovine airway smooth muscle. Eur Respir J 32: 275–284.

30. Ressmeyer AR, Bai Y, Delmotte P, Uy KF, Thistlethwate P, et al. (2010) Human airway contraction and formoterol-induced relaxation is determined by Ca2+ oscillations and Ca2+ sensitivity. Am J Respir Cell Mol Biol 43: 179–191.

31. .Soeller C, Cannell MB (2004) Analysing cardiac excitation-contraction coupling with mathematical models of local control. Prog Biophys Mol Biol 85: 141–162.

32. Thurley K, Skupin A, Thul R, Falcke M (2012) Fundamental properties of Ca2+ signals. Biochim Biophys Acta 1820(8): 1185–1194.

33. Dickinson G, Parker I (2013) Factors determining the recruitment of inositol trisphosphate receptor channels during calcium puffs. Biophys J 105: 2474–2484.

34. Rüdiger S, Shuai JW, Sokolov IM (2010) Law of mass action, detailed balance, and the modeling of calcium puffs. Phys Rev Lett 105(4): 048103

35. .Rüdiger S, Jung P, Shuai J (2012) Termination of Ca2+ release for clustered IP3R channels. PLoS Comput Biol 8(5): e1002485

36. Chandrasekera PC, Kargacim ME, Deans JP, Lytton J (2009) Determination of apparent calcium affinity for endogenously expressed human sarco(endo)plasmic reticulum calcium-atpase isoform serca3. Am J Physiol Cell Physiol 296: C1105–C1114.

37. Rüdiger S, Shuai JW, Huisinga W, Nagaiah C, Warnecke G, et al. (2007) Hybrid stochastic and deterministic simulations of calcium blips. Biophys J 93: 1847–1857.

13

CHAPTER

Canadian-led capacity-building in biostatistics and methodology in cardiovascular and diabetes trials: the CANNeCTIN Biostatistics and Methodological Innovation Working Group

Lehana Thabane1,2,3,4*, George Wells5 , Richard Cook6 , Robert Platt7 , Janice Pogue4 , Eleanor Pullenayegum1,2,3, David Matthews6 , Tara McCready4 , Philip J Devereaux1,4, John A Cairns8 , Salim Yusuf1,4,9, the CANadian Network and Centre for Trials Internationally (CANNeCTIN) Investigators

[1] *Department of Clinical Epidemiology and Biostatistics, McMaster University, 1200 Main Street West, Hamilton, Ontario, L8N 3Z5, Canada.*

[2] *Biostatistics Unit, St Joseph's Healthcare Hamilton, 50 Charlton Avenue East, Hamilton, Ontario, L8N 4A6, Canada.*

[3] *The Centre for Evaluation of Medicines, St Joseph's Healthcare Hamilton, 105 Main St. East, Level P1, Hamilton, Ontario, L8N 1G6, Canada.*

[4] *Population Health Research Institute, Hamilton Health Sciences, 237 Barton Street East, Hamilton, Ontario, L8L 2X2, Canada.*

[5] *University of Ottawa Heart Institute, 40 Ruskin Street, Ottawa, Ontario, K1Y 4W7, Canada.*

[6] *Department of Statistics and Actuarial Science, University of Waterloo, 200 University Avenue West, Waterloo, Ontario, N2L 3G1, Canada.*

[7] *Department of Epidemiology and Biostatistics, McGill University, 1020 Pine Avenue West, Montreal, Quebec, H3A 1A2, Canada.*

[8] *Department of Medicine, University of British Columbia, 2329 West Mall, Vancouver, British Columbia, V6T 1Z4, Canada.*

ABSTRACT

The Biostatistics and Methodological Innovation Working (BMIW) Group is one of several working groups within the CANadian Network and Centre for Trials INternationally (CANNeCTIN). This programme received funding from the Canadian Institutes of Health Research and the Canada Foundation for Innovation beginning in 2008, to enhance the infrastructure and build capacity for large Canadian-led clinical trials in cardiovascular diseases (CVD) and diabetes mellitus (DM). The overall aims of the BMIW Group's programme within CANNeCTIN, are to advance biostatistical and methodological research, and to build biostatistical capacity in CVD and DM. Our program of research and training includes: monthly videoconferences on topical biostatistical and methodological issues in CVD/DM clinical studies; providing presentations on methods issues at the annual CANNeCTIN meetings; collaborating with clinician investigators on their studies; training young statisticians in biostatistics and methods in CVD/DM trials and organizing annual symposiums on topical methodological issues. We are focused on the development of new biostatistical methods and the recruitment and training of highly qualified personnel - who will become leaders in the design and analysis of CVD/DM trials. The ultimate goal is to enhance global health by contributing to efforts to reduce the burden of CVD and DM.

BACKGROUND

Jointly funded beginning in 2008 by the Canadian Institutes of Health Research (CIHR) and the Canada Foundation for Innovation (CFI), the CANadian Network and Centre for Trials INternationally (CANNeCTIN) was among five successful applications under the CIHR-CFI strategic initiative to support clinical research programs, teams and network infra-structure that focused on high-impact, clinically relevant problems [1]. CIHR is the Canadian equivalent of the US National Institutes of Health. It was established by the Canadian federal government in 2000, as the successor to the Medical Research Council and currently supports more than 13,000 health researchers and trainees in universities, teaching hospitals and other health organizations and research centres across the country. CFI is an independent corporation created in 1997 by the Government of Canada to fund research infrastructure. The CFI's mandate is to strengthen the capacity of Canadian universities, colleges, research hospitals, and non-profit research institutions to carry out world-class research and technology development that benefits Canadians.

The focus for CANNeCTIN is to enhance the infrastructure and to build capacity for clinical trials in cardiovascular diseases (CVD) and diabetes mellitus (DM), especially those with a focus on neglected conditions, outcomes and interventions. There is an explicit goal to build capacity by developing young trialists who could emerge to be the leaders of large trials and expanding biostatistical expertise as it relates to clinical trials. Led by Salim Yusuf (Hamilton Health Sciences and McMaster University) and John Cairns (University of British Columbia), and coordinated by the Population Health Research Institute (PHRI) (Hamilton, Ontario), CANNECTIN has engaged more than 100 researchers from 19 universities including all of Canada's 17 medical schools. This network is linked to an international network of over 1500 affiliated hospitals and clinics from 80 countries [1] and is committed to developing links with investigators in developing countries (e.g. South Africa, other African countries, South American countries and India). PHRI was launched as a joint Hamilton Health Sciences and McMaster University research institute in 1999. It is located in the David Braley Cardiac, Vascular and Stroke Research Institute (DBCVSRI) at Hamilton General Hospital. The PHRI provides an education, training, and mentorship environment for learners working on cutting-edge projects with world class scientists, with a vision of world class research for new discoveries solving global health challenges. PHRI's research interests span all frontiers of the globe and include a broad spectrum of health-related issues. Originally a cardiovascular disease research institute, PHRI's programs have expanded to include a broad specrum of medical and societal conditions in varied populations defined by ethnicity or geographic region.

The organizational structure of CANNeCTIN includes Working Groups which are disease/discipline-based (e.g. interventional cardiology, perioperative medicine, cardiac surgery) and technological/programmatic in type (e.g., biostatistics and methodological innovation, pharmacogenomics, developing countries, education, knowledge translation (KT)) collaborative national and international networks and a coordination centre based within the PHRI [1]. A detailed description of the programme, organization, functions and goals is available athttp://www.cannectin.ca.

At the planning stage of the CANNeCTIN program, it was recognized that biostatisticians play a critical role in designing health studies (by helping to formulate research questions and to determine appropriate research designs, data collection procedures and analytic strategies) and in conducting analyses of data from studies to answer scientific questions. The universal shortage of biostatisticians has been documented in many countries including the United States [2] and Australia [3]. In their "Strategy for patient-oriented research" released in February 2010, CIHR acknowledged that in Canada "...the clinical research workforce has not grown since CIHR's creation in 2000, with obvious shortages of *biostatisticians*, health economists, clinical epidemiologists, social scientists, ..." and further noted that "...most academic health science centres conducting clinical research report a critical shortage of *biostatisticians* and *methodologists*" (http://www.cihr-irsc.gc.ca) [emphasis is ours]. Canada needs to train and support the careers of biostatisticians and research methodologists to enhance its capacity to conduct patient-oriented research with the potential to improve health and enhance the sustainability of the Canadian healthcare system. A fundamental goal of CANNeCTIN is to improve this situation.

The objectives of this paper are: 1) to describe the innovative research and training activities of the Biostatistics and Methodological Innovation Working (BMIW) Group in building capacity in biostatistics and clinical trial methods; 2) to disseminate the activities of the BMIW Group to other interested researchers; and 3) to encourage interested biostatisticians and methodologically oriented clinical researchers to join the BMIW Group.

THE BIOSTATISTICS AND METHODOLOGICAL INNOVATION WORKING GROUP

As one of the CANNeCTIN Working Groups, the BMIW Group was created to bring clinical researchers and biostatisticians together from multiple universities across Canada to: a) identify and address complex biostatistical and methodological problems relevant to clinical trials and epidemiologic studies; b) advise clinical trialists regarding these issues; and c) build capacity through practical and interactive training of future biostatisticians and clinician-methodologists in CVD/DM trials.

Innovations in biostatistical methods have already played a major role in health research; however, clinical researchers face increasingly challenging problems requiring further innovation. Unresolved biostatistical challenges include: a) optimal ways to analyze pharmacogenomic data; b) developing new statistical methods in the design and analysis of CVD/DM trials; c) addressing complexities in non-inferiority and adaptive trial designs. Using simulations and existing datasets from large completed studies (see PHRI website for a complete listing of completed and on-going multi-centre studies: http://www.phri.ca/body.cfm?id=22), the BMIW Group is able to empirically test their hypotheses on many of the above biostatistical and methodological issues.

The original core centres in the Group were the University of Waterloo, University of Ottawa, McGill University and McMaster University with PHRI as the coordinating centre. Other centres that have joined the Group include the University of Toronto and University of Western Ontario. Figure 1 shows the key members from each centre.

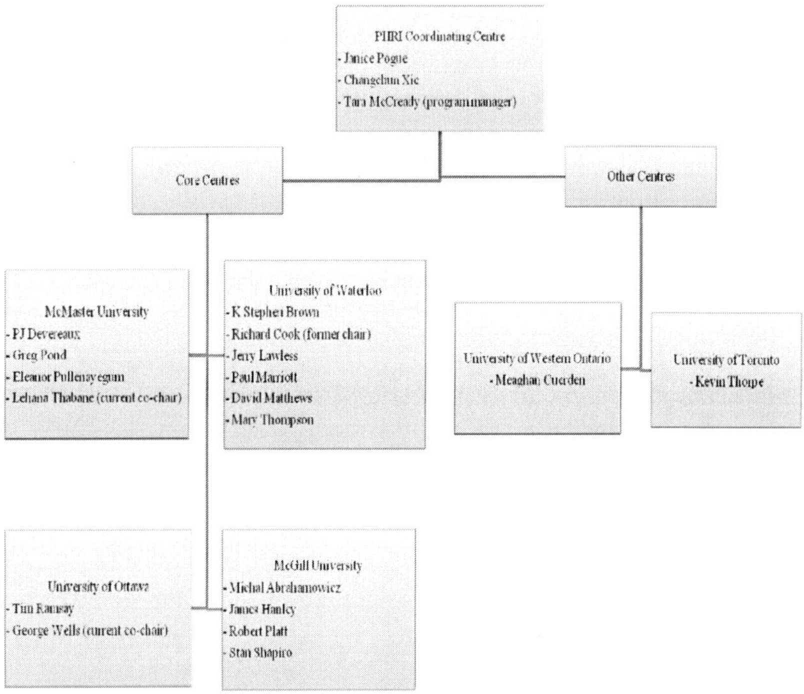

Figure 1. Key Members of the CANNeCTIN Biostatistics and Methodological Innovation Group by Centre.

Innovations in Biostatistical Research and Training

Our innovative program of research and training activities includes: monthly videoconferences on topical biostatistical and methodological issues in CVD/MD clinical studies; providing presentations on methodological issues at the annual CANNeCTIN meetings; recruiting and training young statisticians in biostatistics and methods in CVD/DM trials and organizing annual symposiums on topical methodological issues. These activities were deliberately chosen to share knowledge, provoke interactive discussion, stimulate research ideas, encourage research collaboration and cultivate academic cross-fertilization among biostatisticians, clinicians and trainees.

Monthly video-conferences

The BMIW Group holds regular videoconference/webcast seminars on advanced issues in clinical trials methodology. The seminars take place every second Friday of the month between September to June. Participants can join the live videoconference sites at the Hamilton General Hospital, McMaster University, University of Waterloo, McGill University, and the University of Ottawa Heart Institute or view a live webcast of the presentation through the Ontario Telemedicine Network (OTN) website (http://webcast.otn.ca). The webcasts are archived on the OTN website for two years and then moved to the CANNeCTIN website. Individuals interested in taking part in the videoconferences can email cannectin@phri.ca for information about adding their centres to the live videoconference, join the videoconference in person athttp://www.cannectin.ca/default.cfm?id=66 or watch a live webcast on the OTN website. The seminars have been running for three years and have covered a wide spectrum of issues in clinical studies (see Table 1). The pdf versions and some of the video webcasts of presentations are available online athttp://www.cannectin.ca/default.cfm?id=25 and can form a useful learning resource for individuals both within t and outside of the network.

Table 1. Coverage of topics and issues at monthly videoconferences for 2008-2010

Topic	Issues covered*
Issues in RCTs	• Biases resulting from patient withdrawal in RCTs and how to address them;
	• Design and analysis issues in knowledge translation trials in primary care;
	• Testing for blinding at the end of an RCT [5],
	• Prognostic imbalance in RCTs;
	• Dynamic allocation methods: why the controversy?
	• Statistical issues in the use of composite outcomes clinical trials.
Issues in cluster RCTs	• Clustered measurement in cluster randomized trials;
	• Imputation strategies for missing binary outcomes in cluster randomized trials.
Non-inferiority designs	• What's wrong with non-inferiority designs?
Pragmatic Trials	• A pragmatic-explanatory continuum summary (PRECIS) [6];
Meta-analysis issues	• Empirical priors for between-study heterogeneity in meta-analysis;
	• Precision in meta-analysis;
	• Indirect comparisons for evaluating healthcare interventions [7].
Other issues	• Bias in logistic regression due to omitted covariates;
	• Statistical genetics and coronary artery disease;
	• Longitudinal modeling when the response and time-dependent covariates are measured at distinct time-points.

*Pdf Slides and audio versions of the presentations are available at http:/www.cannectin.ca/default.cfm?id=25.

Presentations at CANNeCTIN annual meetings

To facilitate cross-fertilization between statisticians and clinicians, the BIMW Group regularly engages in interactive discussions with clinicians on methodological issues that arise in CANNeCTIN studies. Clinical investigators are invited to present to their studies to the group at our monthly biostatistics videoconferences and receive input from the group. The group members also give presentations at the annual CANNeCTIN meeting. At the CANNeCTIN Junior investigator meeting held in Winter 2010, the members of the group delivered the following presentations:

- How CANNeCTIN investigators can collaborate with statisticians at PHRI;
- What you need to know about pilot studies: the what, how and why [4];
- Some issues in the design and analysis of RCTs - covering issues in cluster randomization trials and time-to-event outcomes; and
- Common errors in CIHR RCT grants.

These presentations are available at http://www.cannectin.ca/default.cfm?id=116. We plan to continue to foster these interactions in future meetings and to expand the coverage to include more topics. The BMIW Group also participated in the Cutting Edge Symposiums on Pharmacogenomics that took place in May 2009 and Perioperative Medicine held in April 2010, in Hamilton (Ontario, Canada) (http://www.cannectin.ca /body.cfm?id=68). In these symposiums, we collaborate closely with our clinician investigators to discuss the biostatistical and methodological issues arising from different studies. For example, one of the trials - PADIT (Prevention of Arrhythmia Device Trial) [ClinicalTrials.gov identifier #: NCT01002911] involved both the use of both a cross-over design and cluster-randomization. The trial uses "site" as a unit of randomization. The primary objective is to compare conventional pre-operative antibiotics versus conventional intra-operative plus post-operative antibiotics in preventing hospitalization attributed to device infection in patients undergoing cardiac surgery. This raised interesting discussions among biostatisticians and clinicians about the design and analysis of the trial.

The group also takes part in the annual Trout-CANNeCTIN workshop - an intensive, interactive training program led by Dr David Sackett, which guides young researchers in the design, implementation, and analysis of high-quality clinical studies, as well as in effective grant writing and academic career development. Our role includes providing biostatistical feedback and support to the trainees.

Capacity-building through training and mentorship of young biostatisticians

One of our goals is to build capacity in biostatistics within Canada through advanced and practical training of graduate and postgraduate students. This occurs in an interdisciplinary environment, with clinicians and biostatisticians working together on applied problems. As noted earlier, the worldwide need for experienced biostatisticians in many countries is high in all areas of health research [2, 3] and Canada is no exception. Our program is to recruit and train biostatisticians within Canada with the necessary practical experience and skills to work with clinical investigators. The specific objectives of this training and mentorship programme are to promote enthusiasm and commitment to excellence in statistical collaboration in CVD and DM clinical research; to enhance communication of statistical issues to clinician collaborators; to train young statisticians to acquire biostatistical self-sufficiency and develop skills in applied statistics in CVD and DM trials; and to enhance a culture of collaboration among statisticians and clinician researchers. We introduce our trainees to the rewards and challenges of health care research, through practical training obtained by working on real problems that are encountered in ongoing trials. We provide partial funding for all CANNeCTIN biostatistics trainees, who have a primary supervisor at their "home" institution. All supervisors have to be active members of the BMIW Group. The student submits a proposal and receives input from all the members of the group (collective mentoring). By providing hands-on experience in large clinical studies, our training approach complements training programs already existing in many universities and builds biostatistical capacity specific to CVD and DM trials in Canada.

Table 2 provides a summary of our trainees to date (11 trainees), their "home" institution, project title and primary supervisor(s).

Table 2. Current List of CANNeCTIN Biostatistics Trainees

Institution	Trainee	Project	Supervisor
McMaster University	Kristian Thorlund	Methodological improvements in meta-analysis	Drs. Lehana Thabane and PJ Devereaux
	Jinhui Ma	Issues in the Statistical Analysis and Imputation Strategies for Binary outcome from Cluster Randomized Trials in Management of Cardiovascular Risk Factors	Dr. Lehana Thabane
	Rachel Chu	Intraclass correlation in multicentre RCTs and prognostic heterogeneity/imbalance	Dr. Lehana Thabane
	Hoi Suen	Generalised Additive Models for the analysis of health utility data	Dr Eleanor Pullenayegum
University of Waterloo	Haocheng Li	Design of Clinical Trial and Statistical Analysis with Missing Data	Dr. Grace Yi
	Longyang Wu	Design of Clinical Trials with Recurrent Events and Competing Risks	Dr. Richard Cook
	Audrey Boruvka	Event history analysis with incomplete data	Dr. Richard Cook
	Min Chen	Empirical Likelihood Methods for Pretest-Posttest Studies	Drs Mary Thompson and Changbao Wu
University of Ottawa	Robert William Davies	Statistical Issues Which Pertain to the use of GWAS for the Identification, Characterization and Quantification of Genetic Effects in Cardiovascular Disease	Dr. George Wells
McGill University	Maria Esther Perez Trejo	The problem of extra variation induced by double clustering	Dr. Robert Platt
	Michael Regier	Develop causal methods appropriate for repeatedly measured data	Dr. Robert Platt
	Menglan Pan	Marginal Structural Models, Odds Ratios, and Collapsibility	Drs. Robert Platt and Jay Kaufman

Other Activities: Special Invited Sessions at Scientific Meetings and the Annual Biostatistics and Methods Symposium

The BMIW Group has organized some special sessions sponsored by CANNeCTIN at various biostatistical meetings including the Canadian Society for Epidemiology and Biostatistics annual meeting held in Ottawa (Ontario, Canada) in, 2009; and the Statistical Society of Canada annual meeting held in Vancouver (British Columbia, Canada) in 2009. We are currently organizing another invited sessions at the annual meetings of the Statistical Society of Canada (SSC) in Wolfville (Nova Scotia, Canada) in June 2011 and International Society for Clinical Biostatistics (ISCB) in Ottawa (Ontario, Canada) in August 2011. These activities have provided good forums for the group to share their research with national and international statistical communities

The BMIW group plans to organize annual symposiums on challenging and relevant topics in biostatistics in RCTs or observational studies that will involve other experts from Canada and abroad, and be suitable for publication in peer-reviewed journals. Each symposium will focus on answering four key questions: 1) what is the state-of-the-art? ii) what are the outstanding or controversial issues that remain unresolved or need to be addressed? iii) what guidance can we provide to researchers on these issues based on the current knowledge?; and iv) what research needs to be done to fully address the issues?

Topical biostatistical and methodological issues that have been identified so far include composite outcomes, stopping rules, surrogate outcomes, non-inferiority designs, non-compliance, adjustment for baseline imbalance in RCTs, adaptive designs, and large vs. small trials. The first CANNeCTIN Cutting Edge Symposium on Advanced Biostatistics and Methodological Issues in Clinical Trials is planned for Hamilton, Canada for April 28-29, 2011, will focus on outcomes in CVD trials - covering both composite and surrogate outcomes, and adaptive designs. More details on the symposium can be found at http://www.cannectin.ca/default.cfm?id=128.

Lessons Learned

Effective use of information technology (IT) to link different centres through videoconferences has been key to the success of our monthly seminars. Occasionally, we encounter some technical problems in connecting sites, but these problems are always resolved without much difficulty and with some patience. To date, no seminars have been cancelled because of IT challenges.

Mentoring the next generation of biostatisticians in cardiovascular trials has been a worthwhile journey so far. Collectively, we have 11 trainees from four Canadian universities, supervised or mentored by seven BMIW Group biostatisticians. We hope that this effort will continue to expand the training opportunities to more national and international centres.

Interacting and collaborating with clinicians in addressing CVD/DM problems has been a rewarding experience for many of us. The CANNeCTIN programme provides an excellent opportunity to promote academic dialogue among biostatisticians and clinicians (including our trainees). By sharing knowledge, provoking interactive discussion, stimulating research ideas, encouraging collaboration and fostering academic cross-fertilization, we can make our biostatistical research more relevant and applicable to important problems in CVD and DM research.

Some Concluding Remarks

There is a severe shortage of biostatistical expertise in CVD/DM research. Our efforts to reduce the global burden of these diseases depend on the conduct of large well-designed trials to advance our understanding of the key predictors of the disease and the best strategies for prevention, treatment and management. The BMIW Group is making substantial contributions towards the realization of CANNeCTIN's vision to advance global health through building the capacity of the Canadian research community to lead major CVD and DM clinical trials. The long-term contributions of the BMIW Group will include the development of new biostatistical methods and recruitment and training of highly qualified personnel. These personnel will become leaders in collaborative health research through contributions to the design and analysis of CVD/DM trials, and also serve as committee members and reviewers for granting agencies such as CIHR that support clinical research in Canada. We believe that with suitable investments, this is a model that can be useful for building human capacity in other areas of clinical research experiencing similar shortage of biostatistical expertise.

ACKNOWLEDGEMENTS

Dr Thabane is a clinical trials mentor the Canadian Institutes of Health Research. Dr. Cook is Canada Research Chair in Statistical Methods for Health Research and is supported by CIHR and NSERC (Natural Sciences and Engineering Research Council). Dr. Platt is a Senior Chercheur-boursier of the Fonds de la Recherche en Santé du Québec.

CANNeCTIN Lead Investigators: Salim Yusuf (McMaster University, Hamilton, Ontario), John Cairns (University of British Columbia, Vancouver, British Columbia), Sonia Anand (McMaster University), Todd Anderson (University of Calgary, Calgary, Alberta), Malcolm Arnold (University of Western Ontario, London Ontario), Stuart Connolly (McMaster University), Jafna Cox (Dalhousie University, Halifax, Nova Scotia), Gilles Dagenais (Laval University, Quebec City, Quebec), PJ Devereaux (McMaster University), Paul Dorian (University of Toronto, Toronto, Ontario), Vlad Dzavik (University of Toronto), Stephen Fremes (University of Toronto), Hertzel Gerstein (McMaster University), Scott Lear (Simon Fraser University, Vancouver, British Columbia), Finlay McAlister (University of Alberta, Edmonton, Alberta), Michel Nguyen (Universite de Sherbrooke, Sherbrooke, Quebec), Richard Novick (University of Western Ontario, London, Ontario), Robert Roberts (University of Ottawa, Ottawa, Ontario), Thomas Schricker (McGill University, Montreal, Quebec), Ashfaq Shuaib (University of Alberta), Chris Simpson (Queen's University, Kingston, Ontario), Samuel Siu (University of Western Ontario), Bruce Sussex (Memorial University of Newfoundland, St John's, Newfoundland and Labrador), James Tam (University of Manitoba, Winnipeg, Manitoba), Koon Teo (McMaster University), Lehana Thabane (McMaster University), Pierre Theroux (Universite de Montreal, Montreal, Quebec), Jack Tu (University of Toronto), Richard Cook (University of Waterloo, Waterloo, Ontario), George Wells (University of Ottawa), Bernie Zinman (University of Toronto), Kelly Coverett (University of Sasketchewan, Saskatoon, Sasketchewan)

COMPETING INTERESTS

The authors declare that they have no competing interests.

AUTHORS' CONTRIBUTIONS

LT drafted the manuscript. All authors reviewed and edited draft versions of the manuscript and approved the final version.

REFERENCES

1. Cairns JA, Yusuf S, Cook RJ, for CANNeCTIN: Canadian Network and Centre for Trials Internationally (CANNeCTIN): a national network for Canadian-led trials in cardiovascular diseases and diabetes mellitus. Canadian Journal of Cardiology. 2010, 26 (7): 353-8.

2. DeMets DL, Stormo G, Boehnke M: Training of the next generation of biostatisticians: a call to action in the U.S. Statistics in Medicine. 2006, 25: 3415-3429.

3. Simpson JM, Ryan P, Carlin JB: Training a new generation of biostatisticians: A successful consortium model. Journal of Statistics Education. 2009, 17 (2): Last date of access: 2010-11-12,http://www.amstat.org/publications/jse/ v17n2/ simpson.html

4. Thabane L, Ma J, Chu R, Cheng J: A Tutorial on Pilot Studies: The What, Why and How. BMC Medical Research Methodology. 2010, 10: 1

5. Sackett DL: Commentary: Measuring the success of blinding in RCTs: don't, must, can't or needn't?. International Journal of Epidemiology. 2007, 36 (3): 664-5.

6. Thorpe KE, Zwarenstein M, Oxman AD: A pragmatic-explanatory continuum indicator summary (PRECIS): a tool to help trial designers. Canadian Medical Association Journal. 2009, 180 (10): E47-57.

7. Wells GA, Sultan SA, Chen L: Indirect Evidence: Indirect Treatment Comparisons in Meta-Analysis. 2009, Ottawa: Canadian Agency for Drugs and Technologies in Health, Last date of access: 2010-11-04,http://www.cadth.ca/media /pdf/H0462_itc_tr_e.pdf

14
CHAPTER

Comprehensive Biostatistical Analysis of CpG Island Methylator Phenotype in Colorectal Cancer Using a Large Population-Based Sample

Katsuhiko Nosho[1]., Natsumi Irahara[1]., Kaori Shima[1]., Shoko Kure[1]., Gregory J. Kirkner[2], Eva S. Schernhammer[2,3,4], Aditi Hazra[2,4,] David J. Hunter[2,4], John Quackenbush[5,6], Donna Spiegelman[2,4,6], Edward L. Giovannucci[2,4], Charles S. Fuchs[1,2,] Shuji Ogino[1,4,7]

1 Department of Medical Oncology, Dana-Farber Cancer Institute and Harvard Medical School, Boston, Massachusetts, United States of America,

2 Channing Laboratory, Department of Medicine, Brigham and Women's Hospital and Harvard Medical School, Boston, Massachusetts, United States of America,

3 Ludwig Boltzmann-Institute for Applied Cancer Research, and Applied Cancer Research – Institute for Translational Research, Vienna, Austria,

4Department of Epidemiology, Harvard School of Public Health, Boston, Massachusetts, United States of America,

5 Department of Biostatistics, Dana-Farber Cancer Institute and Harvard Medical School, Boston, Massachusetts, United States of America,

6 Department of Biostatistics, Harvard School of Public Health, Boston, Massachusetts, United States of America,

7 Department of Pathology, Brigham and Women's Hospital and Harvard Medical School, Boston, Massachusetts, United States of America

ABSTRACT

Background

The CpG island methylator phenotype (CIMP) is a distinct phenotype associated with microsatellite instability (MSI) and *BRAF* mutation in colon cancer. Recent investigations have selected 5 promoters (*CACNA1G, IGF2, NEUROG1, RUNX3* and *SOCS1*) as surrogate markers for CIMP-high. However, no study has comprehensively evaluated an expanded set of methylation markers (including these 5 markers) using a large number of tumors, or deciphered the complex clinical and molecular associations with CIMP-high determined by the validated marker panel.

Metholodology/Principal Findings

DNA methylation at 16 CpG islands [the above 5 plus *CDKN2A* (p16), *CHFR, CRABP1, HIC1,IGFBP3, MGMT,* MINT1, MINT31, *MLH1*, p14 (*CDKN2A*/ARF) and *WRN*] was quantified in 904 colorectal cancers by real-time PCR (MethyLight). In unsupervised hierarchical clustering analysis, the 5 markers (*CACNA1G, IGF2, NEUROG1, RUNX3* and *SOCS1*), *CDKN2A,CRABP1*, MINT31, *MLH1*, p14 and *WRN* were generally clustered with each other and with MSI and *BRAF* mutation. *KRAS* mutation was not clustered with any methylation marker, suggesting its association with a random methylation pattern in CIMP-low tumors. Utilizing the validated CIMP marker panel (including the 5 markers), multivariate logistic regression demonstrated that CIMP-high was independently associated with older age, proximal location, poor differentiation, MSI-high, *BRAF* mutation, and inversely with LINE-1 hypomethylation and β-catenin (*CTNNB1*) activation. Mucinous feature, signet ring cells, and p53-negativity were associated with CIMP-high in only univariate analysis. In stratified analyses, the relations of CIMP-high with poor differentiation, *KRAS* mutation and LINE-1 hypomethylation significantly differed according to MSI status.

Conclusions

Our study provides valuable data for standardization of the use of CIMP-high-specific methylation markers. CIMP-high is independently associated with clinical and key molecular features in colorectal cancer. Our data also suggest that *KRAS* mutation is related with a random CpG island methylation pattern which may lead to CIMP-low tumors.

INTRODUCTION

Epigenetic aberrations are important mechanisms in human carcinogenesis [1], [2]. A number of tumor suppressor genes are silenced by promoter CpG island methylation [3], [4]. A subset of colorectal cancers exhibit widespread promoter methylation, which is referred to as the CpG island methylator phenotype (CIMP) [4]–[7]. CIMP-high colorectal tumors have been associated with older age, female sex, proximal location, mucinous and poor differentiation, microsatellite instability (MSI), *BRAF* mutation, high LINE-1 methylation level, wild-type *TP53*, stable chromosomes, and inactive WNT/β-catenin [8]–[23]. However, many of these features are interrelated, and thus, it is essential to analyze a large number of tumors by multivariate analysis to decipher the complex relations between CIMP-high and these clinical/tumoral variables.

There is considerable heterogeneity of tumors with regard to CpG island methylation, and not all CpG islands are methylated in a similar manner in colorectal cancer [15]. Thus, choice of CpG islands can substantially influence the features of CIMP. In fact, different CIMP panels used in various studies have caused considerable confusion [7]. Weisenberger et al. [15] have screened 195 CpG islands, and selected 5 loci (*CACNA1G, IGF2, NEUROG1, RUNX3* and*SOCS1*), which can serve as surrogate markers for CIMP-high. We have further validated the use of 8 markers (the above 5 plus *CDKN2A* (p16), *CRABP1* and *MLH1*) as a CIMP-high diagnostic panel [24]. However, no study has comprehensively compared these CIMP-high-specific CpG islands and other CpG islands using a large number of tumors.

In this study, we have assessed 16 CpG islands including the new 5 CIMP markers as well as MINT (methylated in tumor) markers and other CpG islands, utilizing hierarchical clustering analysis on a large number of colorectal cancers. We have also assessed the characteristics of CIMP-high tumors determined by a validated marker panel, and interactions of various clinical and tumoral factors by multivariate logistic regression analysis. This study provides the rationale for standardization of CIMP-high-specific methylation markers.

METHODS

Study Group

We utilized the databases of two large prospective cohort studies; the Nurses' Health Study (NHS, N=121,700 women followed since 1976) [25], [26], and the Health Professionals Follow-up Study (HPFS, N=51,500 men followed since 1986) [26]. A subset of cohort participants developed colorectal cancer during prospective follow-up. Thus, these colorectal cancers represented a population-based, relatively unbiased sample (compared to a single or few-hospital-based sample). Previous studies on the cohorts have described baseline characteristics of cohort participants and incident colorectal cancer cases, and confirmed that our colorectal cancers were well representative as a population-based sample [25], [26]. Clinical information was obtained through chart review by physicians. We collected paraffin-embedded tissue blocks from hospitals where participants had undergone resections of primary colorectal cancers. Based on availability of adequate tissue specimens, a total of 904 colorectal cancer cases (406 from the men's cohort and 498 from the women's cohort) were included. Clinical characteristics of the cases are described in **Table 1** (on the left, under the column heading "All cases"). Among our cohort studies, there was no significant difference in demographic features between cases with tissue available and those without available tissue[26]. Most tumors have previously been characterized for statuses of MSI,

CIMP, *KRAS,BRAF*, p53, β-catenin, LINE-1 methylation and 14 of the 16 methylation markers [19], [21],[24], [27]. However, none of our previous studies have comprehensively analyzed the 16 methylation markers in relation to each other, independent associations of CIMP with various clinical, pathological or tumoral molecular characteristics, or interactions of various factors on the associations with CIMP-high by comprehensive biostatistical methods. This study represents a unique novel study in term of 1) a large sample size; 2) the validated set of CIMP-specific methylation markers; 3) the number of other molecular events analyzed, including 8 CpG islands other than the CIMP-specific markers, MSI, *KRAS*, *BRAF*, p53, LINE-1 methylation and β-catenin; and 4) comprehensive statistical analyses including unsupervised hierarchical clustering, smoothing splines to assess nonlinearity, multivariate logistic regression, and stratified logistic regression. Thus, this study obtained novel data from the existing materials and database, analogous to novel studies using the well-described cell lines or mouse models. Informed consent was obtained from all study subjects. Tissue collection and analyses were approved by the Harvard School of Public Health and Brigham and Women's Hospital Institutional Review Boards.

Pathologic Examination, DNA Extraction and Sequencing of *KRAS* and*BRAF*

For all cases, pathologic features including tumor differentiation, mucinous features and signet ring cells were examined by a pathologist (S.O.). Poor differentiation was defined as the presence of <50% glandular area. Genomic DNA was extracted from paraffin tissue, and PCR and Pyrosequencing targeted for *KRAS* codons 12 and 13, and *BRAF* codon 600 were performed as previously described [28], [29].

Table 1. Clinical, pathologic and molecular characteristics of colon cancer cases according to CIMP status.

Clinical, pathological or molecular feature	All cases	CIMP-low/0	CIMP-high	P value
Total N	904	771	133	
Sex				0.003
Male	406 (45%)	362 (47%)	44 (33%)	
Female	498 (55%)	409 (53%)	89 (67%)	
Mean age±SD	66.3±8.4	65.7±8.5	69.4±6.9	<0.0001#
Tumor location^				<0.0001
Proximal	386 (45%)	270 (37%)	116 (89%)	
Distal (excluding rectum)	282 (33%)	270 (37%)	12 (9.2%)	
Rectum	199 (23%)	196 (27%)	3 (2.3%)	
Tumor stage				<0.0001
I	203 (25%)	188 (28%)	15 (12%)	
II	261 (33%)	193 (29%)	68 (54%)	
III	229 (29%)	203 (30%)	26 (21%)	
IV	106 (13%)	90 (13%)	16 (13%)	
Tumor differentiation				<0.0001
Well/moderate	803 (91%)	710 (94%)	93 (70%)	
Poor	83 (9.4%)	43 (5.7%)	40 (30%)	
Mucinous component				<0.0001
0%	601 (66%)	545 (71%)	56 (42%)	
1–49%	188 (21%)	152 (20%)	36 (27%)	
≥50%	115 (13%)	74 (9.6%)	41 (31%)	
Signet ring cells				<0.0001
0%	844 (93%)	733 (95%)	111 (83%)	
≥1%	60 (6.6%)	38 (4.9%)	22 (17%)	
MSI				<0.0001
Non-MSI-high	748 (85%)	707 (95%)	41 (31%)	
MSI-high	127 (15%)	37 (5.0%)	90 (69%)	
Mean LINE-1 methylation (%)±SD	61.4±9.6	60.7±9.6	65.1±8.3	<0.0001#
BRAF				<0.0001
Wild-type	748 (87%)	697 (95%)	51 (40%)	
Mutated	113 (13%)	36 (4.9%)	77 (60%)	
KRAS				<0.0001
Wild-type	557 (63%)	445 (59%)	112 (85.5%)	
Mutated	326 (37%)	307 (41%)	19 (14.5%)	
p53*				<0.0001
Negative	506 (57%)	403 (53%)	103 (77%)	
Positive	386 (43%)	356 (47%)	30 (23%)	
β-catenin*				<0.0001
Inactive (score 0–2)	499 (64%)	403 (60%)	96 (91%)	
Active (score 3–5)	278 (36%)	269 (40%)	9 (8.6%)	

(%) indicates the proportion of cases with a specific clinical feature within each MSI/CIMP subtype.
^Proximal colon includes cecum to transverse colon, and distal colon includes splenic flexure to sigmoid colon.
*p53 and β-catenin status was determined by immunohistochemistry. Active β-catenin was defined as β-catenin score ≥3, where the β-catenin score was the sum of nuclear (0, 1+ or 2+), cytoplasmic (0, 1+ or 2+) and membrane (0 or 1+ if expression is lost) scores as originally described by Jass et al.[35].
#t-test assuming unequal variances.
CIMP, CpG island methylator phenotype; LINE-1, long interspersed nucleotide element-1; MSI, microsatellite instability; SD, standard deviation.

Microsatellite Instability (MSI) Analysis

MSI status was determined by the MSI panel including D2S123, D5S346, D17S250, BAT25, BAT26, BAT40, D18S55, D18S56, D18S67 and D18S487 (i.e., 10-marker panel) as previously described [24]. A "high degree of MSI" (MSI-high) was defined as the presence of instability in ≥30% of the markers.

Real-time PCR (MethyLight) for Quantitative DNA Methylation Analysis

Sodium bisulfite treatment on DNA and subsequent real-time PCR (MethyLight [30]) was validated and performed as previously described [31]. We quantified DNA methylation in 5 CIMP-specific promoters (*CACNA1G*, *IGF2*, *NEUROG1*, *RUNX3* and *SOCS1*) and 11 other CpG islands [*CDKN2A* (p16), *CHFR*, *CRABP1*, *HIC1*, *IGFBP3*, *MGMT*, MINT1, MINT31,*MLH1*, p14 (*CDKN2A*/ARF), and *WRN*]. *COL2A1* (the collagen 2A1 gene) was used to normalize for the amount of template bisulfite-converted DNA [31]. Primers and probes were previously described [15], [27], except for *IGFBP3*, p14 and *WRN*: IGFBP3-F, 5′-G***TT*** ***T***CG GGC GTG AG***T*** ACG A-3′ (Genbank No. M35878, nucleotide Nos. 1692-1710); IGFBP3-R, G***AA*** TCG ***A***CG CA***A*** ***A***CA CG***A*** CT***A*** C(nucleotide Nos. 1789-1810) and IGFBP3-probe, 6FAM-***T***CG G***TT*** G***TT*** ***T***AG GGC GAA GTA CGG G-BHQ-1(nucleotide Nos. 1760-1784) (bisulfite-converted nucleotides are highlighted by bold face and italics); P14 (CDKN2A/ARF)-F, 5′- ***T***TG GAG GCG GCG AGA A***T***A T-3′ (Genbank No. L41934, nucleotide Nos. 238-256); P14-R, 5′-CCC CGT***AAA*** CCG CG***A*** ***A***AT ***A***-3′ (nucleotide Nos. 332-350); P14-probe, 6FAM-5′- CGG ***TT***C G***T***C GCG AGT GAG GGT T-3′ –BHQ-1 (nucleotide Nos. 299-320); WRN-F, 5′-G***T***A TCG ***TT***C GCG GCG ***TTT*** A***T***-3′ (Genbank No. AY442327, nucleotide Nos. 1827-1846); WRN-R, 5′-***A***CG ***AAA*** CCG***A***T***A*** TCC GAA ***A***TC A -3′ (nucleotide Nos. 1887-1908) and WRN-probe, 6FAM-***TTT*** ***T***T***T*** ***T***TG CGG ***T***CG ***T***TG CGG G-BHQ-(nucleotide Nos. 1855-1876). The PCR condition was initial denaturation at 95°C for 10 min followed by 45 cycles of 95°C for 15 sec and 60°C for 1 min. A standard curve was made for each PCR plate by duplicated PCR amplifications for *COL2A1* on bisulfite-converted human genomic DNA at 4 different concentrations (in a 5-fold dilution series). The percentage of methylated reference (PMR, i.e., degree of methylation) at a specific locus was calculated by dividing the *GENE:COL2A1* ratio of template amounts in a sample by the *GENE:COL2A1* ratio of template amounts in *Sss*I-treated human genomic DNA (presumably fully methylated) and multiplying this value by 100. Methylation positivity was set as PMR≥4 as previously validated [31].

Pyrosequencing to Measure LINE-1 Methylation

In order to accurately quantify relatively high LINE-1 methylation levels, we utilized Pyrosequencing as previously described [21]. LINE-1 methylation level measured by Pyrosequencing has been shown to correlate well with overall 5-methylcytosine level (i.e., genome-wide DNA methylation level) in tumor cells [32], [33].

Immunohistochemistry for p53 and β-catenin

Tissue microarrays (TMAs) were constructed and immunohistochemistry for p53 and β-catenin was performed as previously described [19], [34]. Appropriate positive and negative controls were included in each run of immunohistochemistry. Cytoplasmic and nuclear β-catenin expression was recorded separately as either no expression (0), weak expression (1+), or moderate/strong expression (2+). The β-catenin activation score was calculated as the sum of nuclear score (0–2), cytoplasmic score (0–2) and membrane score (0 if membrane staining was positive, +1 if membrane expression was lost), as originally described by Jass et al. [35]. All immunohistochemically-stained slides were examined by one of the investigator (β-catenin by K.N.; p53 by S.O.) unaware of other data. Random samples of 402 and 118 tumors were re-examined for β-catenin and p53, respectively, by a second observer (β-catenin by S.O., p53 by K.N.) unaware of other data, and the concordances between the two observers were 0.83 for β-catenin (κ=0.65, $p<0.0001$), and 0.87 for p53 (κ=0.75, $p<0.0001$), indicating substantial agreement.

Statistical Analysis

For cluster analysis of biomarkers including the 16 methylation markers, MSI, *KRAS* and*BRAF*, we utilized average linkage hierarchical clustering with a Euclidean distance metric as implemented in MeV (http://www.tm4.org) [36]. The chi square test was used to examine an association between CIMP and other categorical variables of interest. The t-test assuming unequal variances was performed to compare mean age and mean LINE-1 methylation level. The κ coefficient was calculated to assess agreement between each of the 16 markers (positive vs. negative) and the 16-marker CIMP panel (CIMP-high positive vs. negative).

To examine the relations of a given variable and CIMP-high, we utilized unconditional logistic regression models to calculate odds ratios (ORs) for CIMP-high, according to the status of the given variable, unadjusted and adjusted for age, sex, tumor location, stage, differentiation, LINE-1 methylation level, and status of MSI, *KRAS*, *BRAF*, p53 and β-catenin. To adjust for potential confounding, age and LINE-1 methylation level were used as continuous variables, and all of the other variables were used as categorical variables.

For age and LINE-1, we assessed non-linearity by the likelihood ratio test that compared a regression model including a quadratic (or cubic) term with a model excluding it. The likelihood ratio test showed that including the quadratic term did not significantly alter model fit ($p=0.86$ for age, $p=0.078$ for LINE-1), and that including the cubic term did not significantly alter model fit ($p=0.87$ for age, $p=0.084$ for LINE-1). We also examined the possibility of a non-linear relation between age (or LINE-1 methylation) and CIMP-high, non-parametrically with restricted cubic splines [37].

We dichotomized tumor location (proximal vs. distal), tumor differentiation (poor vs. well/moderate), signet ring cells (present vs. absent), MSI (high vs. non-MSI-high), p53 (positive vs. negative), *KRAS* (mutated vs. wild-type), *BRAF* (mutated vs. wild-type) and β-catenin (active vs. inactive). There were 3 categories for mucinous feature (0%, 1–49%, and ≥50%) in the initial main analysis (**Table 2**). We dichotomized mucinous feature (present vs. absent) in secondary stratified analyses and analyses of interactions, because multivariate ORs for CIMP-high were similar across the 1–49% mucinous and ≥50% mucinous categories (in reference to the non-mucinous category). There were 4 categories for stage (I, II, III and IV) in the initial main analysis (**Table 2**). We dichotomized tumor stage (I vs. II–IV) in secondary stratified analyses and analyses of interactions, because multivariate ORs for CIMP-high were similar across stage II–IV (in reference to stage I).

Table 2. Associations with CIMP-high in colorectal cancer by univariate and multivariate analyses.

Clinical, pathological, or molecular characteristics	Univariate OR (95% CI)	P value	OR adjusted for major confounder(s)	Major confounder(s) (in the order of strength of effect)	Multivariate OR (95% CI)	P value
Age (10-year increment)	1.78 (1.40–2.27)	<0.0001	2.53 (1.69–3.78)	*BRAF*, MSI	**3.16 (1.93–5.18)**	**<0.0001**
Female (vs. male)	1.79 (1.22–2.64)	0.003	-	-	1.96 (0.95–4.00)	0.071
Proximal (vs. distal)^	13.3 (7.64–23.3)	<0.0001	5.58 (2.80–11.1)	MSI, *BRAF*	**3.39 (1.57–7.34)**	**0.002**
Tumor stage (vs. I)				tumor location, MSI, *BRAF*		
Stage II	4.42 (2.44–8.00)	<0.0001	2.53 (1.06–6.08)		1.83 (0.69–4.83)	0.23
Stage III	1.61 (0.83–3.12)	0.16	1.91 (0.72–5.12)		1.83 (0.63–5.28)	0.26
Stage IV	2.23 (1.06–4.71)	0.04	2.28 (0.78–6.65)		1.72 (0.53–5.62)	0.37
Poor differentiation	7.28 (4.50–11.8)	<0.0001	2.96 (1.42–6.19)	MSI, *BRAF*	**2.98 (1.15–7.69)**	**0.024**
Mucinous feature (vs. 0%)				MSI, *BRAF*		
1–49%	2.31 (1.46–3.64)	0.0003	1.72 (0.89–3.29)		1.53 (0.71–3.32)	0.28
≥50%	5.39 (3.37–8.63)	<0.0001	2.09 (1.03–4.24)		2.06 (0.81–5.22)	0.13
Signet ring cells, any	3.82 (2.18–6.71)	<0.0001	0.68 (0.32–1.41)	mucin, differentiation	0.98 (0.30–3.17)	0.97
MSI-high	41.9 (25.5–68.9)	<0.0001	27.6 (16.2–47.1)	tumor location	**21.2 (9.79–45.8)**	**<0.0001**
BRAF mutation	29.2 (18.0–47.6)	<0.0001	18.7 (11.0–31.7)	tumor location	**15.9 (6.60–38.4)**	**<0.0001**
KRAS mutation	0.25 (0.15–0.41)	<0.0001	0.71 (0.36–1.40)	*BRAF*, MSI	0.97 (0.44–2.10)	0.93
β-catenin activation*	0.14 (0.07–0.28)	<0.0001	0.21 (0.10–0.44)	tumor location	**0.21 (0.070–0.62)**	**0.005**
LINE-1 hypomethylation (30% decline)	0.20 (0.10–0.39)	<0.0001	0.30 (0.13–0.69)	MSI	**0.27 (0.094–0.75)**	**0.012**
p53 positivity	0.34 (0.22–0.52)	<0.0001	0.66 (0.39–1.13)	MSI	0.73 (0.35–1.51)	0.39

Multivariate logistic regression model includes all of the above variables. Note that female, tumor stage, signet ring cells, mucinous feature, *KRAS* and p53 are not significantly related with CIMP-high after adjusting for other variables.

*β-catenin activation is defined as β-catenin score ≥3. The β-catenin score is the sum of nuclear (0, 1+ or 2+), cytoplasmic (0, 1+ or 2+) and membrane (0 or 1+) scores as originally described by Jass et al.[35].

^Proximal colon includes cecum to transverse colon, and distal colon includes splenic flexure to rectum.

CI, confidence interval; CIMP, CpG island methylator phenotype; LINE-1, long interspersed nucleotide element-1; MSI, microsatellite instability; OR, odds ratio.

When there was missing information on tumor stage (12%), LINE-1 (3.9% missing), MSI (3.2% missing), p53 (1.3% missing), *KRAS* (2.3% missing) or *BRAF* (4.7% missing), we assigned a separate ("missing") indicator variable and included those cases in the multivariate analysis models. We confirmed that excluding cases with a missing variable did not significantly alter results (data not shown). There was no missing information in other variables.

An association of each variable with CIMP-high was also assessed in strata of important clinical or molecular features, including age (<65 year old vs. ≥65 year old), sex, tumor location (proximal vs. distal), MSI status, and *BRAF* status. For stratified analysis, each multivariate logistic regression model included a variable of interest that was stratified by a given stratifying variable (e.g., age) and adjusted for all of the remaining variables (SAS codes available upon request).

An interaction was assessed by including the cross product term of a given variable (e.g., MSI) and another variable of interest in a regression model, and the likelihood ratio test compared a model including the cross product term with that excluding it. In addition to interactions of any given variable with MSI, location, age, sex and *BRAF*, we examined all possible remaining two-way interactions, and found no significant interactions (data not shown).

All statistical analyses except for clustering analysis used SAS version 9.1 (SAS Institute, Cary, NC). All p values were two-sided, and statistical significance was defined as p≤0.05. Nonetheless, multiple hypotheses testing was considered when interpreting the data, especially in examining multiple two-way interactions.

RESULTS

Evaluation of 16 methylation markers

We obtained 904 colorectal cancer specimens and quantified DNA methylation in the 16 loci [*CACNA1G, IGF2, NEUROG1, RUNX3, SOCS1, CDKN2A* (p16), *CRABP1, MLH1, CHFR,HIC1, IGFBP3, MGMT,* MINT1, MINT31, p14 (*CDKN2A*/ARF), and *WRN*] by real-time PCR (MethyLight [30]) assays. The first 5 loci (up to *SOCS1*) were selected as good predictors of CIMP (CpG island methylator phenotype) by screening of 195 CpG islands [15]. The use of the first 8 loci (up to *MLH1*) as a CIMP-high diagnostic panel has been previously validated [24].

To evaluate 16 methylation markers in an unbiased fashion, we conducted an unsupervised hierarchical clustering analysis of the 16 methylation markers and status of MSI (microsatellite instability), and *KRAS* and *BRAF* oncogenes, using 860 tumors with all of these results available (**Figure 1**). The 8 CIMP-high markers (*CACNA1G, CDKN2A* (p16), *CRABP1, IGF2,MLH1, NEUROG1, RUNX3* an d *SOCS1*) were generally clustered together, indicating good concordance of methylation patterns in these markers and supporting these 8 markers as good CIMP-high markers. In addition, p14, MINT31 and *WRN* were also clustered with the 8 markers. The other 5 methylation markers (*MGMT, HIC1, CHFR,* MINT1 and *IGFBP3*) were not clustered closely with each other or the 8 markers. The *BRAF* and MSI variables, which have been known to be associated with CIMP-high [15], [18], [24], were also clustered together with these 8 markers, indicating tight associations with

CIMP-high. Notably, *KRAS* mutation was not clustered with any of the methylation markers, suggesting its association with a random methylation pattern (particularly in CIMP-low tumors which have been associated with*KRAS* mutation [29]; see also **Supplemental Figure S1**). We used clustering analysis only for the examination of marker clustering, but not for tumor classification. That was because clustering of markers was very stable with the large number of tumors (i.e., excluding a few tumors did not substantially influence results) while tumor classification by clustering analysis based on the 16 markers was not stable.

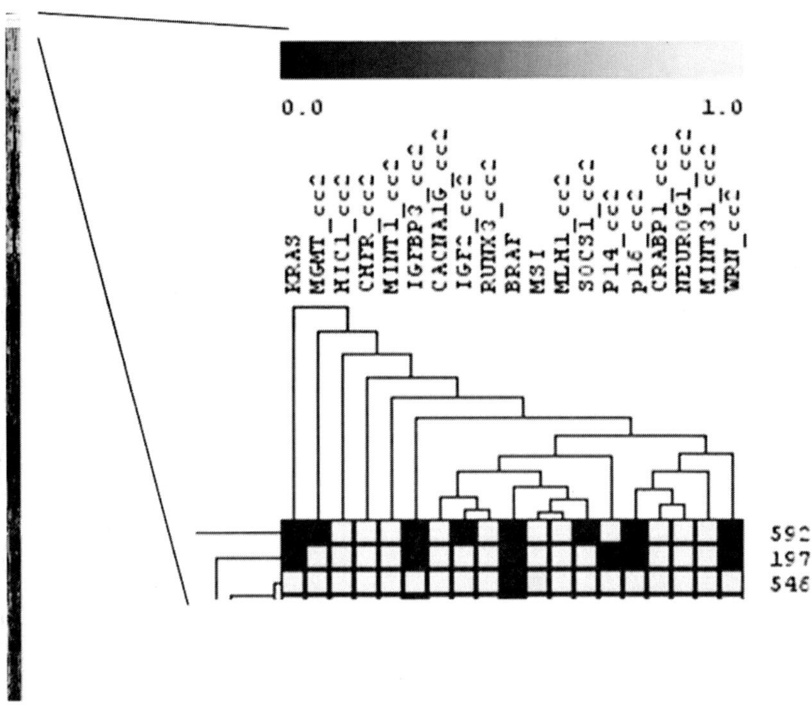

Figure 1. Hierarchical clustering analysis of 16 methylation makers, MSI, *KRAS*and *BRAF* in colorectal cancers.

Horizontal and vertical axes represent markers and cases, respectively. The expanded view of clustering tree for the markers is shown on the right. The 8 markers in our CIMP-high diagnostic panel

(*CACNA1G, IGF2, RUNX3, MLH1, SOCS1, CDKN2A* (p16),*CRABP1* and *N EUROG1*) are clustered closely, supporting that these markers are good CIMP-high markers. Also note the close relationship between MSI, *BRAF* and the 8 CIMP-high markers. *KRAS* mutation is not clustered with any of the methylation markers analyzed, suggesting that *KRAS* mutation (which is associated with CIMP-low[24], [29]; see Supplemental Figure) is probably associated with a random methylation pattern.

To describe performance of each of the 16 markers in an unbiased way, we calculated κ coefficient (for agreement statistics), sensitivity and specificity of each maker for CIMP-high diagnosis determined by the 16 markers (**Supplemental Table S1**). The cutoff for CIMP-high was set as ≥11/16 or ≥10/16 methylated markers based on the distribution of *KRAS* and *BRAF*mutations (**Supplemental Figure**), and on the previous findings that CIMP-high is associated with *BRAF* mutation and CIMP-low is associated with *KRAS* mutation [24], [29]. Sensitivity and specificity of each marker reflected overall concordance of a methylation pattern with the remaining 15 markers. It was evident that performance of the 8 CIMP-panel markers (*CACNA1G, CDKN2A, CRABP1, IGF2, MLH1, NEUROG1, RUNX3* and *SOC S1*) was generally good. The κ coefficient was greater than 0.5 for all of these 8 markers. *RUNX3* was the single best marker for CIMP-high diagnosis. Among the other 8 markers (*CHFR, HIC1, IGFBP3,MGMT,* MINT1, MINT31, p14 and *WRN*), only MINT31 and p14 consistently showed the κ coefficient greater than 0.5, and good sensitivity/specificity. This was in agreement with clustering analysis, which showed that MINT31 and p14 clustered with the 8 CIMP-panel markers.

We also compared the all-16-marker panel with the 8-marker CIMP panel. Using the 8-maker panel, or the 16-maker panel, CIMP-high was defined as ≥6/8 or ≥11/16 methylated markers, respectively. Among the 904 cases, 879 cases (97.2%) showed concordant diagnosis of CIMP status between the 16-marker panel and the 8-marker panel (κ=0.89, p<0.0001). When the 16-marker CIMP panel was used, the associations of CIMP-high with clinical and molecular features were very similar to the CIMP-high associations by the 8-marker CIMP panel (data not shown). We also confirmed a high degree of agreement (98.6% concordant; κ=0.94) between the 8-

marker panel and the 5-marker panel described by Weisenberger et al. [15]. Thus, in subsequent analyses, we used the 8-marker CIMP panel which we had extensively validated[24].

CIMP-high in colorectal cancer

We assessed clinical, pathologic and molecular features of CIMP-high colorectal cancer (**Table 1**). By univariate analysis, CIMP-high was associated with female sex, older age, proximal location, poor differentiation, mucin, signet ring cells, MSI-high and *BRAF* mutation, and inversely with stage I, *KRAS* mutation, LINE-1 hypomethylation, positive p53, and active β-catenin (all $p<0.004$).

Age was linearly associated with CIMP-high in logistic regression analysis (p for trend <0.0001). We did not show significant non-linearity by the likelihood ratio test that compared a model including a quadratic (or cubic) term with a model excluding it ($p>0.85$). Likewise, LINE-1 hypomethylation was inversely linearly associated with CIMP-high (p for trend <0.0001), and there was no significant non-linearity by the likelihood ratio test, using a quadratic (or cubic) term ($p \geq 0.078$). Non-parametric restricted cubic splines also supported a linear relation between age and CIMP-high (**Figure 2**) and an inverse linear relation between LINE-1 hypomethylation and CIMP-high (**Figure 3**).

Log_e(OR for CIMP-high) (y axis) according to age (x axis) is shown (with young age as a referent). Broken lines indicate 95% confidence interval. Note the linear relation between age and CIMP-high. CIMP, CpG island methylator phenotype; OR, odds ratio.

Log_e(OR for CIMP-high) (y axis) according to LINE-1 methylation (x axis) is shown (with high-level LINE-1 methylation as a referent). Broken lines indicate 95% confidence interval. Note the inverse linear relation between LINE-1 hypomethylation and CIMP-high. CIMP, CpG island methylator phenotype; LINE-1, long interspersed nucleotide element-1; OR, odds ratio.

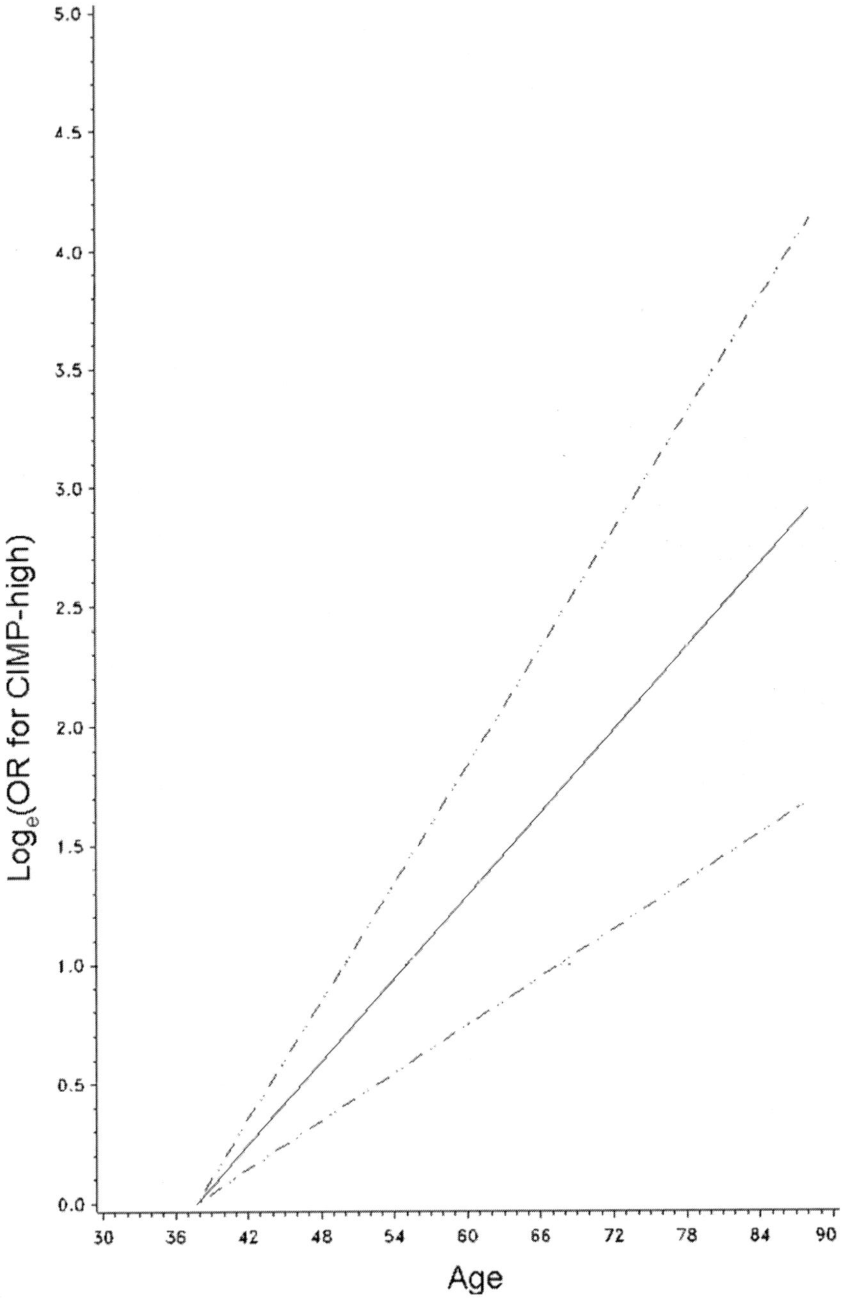

Figure 2. Smoothing spline for the age/CIMP-high association.

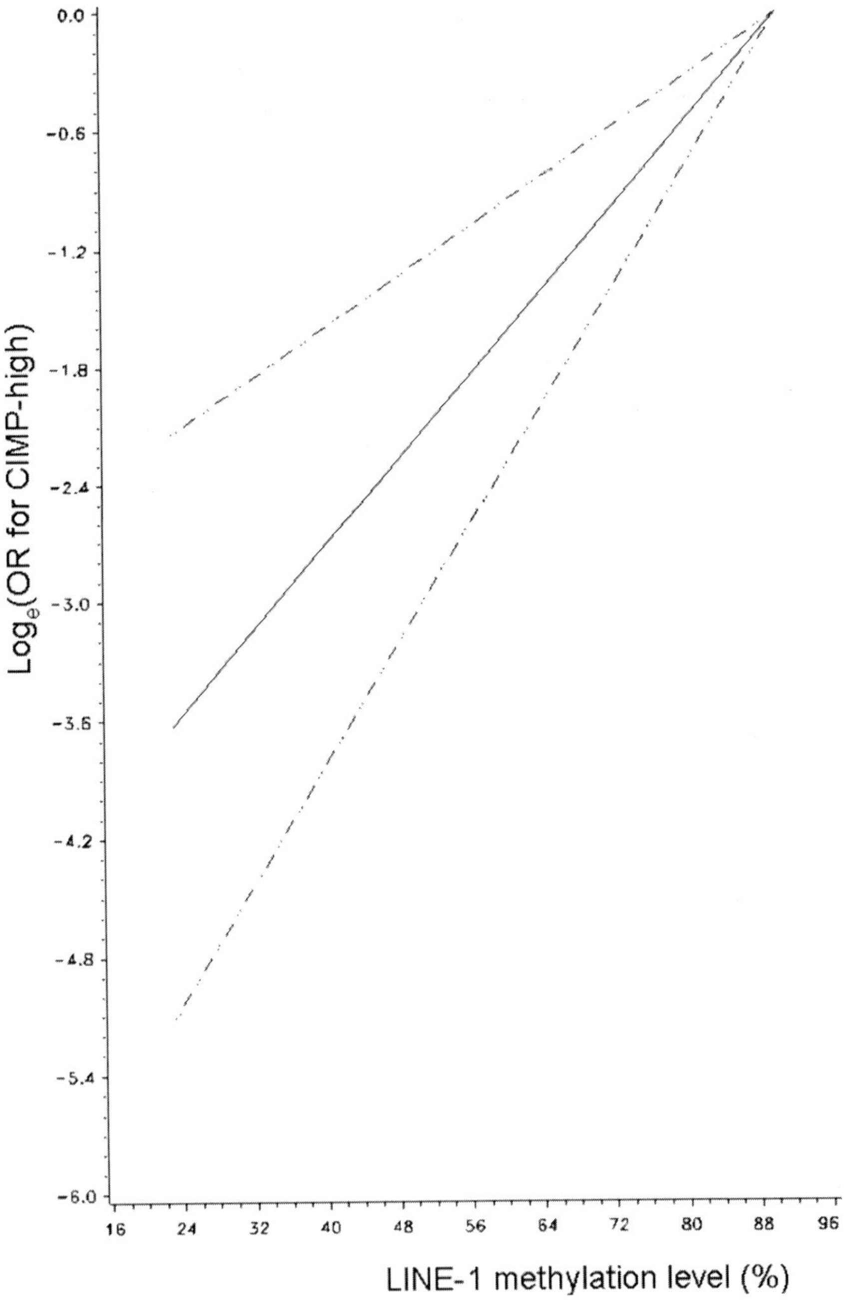

Figure 3. Smoothing spline for the LINE-1/CIMP-high association.

In multivariate logistic regression analysis, CIMP-high was significantly associated with older age, proximal location, poor differentiation, MSI-high and *BRAF* mutation, and inversely with active β-catenin and LINE-1 hypomethylation (**Table 2**). However, all of the other features (female, stage, mucin, signet ring cells, *KRAS* and p53) were no longer significantly associated with CIMP-high in multivariate analysis. We further examined for potential confounders in the association of each variable with CIMP-high. Except for sex, all of the other variables showed substantial changes in odds ratio (OR) for the association with CIMP-high after adjusting for MSI, *BRAF* and/or tumor location (or other variables) (**Table 2**). These results indicated the existence of complex relations between clinical and molecular features (including CIMP) in colorectal cancer, which are summarized in **Figure 4**.

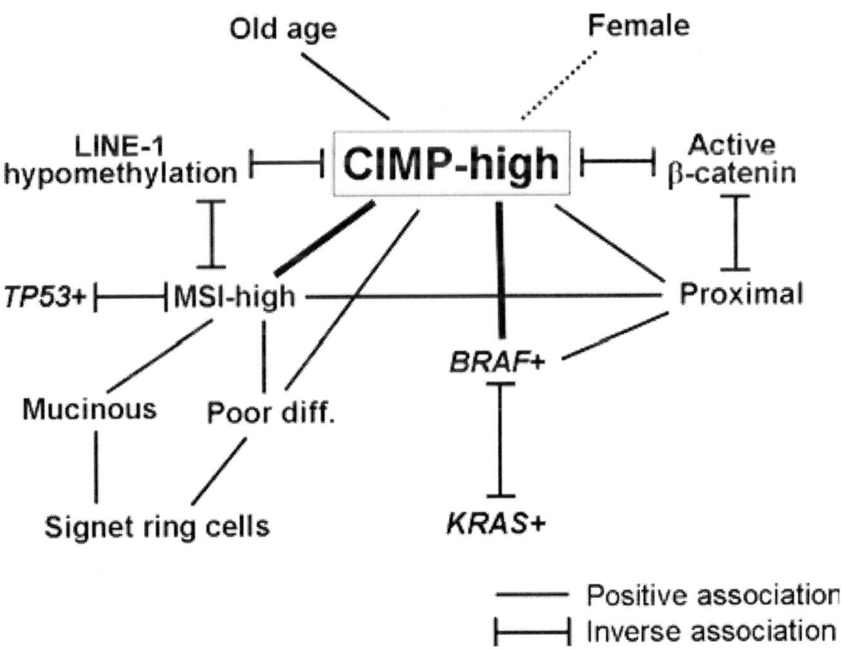

Figure 4. Summary of associations of CIMP-high with clinical and molecular features. The broken line indicates the relatively weak association.

Associations with CIMP-high in strata of MSI

Molecular classification by MSI status is increasingly important in colorectal cancer [38]–[40]. Thus, we examined the relations of clinical and tumoral variables with CIMP-high in MSI-high tumors and non-MSI-high tumors (**Table 3**). Older age, proximal location and *BRAF* mutation were significantly associated with CIMP-high in both MSI-high and non-MSI-high tumors. In contrast, the relations of CIMP-high with poor differentiation, *KRAS* mutation and LINE-1 hypomethylation appeared to be different according to MSI status (p for interaction <0.005). CIMP-high was associated with poor differentiation and inversely with *KRAS* mutation in MSI-high tumors, but not in non-MSI-high tumors. LINE-1 hypomethylation was inversely associated with CIMP-high in non-MSI-high tumors, but not in MSI-high tumors.

Table 3. Associations with CIMP-high in MSI-high and non-MSI-high colorectal cancers.

Clinical, pathological, or molecular characteristics	P for interaction with MSI	Among non-MSI-high tumors		Among MSI-high tumors	
		Multivariate OR (95% CI)	P value	Multivariate OR (95% CI)	P value
Age (10-year increment)	0.033	2.12 (1.23–3.65)	0.007	6.14 (2.49–15.1)	<0.0001
Female (vs. male)	0.46	1.41 (0.57–3.47)	0.45	2.03 (0.69–6.06)	0.20
Proximal (vs. distal)^	0.33	3.01 (1.22–7.40)	0.016	7.17 (1.74–29.5)	0.006
Tumor stage II–IV (vs. I)	0.064	0.97 (0.35–2.68)	0.95	4.92 (1.18–20.5)	0.029
Poor differentiation	**0.002**	0.84 (0.21–3.30)	0.80	**25.6 (3.43–191)**	**0.002**
Mucinous feature, any	0.29	2.02 (0.86–4.74)	0.11	0.95 (0.30–2.99)	0.93
Signet ring cells, any	0.22	1.65 (0.44–6.17)	0.46	0.42 (0.065–2.71)	0.36
BRAF mutation	0.21	11.7 (4.34–31.6)	<0.0001	49.8 (4.71–527)	0.001
KRAS mutation	**0.004**	2.24 (0.81–6.17)	0.12	**0.17 (0.039–0.78)**	**0.022**
p53 positivity	0.65	0.72 (0.31–1.70)	0.46	0.50 (0.12–2.00)	0.33
LINE-1 hypomethylation (30% decline)	**0.002**	**0.095 (0.026–0.34)**	**0.0003**	3.20 (0.47–22.0)	0.24
β-catenin activation*	0.18	0.32 (0.097–1.04)	0.058	0.063 (0.008–0.51)	0.009

Each multivariate logistic regression model assesses a variable of interest (stratified by MSI status in a given model), adjusting for all of the above remaining variables. An interaction was assessed by the likelihood ratio test that compares a model including a cross product term (of the MSI variable and another variable of interest) with a model excluding it.

*β-catenin activation is defined as β-catenin score ≥3, where the β-catenin score is the sum of nuclear (0, 1+ or 2+), cytoplasmic (0, 1+ or 2+) and membrane (0 or 1+) scores as originally described by Jass et al.[35].

^Proximal colon includes cecum to transverse colon, and distal colon includes splenic flexure to rectum.

CI, confidence interval; CIMP, CpG island methylator phenotype; LINE-1, long interspersed nucleotide element-1; MSI, microsatellite instability; OR, odds ratio.

Associations with CIMP-high in strata of tumor location

There is accumulating evidence for a molecular difference between proximal and distal colorectal cancers [38], [41]. Therefore, we examined the relations of clinical and tumoral variables with CIMP-high in proximal tumors and distal tumors (**Table 4**). The relations of CIMP-high with the variables did not appear to differ according to tumor location (all p for interaction >0.23).

Table 4. Associations with CIMP-high in proximal and distal colorectal cancers.

Clinical, pathological, or molecular characteristics	P for interaction with location	Among proximal tumors^		Among distal tumors^	
		Multivariate OR (95% CI)	P value	Multivariate OR (95% CI)	P value
Age (10-year increment)	0.32	2.62 (1.58–4.34)	0.0002	4.62 (1.61–13.2)	0.004
Female (vs. male)	0.71	1.93 (0.87–4.30)	0.11	1.21 (0.32–4.58)	0.78
Tumor stage II–IV (vs. I)	0.31	2.48 (0.79–7.79)	0.12	1.00 (0.24–4.15)	0.99
Poor differentiation	0.46	2.54 (0.91–7.10)	0.075	5.81 (0.89–37.8)	0.066
Mucinous feature, any	0.24	1.25 (0.58–2.72)	0.57	3.14 (0.79–12.5)	0.10
Signet ring cells, any	0.56	0.86 (0.25–2.94)	0.81	2.01 (0.18–22.6)	0.57
MSI-high	0.33	31.0 (13.2–73.2)	<0.0001	14.3 (3.28–62.5)	0.0004
BRAF mutation	0.56	13.7 (5.21–36.1)	<0.0001	22.8 (4.78–109)	<0.0001
KRAS mutation	0.39	1.20 (0.48–2.99)	0.70	0.57 (0.13–2.44)	0.44
p53 positivity	0.37	0.89 (0.39–2.06)	0.79	0.37 (0.083–1.63)	0.19
LINE-1 hypomethylation (30% decline)	0.26	0.19 (0.055–0.63)	0.007	0.65 (0.098–4.24)	0.65
β-catenin activation*	-#	0.35 (0.11–1.13)	0.070	0#	-#

Each multivariate logistic regression model assesses a variable of interest (stratified by tumor location in a given model), adjusting for all of the above remaining variables. An interaction was assessed by the likelihood ratio test that compares a model including a cross product term (of the location variable and another variable of interest) with a model excluding it.

*β-catenin activation is defined as β-catenin score ≥3, where the β-catenin score is the sum of nuclear (0, 1+ or 2+), cytoplasmic (0, 1+ or 2+) and membrane (0 or 1+) scores as originally described by Jass et al.[35].

^Proximal colon includes cecum to transverse colon, and distal colon includes splenic flexure to rectum.

#Because there was no CIMP-high β-catenin-active tumors in distal colon, stable p for interaction and 95% CI for OR could not be estimated.

CI, confidence interval; CIMP, CpG island methylator phenotype; LINE-1, long interspersed nucleotide element-1; MSI, microsatellite instability; OR, odds ratio.

Associations with CIMP-high in other stratified analyses

We examined the relations of clinical and tumoral variables with CIMP-high in strata of sex, age (<65 year old vs. ≥65 year old) and *BRAF* status. Considering multiple hypotheses testing (12-hypotheses testing each), the effect of the variables did not appear to significantly differ according to age (all p for interaction >0.03) and sex (all p for interaction >0.02). Notably, the effect of LINE-1 hypomethylation did appear to differ according to *BRAF* status (p for interaction=0.001) (**Table 5**). A significant inverse association of LINE-1 hypomethylation with CIMP-high was present in *BRAF*-mutated tumors [adjusted OR=0.022; 95% confidence interval (CI), 0.003–0.17], but not in *BRAF*-wild-type tumors (adjusted OR=0.87; 95% CI, 0.25–3.06).

Table 5. Associations with CIMP-high in *BRAF*-wild-type and *BRAF*-mutated colorectal cancers.

Clinical, pathological, or molecular characteristics	P for interaction with *BRAF*	Among *BRAF*-wild-type tumors		Among *BRAF*-mutated tumors	
		Multivariate OR (95% CI)	P value	Multivariate OR (95% CI)	P value
Age (10-year increment)	0.13	3.60 (2.02–6.43)	<0.0001	1.80 (0.81–4.02)	0.15
Female (vs. male)	0.23	2.27 (1.01–5.09)	0.047	0.70 (0.14–3.51)	0.67
Proximal (vs. distal)^	0.56	3.87 (1.57–9.50)	0.003	2.33 (0.52–10.4)	0.27
Tumor stage II–IV (vs. I)	0.043	2.79 (0.92–8.45)	0.69	0.37 (0.070–1.94)	0.24
Poor differentiation	0.27	3.84 (1.27–11.6)	0.017	1.43 (0.32–6.49)	0.64
Mucinous feature, any	0.98	1.56 (0.69–3.56)	0.29	1.54 (0.45–5.30)	0.50
Signet ring cells, any	0.25	0.67 (0.15–3.09)	0.61	2.55 (0.40–16.3)	0.32
MSI-high	0.21	21.6 (9.56–48.6)	<0.0001	82.6 (8.48–804)	0.0001
KRAS mutation	0.37	1.02 (0.44–2.35)	0.96	0.18 (0.005–6.69)	0.35
p53 positivity	0.52	0.55 (0.21–1.40)	0.21	0.90 (0.26–3.06)	0.86
LINE-1 hypomethylation (30% decline)	**0.001**	0.87 (0.25–3.06)	0.83	0.022 (0.003–0.17)	0.0003
β-catenin activation*	0.44	0.20 (0.052–0.76)	0.018	0.49 (0.076–3.21)	0.46

Each multivariate logistic regression model assesses a variable of interest (stratified by *BRAF* status in a given model), adjusting for all of the above remaining variables. An interaction was assessed by the likelihood ratio test that compares a model including a cross product term (of the *BRAF* variable and another variable of interest) with a model excluding it.

*β-catenin activation is defined as β-catenin score ≥3, where the β-catenin score is the sum of nuclear (0, 1+ or 2+), cytoplasmic (0, 1+ or 2+) and membrane (0 or 1+) scores as originally described by Jass et al.[35].

^Proximal colon includes cecum to transverse colon, and distal colon includes splenic flexure to rectum.

CI, confidence interval; CIMP, CpG island methylator phenotype; LINE-1, long interspersed nucleotide element-1; MSI, microsatellite instability; OR, odds ratio.

We also examined all of the remaining potential two-way interactions by the available clinical and tumoral variables, and found no significant interactions with regard to the associations with CIMP-high (data not shown).

DISCUSSION

In this study utilizing a large sample size, we evaluated 16 methylation makers in an unbiased fashion. The 16 methylation markers included the 5 markers (*CACNA1G, IGF2, NEUROG1,RUNX3* and *SOCS1*) that were selected by screening of 195 CpG islands [15] and further validated to be included in the CIMP-high diagnostic panel (the above 5 plus *CDKN2A,CRABP1* and *MLH1*) [24]. By unsupervised hierarchical clustering analysis, the 5 methylation markers were clustered with each other as well as with MSI (microsatellite instability) and*BRAF* mutation. Analysis of κ coefficient, sensitivity and specificity also demonstrated good performance of the 5 methylation markers with generally concordant methylation pattern. Utilizing the validated CIMP panel, we have deciphered the complex relations of

CIMP-high with various clinical, pathologic and molecular features in colorectal cancer. Our data provide a rationale for the of the validated CIMP-specific methylation marker panel.

This study is the first extensive investigation to compare the 5 new CIMP-high markers [15]with MINT1, MINT31 and other CpG islands, using a large sample size. Performance of the 5 new markers (*CACNA1G, IGF2, NEUROG1, RUNX3,*
and *SOCS1*), *CRABP1* and *MLH1* was consistently superior to that of *WRN*, MINT1, *CHFR, IGFBP3, HIC1* and *MGMT*. MINT31,*CDKN2A*, and p14 showed intermediate performance characteristics, and in hierarchical clustering analysis, were generally clustered with the new 5 CIMP markers, MSI and *BRAF*mutation. We have provided valuable data for standardization of methylation markers for the detection of CIMP-high in colorectal cancer.

Studying epigenetic and genetic aberrations is important in cancer research [42]–[46]. We used quantitative PCR assays (MethyLight [30]) to determine the degree of DNA methylation, which is robust enough to reproducibly differentiate low-level methylation from high-level methylation[31]. Our resource of a large colorectal cancer sample obtained from two large prospective cohorts (representing a relatively unbiased sample compared to a single-hospital-based sample) has provided a sufficient power to evaluate the 16 methylation markers, and to simultaneously assess independent relations of CIMP-high with multiple clinical and tumoral molecular variables.

Interestingly, unsupervised clustering analysis using a large number of tumors revealed that*KRAS* mutation was not clustered with any of the 16 methylation markers. However, as shown in our previous studies [24], [29], *KRAS* mutation was more common in CIMP-low tumors compared to CIMP-high and CIMP-0 tumors. Although these findings appeared to be discrepant, we believe that *KRAS* mutation is perhaps associated with a random pattern of CpG island methylation, indicated by the non-clustering phenomenon in clustering analysis. In contrast, our clustering analysis has clearly shown that *BRAF* mutation is clustered with CIMP-high specific markers, indicating that *BRAF* mutation is perhaps associated with a non-random pattern of CpG island methylation.

Previous studies identified various factors associated with CIMP-high, including old age, female, proximal location, poor differentiation, mucin, signet ring cells, MSI-high, *BRAF*mutation, wild-type *KRAS*, inactive β-catenin, wild-type *APC*, high LINE-1 methylation level, and wild-type *TP53* [9]–[19], [21], [47], [48]. However, many of these factors are interrelated. Thus, in order to properly decipher the relations with CIMP-high, it is necessary to use a large number of tumors, determine a number of molecular features, and perform comprehensive biostatistical analysis. We were able to utilize a large colorectal cancer sample that has been examined for multiple molecular events, and appropriate biostatistical methods. **Figure 3**summarizes our current knowledge on the associations of clinical, pathologic and molecular features including CIMP in colorectal cancer. It is very important to keep in mind these relations, when analyzing the association between any of these factors and an outcome (e.g., molecular changes in colorectal cancer, patient mortality, etc.). These factors may confound the relationship of interest. Indeed, we have demonstrated confounding effects of MSI, *BRAF*and tumor location in a number of the associations in **Table 2**. In particular, signet ring cells,*KRAS* and p53 were no longer associated with CIMP-high after adjusting for the confounders.

We have shown that the relations of CIMP-high with tumor differentiation, *KRAS* mutation and LINE-1 hypomethylation appear to differ according to MSI status. MSI is a major molecular classifier in colorectal cancer [38]–[40]. MSI-high tumors have been shown to exhibit widespread mutations in nucleotide repeat sequences such as those in *TGFBR2* and *BAX*[49], [50]. Thus, it is likely that overall genomic changes in MSI-high tumors are dissimilar to those of non-MSI-high tumors. That may explain why there are some pathologic and molecular features that are differentially associated with CIMP-high according to MSI status.

In summary, using the 16 methylation markers and a large population-based sample, we have evaluated performance of each of the 16 methylation markers in an unbiased fashion. Our current study provides valuable data for standardization of the use of CIMP-high-specific markers. Using the validated CIMP-specific methylation marker panel, we have comprehensively analyzed the clinical, pathologic and molecular features of CIMP-high colorectal cancer by comprehensive biostatistical methods. We have provided the rationale to use the validated CIMP-high-specific methylation marker panel in clinical and research settings. Further studies are necessary to elucidate fundamental molecular defects that lead to CIMP-high colorectal cancer.

ACKNOWLEDGMENTS

We deeply thank the Nurses' Health Study and Health Professionals Follow-up Study cohort participants who have generously agreed to provide us with biological specimens and information through responses to questionnaires; hospitals and pathology departments throughout the U.S. for generously providing us with tumor tissue materials; Frank Speizer, Walter Willett, Graham Colditz, Susan Hankinson, and many other staff members who implemented and have maintained the cohort studies.

AUTHOR CONTRIBUTIONS

Conceived and designed the experiments: CF SO. Performed the experiments: KN NI KS SK GJK JQ SO. Analyzed the data: KN NI KS SK GJK ESS AH DJH JQ DS EG CF SO. Contributed reagents/materials/analysis tools: GJK ESS AH JQ DS SO. Wrote the paper: KN NI KS SK DJH JQ EG CF SO.

REFERENCES

1. Jones PA, Baylin SB (2007) The epigenomics of cancer. Cell 128: 683–692.

2. Esteller M (2008) Epigenetics in cancer. N Engl J Med 358: 1148–1159.

3. Baylin SB, Ohm JE (2006) Epigenetic gene silencing in cancer – a mechanism for early oncogenic pathway addiction? Nat Rev Cancer 6: 107–116.

4. Issa JP (2004) CpG island methylator phenotype in cancer. Nat Rev Cancer 4: 988–993.

5. Toyota M, Ahuja N, Ohe-Toyota M, Herman JG, Baylin SB, et al. (1999) CpG island methylator phenotype in colorectal cancer. Proc Natl Acad Sci U S A 96: 8681–8686.

6. Grady WM (2007) CIMP and colon cancer gets more complicated. Gut 56: 1498–1500.

7. Teodoridis JM, Hardie C, Brown R (2008) CpG island methylator phenotype (CIMP) in cancer: Causes and implications. Cancer Lett 268: 177–186.

8. Toyota M, Ohe-Toyota M, Ahuja N, Issa JP (2000) Distinct genetic profiles in colorectal tumors with or without the CpG island methylator phenotype. Proc Natl Acad Sci U S A 97: 710–715.

9. van Rijnsoever M, Grieu F, Elsaleh H, Joseph D, Iacopetta B (2002) Characterisation of colorectal cancers showing hypermethylation at multiple CpG islands. Gut 51: 797–802.

10. Whitehall VL, Wynter CV, Walsh MD, Simms LA, Purdie D, et al. (2002) Morphological and molecular heterogeneity within nonmicrosatellite instability-high colorectal cancer. Cancer Res 62: 6011–6014.

11. Hawkins N, Norrie M, Cheong K, Mokany E, Ku SL, et al. (2002) CpG island methylation in sporadic colorectal cancers and its relationship to microsatellite instability. Gastroenterology 122: 1376–1387.

12. Kambara T, Simms LA, Whitehall VLJ, Spring KJ, Wynter CVA, et al. (2004) BRAF mutation is associated with DNA methylation in serrated polyps and cancers of the colorectum. Gut 53: 1137–1144.

13. Nagasaka T, Sasamoto H, Notohara K, Cullings HM, Takeda M, et al. (2004) Colorectal cancer with mutation in BRAF, KRAS, and wild-type with respect to both oncogenes showing different patterns of DNA methylation. J Clin Oncol 22: 4584–4594.

14. Iacopetta B, Grieu F, Li W, Ruszkiewicz A, Caruso M, et al. (2006) APC gene methylation is inversely correlated with features of the CpG island methylator phenotype in colorectal cancer. Int J Cancer 119: 2272–2278.

15. Weisenberger DJ, Siegmund KD, Campan M, Young J, Long TI, et al. (2006) CpG island methylator phenotype underlies sporadic microsatellite instability and is tightly associated with BRAF mutation in colorectal cancer. Nat Genet 38: 787–793.

16. Goel A, Nagasaka T, Arnold CN, Inoue T, Hamilton C, et al. (2007) The CpG Island Methylator Phenotype and Chromosomal Instability Are Inversely Correlated in Sporadic Colorectal Cancer. Gastroenterology 132: 127–138.

17. Ogino S, Cantor M, Kawasaki T, Brahmandam M, Kirkner G, et al. (2006) CpG island methylator phenotype (CIMP) of colorectal cancer is best characterised by quantitative DNA methylation analysis and prospective cohort studies. Gut 55: 1000–1006.

18. Samowitz W, Albertsen H, Herrick J, Levin TR, Sweeney C, et al. (2005) Evaluation of a large, population-based sample supports a CpG island methylator phenotype in colon cancer. Gastroenterology 129: 837–845.

19. Kawasaki T, Nosho K, Ohnishi M, Suemoto Y, Kirkner GJ, et al. (2007) Correlation of beta-catenin localization with cyclooxygenase-2 expression and CpG island methylator phenotype (CIMP) in colorectal cancer. Neoplasia 9: 569–577.

20. Shen L, Toyota M, Kondo Y, Lin E, Zhang L, et al. (2007) Integrated genetic and epigenetic analysis identifies three different subclasses of colon cancer. Proc Natl Acad Sci U S A 104: 18654–18659.

21. Ogino S, Kawasaki T, Nosho K, Ohnishi M, Suemoto Y, et al. (2008) LINE-1 hypomethylation is inversely associated with microsatellite instability and CpG methylator phenotype in colorectal cancer. Int J Cancer 122: 2767–2773.

22. Derks S, Postma C, Carvalho B, van den Bosch SM, Moerkerk PT, et al. (2008) Integrated analysis of chromosomal, microsatellite and epigenetic instability in colorectal cancer identifies specific associations between promoter methylation of pivotal tumour suppressor and DNA repair genes and specific chromosomal alterations. Carcinogenesis 29: 434–439.

23. Barault L, Charon-Barra C, Jooste V, de la Vega MF, Martin L, et al. (2008) Hypermethylator phenotype in sporadic colon cancer: study on a population-based series of 582 cases. Cancer Res 68: 8541–8546.

24. Ogino S, Kawasaki T, Kirkner GJ, Kraft P, Loda M, et al. (2007) Evaluation of markers for CpG island methylator phenotype (CIMP) in colorectal cancer by a large population-based sample. J Mol Diagn 9: 305–314.

25. Colditz GA, Hankinson SE (2005) The Nurses' Health Study: lifestyle and health among women. Nat Rev Cancer 5: 388–396.

26. Chan AT, Ogino S, Fuchs CS (2007) Aspirin and the Risk of Colorectal Cancer in Relation to the Expression of COX-2. New Engl J Med 356: 2131–2142.

27. Kawasaki T, Ohnishi M, Nosho K, Suemoto Y, Kirkner GJ, et al. (2008) CpG island methylator phenotype-low (CIMP-low) colorectal cancer shows not only few methylated CIMP-high-specific CpG islands, but also low-level methylation at individual loci. Mod Pathol 21: 245–255.

28. Ogino S, Kawasaki T, Brahmandam M, Yan L, Cantor M, et al. (2005) Sensitive sequencing method for KRAS mutation detection by Pyrosequencing. J Mol Diagn 7: 413–421.

29. Ogino S, Kawasaki T, Kirkner GJ, Loda M, Fuchs CS (2006) CpG island methylator phenotype-low (CIMP-low) in colorectal cancer: possible associations with male sex and KRAS mutations. J Mol Diagn 8: 582–588.

30. Eads CA, Danenberg KD, Kawakami K, Saltz LB, Blake C, et al. (2000) MethyLight: a high-throughput assay to measure DNA methylation. Nucleic Acids Res 28: E32.

31. Ogino S, kawasaki T, Brahmandam M, Cantor M, Kirkner GJ, et al. (2006) Precision and performance characteristics of bisulfite conversion and real-time PCR (MethyLight) for quantitative DNA methylation analysis. J Mol Diagn 8: 209–217.

32. Yang AS, Estecio MR, Doshi K, Kondo Y, Tajara EH, et al. (2004) A simple method for estimating global DNA methylation using bisulfite PCR of repetitive DNA elements. Nucleic Acids Res 32: e38.

33. Estecio MR, Gharibyan V, Shen L, Ibrahim AE, Doshi K, et al. (2007) LINE-1 hypomethylation in cancer is highly variable and inversely correlated with microsatellite instability. PLoS ONE 2: e399.

34. Ogino S, kawasaki T, Kirkner GJ, Yamaji T, Loda M, et al. (2007) Loss of nuclear p27 (CDKN1B/KIP1) in colorectal cancer is correlated with microsatellite instability and CIMP. Mod Pathol 20: 15–22.

35. Jass JR, Biden KG, Cummings MC, Simms LA, Walsh M, et al. (1999) Characterisation of a subtype of colorectal cancer combining features of the suppressor and mild mutator pathways. J Clin Pathol 52: 455–460.

36. Saeed AI, Bhagabati NK, Braisted JC, Liang W, Sharov V, et al. (2006) TM4 microarray software suite. Methods Enzymol 411: 134–193.

37. Durrleman S, Simon R (1989) Flexible regression models with cubic splines. Stat Med 8: 551–561.

38. Jass JR (2007) Classification of colorectal cancer based on correlation of clinical, morphological and molecular features. Histopathology 50: 113–130.

39. Ogino S, Goel A (2008) Molecular classification and correlates in colorectal cancer. J Mol Diagn 10: 13–27.

40. Popat S, Hubner R, Houlston RS (2005) Systematic Review of Microsatellite Instability and Colorectal Cancer Prognosis. J Clin Oncol 23: 609–618.

41. Sugai T, Habano W, Jiao YF, Tsukahara M, Takeda Y, et al. (2006) Analysis of molecular alterations in left- and right-sided colorectal carcinomas reveals distinct pathways of carcinogenesis: proposal for new molecular profile of colorectal carcinomas. J Mol Diagn 8: 193–201.

42. Sengupta K, Upender MB, Barenboim-Stapleton L, Nguyen QT, Wincovitch SM Sr, et al. (2007) Artificially introduced aneuploid chromosomes assume a conserved position in colon cancer cells. PLoS ONE 2: e199.

43. Abraham JM, Sato F, Cheng Y, Paun B, Kan T, et al. (2007) Novel decapeptides that bind avidly and deliver radioisotope to colon cancer cells. PLoS ONE 2: e964.

44. Chung W, Kwabi-Addo B, Ittmann M, Jelinek J, Shen L, et al. (2008) Identification of novel tumor markers in prostate, colon and breast cancer by unbiased methylation profiling. PLoS ONE 3: e2079.

45. Muleris M, Chalastanis A, Meyer N, Lae M, Dutrillaux B, et al. (2008) Chromosomal instability in near-diploid colorectal cancer: a link between numbers and structure. PLoS ONE 3: e1632.

46. Firestein R, Blander G, Michan S, Oberdoerffer P, Ogino S, et al. (2008) The SIRT1 deacetylase suppresses intestinal tumorigenesis and colon cancer growth. PLoS ONE 3: e2020.

47. Samowitz WS, Slattery ML, Sweeney C, Herrick J, Wolff RK, et al. (2007) APC mutations and other genetic and epigenetic changes in colon cancer. Mol Cancer Res 5: 165–170.

48. Suehiro Y, Wong CW, Chirieac LR, Kondo Y, Shen L, et al. (2008) Epigenetic-Genetic Interactions in the APC/WNT, RAS/RAF, and P53 Pathways in Colorectal Carcinoma. Clin Cancer Res 14: 2560–2569.

49. Markowitz S, Wang J, Myeroff L, Parsons R, Sun L, et al. (1995) Inactivation of the type II TGF-beta receptor in colon cancer cells with microsatellite instability. Science 268: 1336–1338.

50. Rampino N, Yamamoto H, Ionov Y, Li Y, Sawai H, et al. (1997) Somatic frameshift mutations in the BAX gene in colon cancers of the microsatellite mutator phenotype. Science 275: 967–969.

Index

M

O

P

S

T